Maulana Azad

Also by S. Irfan Habib

Inquilab: Bhagat Singh on Religion & Revolution

Indian Nationalism: The Essential Writings

Domesticating Modern Science: A Social History of Science and Culture in Colonial India (with Dhruv Raina)

To Make the Deaf Hear: Ideology and Programme of Bhagat Singh and His Comrades

Jihad or Itjihad? Religious Orthodoxy and Modern Science in Contemporary Islam

Situating the History of Science: Dialogues with Joseph Needham (edited with Dhruv Raina)

Maulana AZAD

A Life

S. IRFAN HABIB

ALEPH

ALEPH BOOK COMPANY
An independent publishing firm
promoted by Rupa Publications India

First published in India in 2023
by Aleph Book Company
7/16 Ansari Road, Daryaganj
New Delhi 110 002

ISBN: 978-93-93852-18-2

3 5 7 9 10 8 6 4 2

Printed in India.

This book is dedicated to all Indians who are indefatigably committed to an indivisible and compassionate nationalism.

To all those who are struggling hard in the universities, media, and everywhere else to keep us Indians together as one loving and caring nation.

—A vision Maulana Azad strived to achieve all his life, through his faith as well as in politics.

CONTENTS

PREFACE

As a student of modern Indian history, I had always found Maulana Abul Kalam Azad a fascinating figure. He was a profound intellectual and an unrelenting nationalist. He lived with this unblemished reputation all his life and did not falter even during the most challenging of times. Azad can easily be rated as one of the most erudite auto-didacts we have seen. He taught himself everything, from Islam, philosophy, and science to culture and art. His idea of nationalism was also defined through his diverse intellectual readings as well as travel through other colonized nations.

Maulana Azad, once he had decided to be part of the integrative politics of India, was among those nationalist leaders who consciously avoided identifying with just communitarian concerns. He was among leaders such as Hakim Ajmal Khan, Dr M. A. Ansari, Khan Abdul Ghaffar Khan, Hasrat Mohani, Yusuf Meherali, and others, who were 'averse to being labelled as "Muslim Leaders", a category which took no account of their distinct and unique positions and in fact obscured their fundamental differences with, say, the Muslim League and the Jamat-e-Islami.'[1] They were all committed Muslims but never brought their faith into the public domain, except during the short-lived Khilafat Movement. It is pertinent to mention these names and remember this quote from Maulana Azad in today's India, where faith-based nationalism has become part of mainstream political discourse:

> It is one of the greatest frauds on the people to suggest that religious affinity can unite areas which are geographically, economically, linguistically, and culturally different. It

> is true that Islam sought to establish a society which transcends racial, linguistic, economic, and political frontiers. History has however proved that after the first few decades, or at most after the first century, Islam was not able to unite all Muslim countries into one State on the basis of Islam alone.[2]

I had always admired Azad, both as a scholar of Islam and a committed nationalist. However, I focused my attention on Maulana Azad in 2008 when I was invited to join as Maulana Azad Chair at the National University of Educational Planning and Administration (NUEPA), New Delhi. Being the university chair facilitated my understanding of Azad through seminars, lectures, and plays that I organized, particularly on his birthday, 11 November, which we observe as National Education Day. One of our most creative and prolific theatre directors, Sayeed Alam, wrote a play *Maulana Abul Kalam Azad*, which the late Tom Alter brought to life on stage in a stellar solo performance in 2009. This was followed by two other plays about Azad by the same team.

I must acknowledge here the contribution of Shiju Sam Varughese, who not only accessed the archival material I've used in this book but also engaged in several rounds of initial discussions based on these archival resources. Professor R. Govinda, vice-chancellor of the university, was forthcoming with his support and with his ideas about the national education system. My colleagues Sudhanshu Bhushan and K. Ramachandran were always available for animated discussions and much needed tea breaks. I owe a lot of the insights in the book to many discussions with Rizwan Qaiser, whom we sadly lost during the Covid-19 pandemic. My old friend, the Urdu poet Gauhar Raza, helped me decipher some complicated Urdu expressions of Maulana Azad. I cannot forget the Nehru Memorial Museum and Library for facilitating the foundational work, as had been the case in my earlier works as well.

Most of this book was written in the India International Centre library, so I am grateful to its rich collection and the ever-supporting staff. I thank Professor Neera Chandhoke for several informal yet insightful discussions in the IIC lounge. I must thank my editor at Aleph, Pujitha Krishnan, for her skilful reading of the manuscript. I will forever stay grateful for the unstinting support and care of my wife, Atiya, and some welcome distractions from our grandson, Amaan.

This book project faced unprecedented roadblocks because access to some research material was delayed due to the pandemic. There were moments of depression, when writing and thinking seemed meaningless, as friends and family were struggling to cope with life and death situations. It was one of the most challenging tasks for me, both personally as well as professionally. It also led to many missed deadlines, which is definitely not the way I've worked over the past four decades. However, this modest attempt to comprehend Maulana Azad's life and career shall bring out, I hope, many facets that will help us understand both his Islam as well as his idea of India.

S. Irfan Habib
August 2022
New Delhi

INTRODUCTION

It is not an easy task to write about someone whose life was a miscellany of sorts, ranging from journalism, religion, politics, and philosophy to education. Maulana Abul Kalam Azad's interests were as diverse as the country he fought to liberate and build afresh. There are some profiles of this man who occupied centre stage in our struggle for freedom for over four decades. Many of them are in Urdu and thus offer limited access to those who want to understand this charismatic man. Azad loved his solitude and seldom opened up in public, particularly about his personal life. He was aloof, cold, and detached, much like his arch-rival, Muhammad Ali Jinnah. A reticent man, he was unwilling to write about himself. Whenever he did so, it was under strong inducements and pressure from others, which, due to his courteous nature, he could not always resist.[1] So it is not an easy task for researchers to put together a detailed biographical account.

There are a few sources that have been used by most of his biographers, though all of them are suspect in one way or the other. The best known is *India Wins Freedom*, which was not penned by him—it was dictated by Azad to the novelist and politician Humayun Kabir. Another work is *Tazkirah*, which has a lot about Azad's ancestors, but says precious little about Azad himself. It was published by Azad's friend Fazluddin Ahmad, but it did not have Azad's approval and he was not happy that it had been made public. However, M. Mujeeb*, an Urdu scholar and educator, had a different

*Professor M. Mujeeb (1902–85) was a scholar of Urdu and English literature, an educationist, and one of the vice-chancellors of Jamia Milia Islamia University, New Delhi.

take: 'The *Tazkirah* cannot be fully understood unless one begins at the end, with the author's discussion of himself. This would explain not only his attitude but also his style, for his vigour and fluency, his symbolism, his lordship of the heaven and earth of the Urdu language are not literary attainments only, but the overflow of a spiritual force, the result of an illumination that is not of the light of this world.'[2] Mujeeb finds that the book is spontaneous and thus offers a more credible account of Azad's life and family. The third book is *Azad ki Kahani Khud Azad ki Zubani*. It was published by Abdur Razzaq Malihabadi after Azad's death in 1958 and no one saw the original manuscript. Thus, these sources can be used only if the facts therein are corroborated by other available sources—serious scholars like V. N. Datta have used this method and I have tried to follow the same.

I must also refer to two biographies of Azad which were published during his lifetime. One was by Mahadev Desai, titled *Maulana Abul Kalam Azad: The President of Indian National Congress, A Biographical Memoir*, published in 1941, which delved into his ancestry and political career to justify his election as Congress president in 1940. *Maulana Abul Kalam Azad*, published in 1946 by A. B. Rajput, was again a hagiographical account and not a scholarly work.

However, despite all these limitations, there have been some serious biographies, like the ones by V. N. Datta, Ian Henderson Douglas, Malikzada Manzoor Ahmad, and Syeda Saiyidain Hameed. There is also an interesting and detailed account of his political struggle, mainly his fight against communal politics, by Rizwan Qaiser. There are quite a few scholars in Pakistan as well, like Abu Salman Shahjahanpuri, who devoted many years unravelling Azad's work on Islam and little else. With this work, my attempt is to create an exhaustive biographical account of Azad, delving deep into the decisive moments in his life that have a direct bearing on our present. This book is not a chronological account of his life, so I go back and forth to reflect on his thoughts on issues of religion, politics, as well as on other crucial matters.

I want to understand Maulana Azad against the current Islamic and national context, as well as a historical figure. To this end, I have tried to locate Azad in terms of ideas—theological, political, and philosophical. I have deliberately left out many details about his journalistic career, which have been dealt with in detail by Datta, and his detailed political profile that has been the subject of Rizwan Qaiser's book, *Resisting Colonialism and Communal Politics: Maulana Azad and the Making of the Indian Nation* (2011). While I have not looked at these aspects in depth, I have not left them totally untouched.

◆

Azad belonged to a family that had its roots in Delhi from the time of the Mughals. His father, Maulana Khairuddin (1831–1908) had migrated from India to Arabia (present-day Saudi Arabia) with his family a few years before the 1857 revolt. This emigration was not unusual—many Muslim families did the same, anticipating the end of Mughal rule and the subsequent decline in patronage for them under the British regime. The scholarly families chose Hejaz as their destination, where the holy cities of Mecca and Medina are located. Maulana Khairuddin's family also reached Hejaz under the care of his maternal grandfather, Maulana Munawaruddin (1787–1861).

Maulana Khairuddin (1831–1908) became a reputed scholar of Arabic and Islamic theology and was a passionate believer in the Qadariya Sufi order. He married Aliya Begam, who was the niece of Sheikh Mohammad Zahir Watri, the mufti of Mecca and a renowned scholar. Khairuddin travelled widely in the Islamic world and was closely associated with the Ottoman elite in Constantinople (present-day Istanbul).

Azad was born Mohiuddin Ahmad on 11 November 1888, seventeen years after his parents got married, in Qidwah in the holy city of Mecca. The house in which he was born was located near the Baab-al-Salaam, one of the gates of the Great Mosque of Mecca.* Azad was the youngest of five children—he had three sisters and a brother. After spending a few decades in Hejaz, Khairuddin returned to India with his family in 1895 and chose Calcutta as his home at the insistence of many of his rich murids (disciples), who promised him support if he moved to their city. At this time, he was around sixty, tall, and walked with a limp due to a knee injury. He was a learned man whose life was governed by Islam and its moral code. Azad was seven years old at the time of the move. His eldest sister, Zainab, had been born in Constantinople; his other sisters were Fatima, who was a poet and used 'Arzoo' as her takhallus (poetic name), and Hanifa, also a poet whose takhallus was 'Abroo'. Ghulam Yasin, his brother, became known in the literary world as Abu Nasr 'Aah'. The youngest, Mohiuddin Ahmad, later named himself Abul Kalam Azad.

Azad (as he came to be known) did not attend any madrassa or university but was taught at home, with his father being his first teacher. Khairuddin carefully chose other teachers for the young Azad—Maulvi Mohammad Yaqub of Delhi, and later Maulana Saadat Hasan of Aliya Madrassa, Calcutta. Azad completed his early education by the age of twelve, at which time he was competent in Persian and had a rudimentary knowledge of Arabic. He gained proficiency in Persian literature through the teachings of Mirza Mohammad Husain, who had come to Calcutta from Iran.[3] Azad became so proficient that he began work on his Persian dictionary before he was ten years old.[4] Azad got married in 1901 to

*Baab-al-Salaam, means 'Gate of Peace'. Azad's exact date of birth is shrouded in mystery, though the year 1888 was confirmed by Azad in *India Wins Freedom* but he was not sure of the exact date. According to Ghulam Rasool Mehr, Azad was born on 17 or 18 August 1888. V. N. Datta, *Maulana Azad*, New Delhi: Manohar Publishers and Distributors, 1990, p. viii.

Zulaikha, the daughter of Aftab Ahmad, one of his father's disciples in Calcutta; he was about thirteen while his wife was seven years old.

His life began with a struggle against the family milieu, particularly his father, a Sufi pir (guide) who was surrounded by murids (disciples) who would kiss his hands and touch his feet. Disgusted by this cohort of followers that was blind in its devotion to his father, Azad turned to rationalism, inspired by the writings of Sir Syed Ahmad Khan, the nineteenth-century reformer and philosopher. According to the scholar Mohammad Habib, 'it is impossible to deny that he passed through an acute, though short-lived, period of tension during which his old ideas were completely shaken and he adopted that progressive attitude which distinguished him to the end of his life.'[5] Azad revered his father and learnt much from his life and scholarship, yet he instinctively knew the point at which he diverged from his father's beliefs. I have tried to unravel that early phase of his life which had a lasting impact on his later intellectual and public career. I have also attempted to study Wahhabism and its emergence in the late eighteenth-century Arab world. Khairuddin's antipathy for this version of Islam taught young Azad many lessons.

Later, in his twenties, Azad's travels to West Asia brought about a huge shift in his political understanding of the world and of Islam. He understood the realities of colonial oppression and territorial nationalism. All this stimulated Azad to launch a similar tirade against the oppressive colonial regime in India.

He fought this fight, at first, through his paper *Al-Hilal* in 1912, which became very popular, especially with Muslim readers. At this time, Azad distanced himself from Sir Syed Ahmad Khan's influence as well.

Al-Hilal truly reflected Maulana Azad's understanding of Islam as well as his anti-imperialist urge, which soon blossomed into action at the national level. He used his own scanty resources to publish it and did not even accept advertisements to raise funds. As a result, the colonial government saw the independently-run publication as seditious and mounted attacks in the form of fines and security deposits. In the face of mounting attacks, Maulana decided to shut down the paper and launched a fresh one called *Al-Balagh* on 12 November 1915, which continued till 13 March 1916. Maulana had to stop this paper as well because the government exiled him to Moorabadi, a small tribal village near Ranchi.

Anti-colonial sentiments began to rise during Azad's house arrest near Ranchi, which lasted more than three years. India had already seen two Home Rule League agitations led by Bal Gangadhar Tilak and Annie Besant. Mahatma Gandhi had experimented with two mass movements in Champaran and Kheda in 1917–18. The British government had brought in the repressive Rowlatt Act, which led to a mass upsurge and ultimately culminated in the tragic massacre of the innocent and peaceful crowd in Jallianwala Bagh on 13 April 1919. Mahatma Gandhi had already extended his support to the Khilafat Movement with the intention of getting more support for the anti-colonial struggle in the subcontinent. Azad was released during this period of significant political developments on 27 December 1919, but he stayed in Ranchi until the beginning of January 1920.

On his release, Azad had to decide between himself a secluded corner where he could read and write or throwing his weight behind the freedom struggle. 'It was a torrent in consonance with my will and intent, a torrent in which I could hear the voice of heavens, calling a man to accept God's will instead of his own.'[6] Ultimately, Azad upheld 'God's will' and surrendered his own, thus making a sacrifice for the cause of the country.[7] It was soon after his release from jail that Azad first met Gandhi on 18 January 1920. The meeting seemed to have had a profound impact on both men. Gandhi had tried meeting Azad in Ranchi while he was interned there, but the government did not permit this.[8] Azad entered the nationalist struggle through the Khilafat agitation and was later closely involved with most of the mass movements that we shall briefly discuss. Soon after coming out of exile, he presided over the Khilafat Committee meeting in Calcutta in February 1920, where he presented the programme of non-cooperation,[9] which was adopted by the All India Khilafat Committee four months before the Congress did.[10] In a way, Azad was responsible, along with Mahatma Gandhi, for the adoption of the non-cooperation programme,[11] though the latter became the sole exponent and practitioner of the idea.

It is pertinent here to refer briefly to Maulana's role as Congress president twice—both occasions were equally challenging. Maulana was released from prison on 1 January 1923 after the Khilafat-Non-cooperation protests but found the political climate in the country rather dismal. The Congress party was on the verge of a split on the issue of council entry, the two groups were 'No-Changers' and 'Pro-Changers' and the senior Congress leadership was divided on the issue. Azad was asked to chair the special session of the Congress in Delhi on 15 December 1923. This speaks volumes about Azad's stature, as he was accepted by all despite being just thirty-five-years old. He did succeed in reconciling the two Congress factions, thus preventing the catastrophic split.

The second challenge came in 1940 when the Congress party decided to field Maulana Azad for the position of Congress president, again in a very volatile political situation. Once Gandhi threw his weight behind Azad, there was hardly any contest. Azad polled 1,841 votes against his rival M. N. Roy, who got only 181 votes.[12] The Muslim League and Jinnah had been vociferous in their demand for a separate Muslim nation earlier that year, so Azad had a huge task ahead of him—he had to convince Jinnah that after living together for centuries, 'We all are an indivisible nation. No vision of separation from each other can ever fructify.'[13] Jinnah and the Muslim League saw Azad's stance as a major challenge to

Muslim consolidation, which was a crucial factor in lobbying for a separate state successfully. Jinnah's hostility towards Azad was palpable:

> I refuse to discuss with you by correspondence or otherwise as you have completely forfeited the confidence of Muslim India. Cannot you realize that you are made a Muslim Show Boy Congress President? You represent neither Muslims nor Hindus. The Congress is a Hindu body. If you have self respect resign at once. You have done your worst against the League so far. I know you have hopelessly failed. Give it up.[14]

Azad remained steadfast in his role as the president of the Congress during these turbulent political times, which finally led to the historic Quit India resolution during the AICC meeting in Bombay during 7–9 August 1942. Gandhi declared that the Quit India Movement had to be based on non-violence, just as his previous movements had been. In a last bid to quell dissent, all senior leaders of the Congress were arrested soon after this by colonial authorities, including Maulana Azad, who was sent to the Ahmednagar Fort prison. Azad was released after three years in June 1945, during which he lost his wife. The Muslim League used this opportunity, when most of the Congress leaders were incarcerated, to communalize the polity to an irreversible degree.

◆

I have tracked Maulana Azad's evolution as a religious scholar and as a nationalist through his own writings as well as by looking at his contribution to the freedom struggle. His task was not just to be involved in the attempts to emancipate India from imperialist bondage but to keep the country united despite the nefarious designs of fissiparous forces. In most of his writings 'whatever the subject dealt with, the dual purpose was always kept in view, viz., fighting British imperialism on the one hand, and Moslem medievalism on the other.'[15] He had to argue against both Hindu and Muslim communalists. Azad was prophetic in his observations, particularly in the context of identity and nationalism, which is reflected repeatedly in several of his writings. It will be instructive to read what he said to a group of Muslims from United Provinces who had decided to leave for Pakistan in 1947:

> You are leaving your motherland. Do you know what the consequences will be? Your frequent exoduses such as this will weaken the Muslims of India. A time may come when the various Pakistani regions start asserting their separate identities, Bengali, Punjabi, Sindhi, Baloch may declare themselves separate qaums. Will your position in Pakistan be anything more than uninvited guests? The Hindu can be your religious opponent but not your regional and national opponent. You can deal with this situation. But in Pakistan, at any time you will have to face regional and national opposition. Before this opposition, you will be helpless![16]

Azad was truly prescient in his observations. Most of those who migrated from India are still not fully assimilated, they are all dubbed 'muhajirs' who decided to move to the so-called 'Land of the Pure'.

While Azad was pre-occupied with his mission of bringing as many Muslims as possible into the Congress fold, Hindu and Muslim communal forces continued to fan religious hatred. While disagreeing about most things, they concurred on the issue of the two-nation theory. Savarkar's presidential address at the nineteenth Hindu Mahasabha session at Ahmedabad affirmed this:

> As it is, there are two antagonistic nations living side by side in India, several infantile politicians commit the serious mistake in supposing that India is already welded into a harmonious nation, or that it could be welded thus

> for the mere wish to do so. These were well meaning but unthinking friends taking their dreams for realities. That is why they are impatient of communal tangles and attribute them to communal organisations.[17]

Savarkar was condescending when he called national leaders 'infantile politicians'. He also ended up defending the Muslim League's demand for a separate nation when he reduced Hindu–Muslim relations in the country as simply antagonistic. He goes further and says:

> But the solid fact is that the so-called communal questions are but a legacy handed down to us by centuries of cultural, religious, and national antagonism between the Hindus and Muslims.... Let us bravely face unpleasant facts as they are. India cannot be assumed today to be unitarian and homogenous nation, but on the contrary, there are two nations in the main: the Hindus and the Muslims, in India.[18]

Once the colonial authorities began characterizing India's past through a communal lens, it became convenient for Hindu communalists to sow the seeds of discord. For Hindu nationalists, the British were saviours who had rescued them from Muslim 'barbarism'. Colonial historians documented and depicted our medieval past as an endlessly blood-soaked period where Hindus had been subjugated and oppressed for centuries. This facilitated the colonial as well as communalist agenda and made the task of leaders like Azad even more difficult. The same communal agenda and arguments continue even now, making the task of defending our inherited composite nation more complicated. Another important aspect of this biography is to challenge several stereotypes and made-up facts about our past that are today being peddled as history.

This book also aims to explore another important facet of Azad's life that deals with his engagement and interpretation of the Quran and its significance today. Azad went through a phase of unbelief as well. Eventually, after this prolonged phase of unbelief ended, a somewhat refurbished faith came back to Azad, but the scepticism never left him. Azad always stressed on the use of critical faculties, which, he believed, God gifted to humans to make them ashraful makhluqat, or the best of God's creations. His *Tarjuman al-Quran* was an interpretation of faith with a comparative religious perspective and not an attempt to place Islam on a higher pedestal.

> If humanity is to be brought together it will only be on the basis of mutual understanding, especially in matters of fundamental belief. The philosophical understanding of the nature of ultimate reality, and the practice of love, regardless of the distinction of creed, community, and nationality, these are the basic teachings of the Quran.[19]

This was the spirit of the faith he practised and preached all his life. It inspired his politics and his definition of identity and nationalism as well. It was humanism that remained supreme, taking precedence over religious or national identity.

Maulana's internment in the Ahmednagar Fort prison in 1942 for three years brought out an unusual and interesting aspect of his life in the form of epistolary essays published as *Ghubar-i-Khatir* (*The Dust of Memories*). I have devoted a chapter to discuss some of these serious as well as not so serious essays on diverse subjects ranging from history, philosophy, ornithology, and tea to music. *Ghubar-i-Khatir* is an important source, for it provides readers with unbridled access to Azad's family, his education, his likes and dislikes, and his general sensibilities, and thus is an authentic source for his biographical account. This book also represents a shift in Azad's writing style from his early writings. Azad began writing very early in the twentieth century in various journals and newspapers such as *Lisan al-Sidq*, *Al-Nadwa*, and *Al-Hilal* etc. But in *Ghubar-i-Khatir*, his prose was measured, much less verbose, and unlike his earlier works. *Ghubar-i-Khatir* was published in 1946 and sold out fast—a second edition had to be printed by Hali Publishing House that same year. It was sought after not only because Azad had published a book after a long gap but also because it was an unusual book. The third edition of the book was published from Lahore in 1947 by an old admirer of Azad, Lala Pindi Das*. It carried an important letter on music which was missing in the first two editions. After his magnum opus *Tarjuman al-Quran*, *Ghubar-i-Khatir* is an important text that reveals diverse hidden aspects of Maulana's life and his intellectual and social concerns.

Another significant issue that is relevant and necessary to raise and talk about in detail is the idea of nationalism—something we confront every day in our lives and not always in a peaceful manner. Maulana wrote and spoke extensively on this issue, both in the Islamic as well as national context. He travelled to Egypt and other West Asian countries in 1908–1909, an experience that expanded his horizon of what constitutes a 'national identity'. Azad was greatly influenced by Egyptian nationalist leaders like Mustafa Kamil Pasha, who spoke of a territorial nationalism where the collaboration of Coptic Christians and Muslims was indispensable to build a viable nationalist force against colonial oppressors. Thus, Maulana Azad saw himself as a Muslim, but at the same time he also declared himself a proud Indian and an important part of the indivisible unity called Indian nationality. It was a precious part of his being, which he was not prepared to surrender at any cost. Azad declared in 1921 that 'the need

*Lala Pindi Das was one of the old revolutionaries of Punjab. He was a founder of the first revolutionary organization, Bharat Mata Sabha. Lala Lajpat Rai was also one of the founding members of this sabha and it was one of the first organizations that led a peasants' struggle in Punjab in the early twentieth century. Maulana Azad is also known to have travelled to Punjab during his short revolutionary phase and met Sardar Ajit Singh and Sufi Amba Prasad in 1906–1907. This is an updated note in Malik Ram's by introduction to *Ghubar-i-Khatir*, p. 13 in the English edition *Sallies of Mind*, translated by D. R. Goyal, New Delhi: Shipra Publications, 2003.

of the hour is that the seven crore Muslims living in India should establish such close ties and develop such fellow feeling with the twenty-two crore Hindus that they may henceforth be reckoned as one single nation and country, as inseparable parts of one combined and indivisible whole.'[20] He wanted Hindus and Muslims to be part of one homogenous group which he called Ummat-i-Wahida, or one nation. This was the spirit that permeated his idea of India and of Indian nationalism which I have attempted to explain in one of the chapters of this book.

After Independence, Azad took over as the minister of education, science, and culture, with the task of reconstructing an India that had suffered severe blows to its cultural and social fabric for over two hundred years under colonial rule. As he took charge of the first education ministry, Azad had numerous challenges ahead of him. He had to mend fences between the Hindus and Muslims after the tragic Partition and simultaneously rebuild an independent India. He had to cope with the uneven spread of education among India's masses. He was also aware of a huge adult population which needed to be educated outside the formal school education system. He saw it as an imperative task, intrinsic to democratic governance, 'the problem of adult education has become even more important than it was in the past'. Adults needed not only literacy but a broad and holistic social education to contribute to a newly independent society, he felt. He also had to firm up the higher education system and thus set up an Education Commission in 1948, which was chaired by Dr Radhakrishnan. The Commission submitted its report within a year in 1949, focusing mainly on higher education, though secondary education was also covered in its recommendations. It was Azad's recommendations that led to the founding of the University Grants Commission as a controlling body of university education in India; it remains an important statutory body even today. Several crucial steps were taken regarding many Delhi university colleges—Shantiniketan, Jamia Millia Islamia, and others, during Azad's tenure.

Azad was one with Nehru in his faith in the industrial and technological progress of the country, something which had to be accomplished on a priority basis given the exploitative colonial regime that had ignored such developmental aspects. As a result, a network of institutions focusing on technological education came up in the 1950s—the Indian Institutes of Technology (IITs) and the diverse laboratories under the Council of Scientific and Industrial Research (CSIR), although the CSIR had been founded by the British as a wartime facility in 1942. The All India Council of Technical Education was refurbished and the Indian Institute of Science, Bangalore, made rapid progress. This decade can be seen as a foundational one in the context of much needed advancements in technical and scientific education as well as research in India.

There is a lot to admire in Maulana Azad's life, even from his childhood, yet we do need an objective gaze to comprehend such an eventful and complex life. The majority of the works about Azad concentrate on evaluating him as a man of letters and as an Islamic scholar. I believe that we need to understand his engagement with his faith in the radically altered global Islamic context. Thus, I have attempted to locate him in a milieu where most of the critical space within Islam has been reduced to a sort of dogmatic ritualism. Azad took up the arduous project of interpreting and translating the Quran to challenge the detractors of the faith within as well as outside. This task is more urgently required now, though I have noted that Azad's intellectual concerns were not taken seriously even during his own life time. I stress again, as I have done before, that this book is a modest attempt to locate Maulana Azad in the present context of Islam as well as nationalism, as both are not only being misinterpreted but even vandalized today. I will end this section with quite an apt description of Azad by Humayun Kabir:

> With so many gifts and such sensitiveness, it was inevitable that a man like Maulana Azad was lonely in spirit.... Courteous, kindly and a man of infinite charm, he yet breathed an atmosphere of reserve which few could penetrate. He lived in his own world of thought, and out of his musings derived the strength to endure the giant agony of the world. With all his exquisite sense of human suffering, there was in him a courage of endurance and an optimism about the essential goodness of man which sustained him in the midst of all his sufferings.[21]

My attempt in the following chapters is to understand Azad with all the strengths and weaknesses pointed out in the above passage. His faith in the essential goodness of man is reflected in his magnanimity and courtesy towards all those Muslim Leaguers who derided and even abused him all the time. He remained firm in his faith in composite nationalism but never stooped to cross the limits of civility. Despite being mocked, jeered, and dismissed, Azad ignored Jinnah's abusive retorts, even when he dubbed him the showboy of the Congress and an agent of the Hindus.

ONE

THE EARLY YEARS

Mohinuddin Ahmad* was born in Arabia (Mecca) in 1888 to an Arab mother and Indian father. His chronogrammatic name was Feroz Bakht:

> My father gave me the *tarikhi* (calender) name Feroz Bakht; and derived my birth date according to the Hijri calendar from the following line of a couplet:
>
> Jawan Bakht o Jawan Talae, Jawan-baad
> Of exalted destiny, brilliant future, strong support†

His family had migrated from Delhi to Arabia just before the 1857 upsurge. They moved again, when he was between the ages of seven and nine, to Calcutta, and Azad spent his early life there. A precocious child, he did not have much of a childhood, instead stepping into adulthood straight away.

It is a difficult task for any biographer to write a detailed account of Azad's early life and childhood. He seldom wrote or spoke about that period, and most of his biographers have extrapolated based on his writings. Doing this is not only an arduous task, it can also be a little risky as the author may

*He changed his name to Abul Kalam (Father of the Word) when he was very young, and later added 'Azad' when he started writing around the age of eleven.

†It was common practice to calculate the numerical value of each alphabet and compose a line or couplet to commemorate special events like births and deaths. Mohammad Mujeeb, 'The Tadhkirah: A biography in Symbol', in Humayun Kabir (ed.), *Maulana Abul Kalam Azad: A Memorial Volume*, New Delhi: Asia Publishing House, 1959, p. 310. Cited in Syeda Saiyidain Hameed, *Islamic Seal on India's Independence: Abul Kalam Azad-A Fresh Look*, Karachi: Oxford University Press, 1998, p. 4–5.

end up interpreting using their own experiences and biases.

Azad's family belonged to a city that had witnessed many periods of rise and decline in history. And this was not limited to mere political ups and downs but also manifested in the city's cultural and religious life. Very few are aware that Maulana Azad's family had a deep connection with Delhi. And this connection goes back to the Mughal period, something that he has referred to in his autobiographical account, *Tazkirah*. Azad's ancestors came to Delhi from Central Asia during the Sultanate period, and some of them acquired reputations as scholars of Islam during the Mughal Age.

As I have mentioned, Azad's father, Maulana Khairuddin, left Delhi with his maternal grandfather just before the 1857 revolt. Many foresaw the imminent crisis taking shape around the city; in addition, they had been affected by the decline in Mughal fortunes and the rise of the East India Company. As a result, many Muslim scholars and members of the elite class began leaving India, and most of them chose Hejaz as their destination. Azad gives an account of his maternal home in his *Tazkirah*:

> My native city is Delhi...but my mother came from the city built on sacred ground, the city to which the Prophet migrated, the city of his Prophethood, of Revelation (Medina). It is the city to which the worshippers of love turn. It is the Ka'aba for those who live in the ecstasies of prayer.[1]

Before I discuss his familial background and its influences, let me share Azad's observations about race and family. He wrote in *Ghubar-i-Khatir* that 'everyone's moral and social framework is created from the dust of his race and family and I know that my case is no different. Every family develops an individuality through its traditional life which gets transferred from generation to generation.'[2] He was aware that his family background had a tremendous influence on his life: 'The family effect is manifest in all my moves, habits, behaviour, and tastes. These traditions I have inherited from both the maternal and paternal sides. Both were dyed in tradition and its continuity that came to be my inheritance.' However, he goes on to express discomfort with this inheritance: 'I do not find anything—family, education, and [my] early environment in tune with me. Whatever condition and environment that could influence my ideas I think of, none had any place for me; I search but don't find myself anywhere!'[3]

The *Tazkirah* starts with a brief reference to Maulana Azad's family. 'In my family three different lines have converged and all these three families had produced men of wisdom, with gifts of spiritual leadership. No member of any of these families had any desire for worldly fame and eminence, but the world was always offering them honour and authority, which they sometimes accepted and sometimes refused.'[4] However, he was conscious that mere familial connection did not matter and he did not want, even for a moment, to promote himself as someone who belongs to an illustrious family. He says: 'Islam demolished all distinctions and familial associations, and emphasized only on one nisbat (relationship) which is just human. Is there any other relationship possible that a Muslim may like to seek?'[5] Despite immense admiration and respect for his family and their achievements, Azad was clear that what matters is the knowledge achieved through one's own struggle and not what has been inherited through family association.

Pride in the family is one of the many remnants (idols) of the jahiliyya phase (the period preceding the revelation of the Quran), which Islam demolished. It is possible that a new Muslim from an untouchable caste may, through the dint of his hard work, excel more than the families of shaykh al-Islams, the Ottoman-era scholars of Islamic sciences. Azad was quite prophetic when he said that 'it may happen tomorrow though we see even today that the "angel of action" (amal ka farishta) reduces many from big to small and many others from small to big.'[6]

We see in both *Tazkirah* and *Kahani* that Azad indulges in profuse admiration for some of his ancestors. One of the most prominent people Maulana Azad talks about in *Tazkirah* is a maternal ancestor of his father's, Maulana Sheikh Jamaluddin alias Sheikh Bahlol of Delhi. Sheikh Jamaluddin was one of the best-known Islamic scholars of Mughal emperor Akbar's age, a time of great intellectual and theological churning. Understanding the lives of Azad's early ancestors is indispensable to understanding his own intellectual and Islamic personality. We can see quite distinctly that his mind was shaped by his ancestry. Yet he felt that 'one should not establish one's reputation by vaunting the accomplishments of one's ancestors. Rather one should prove oneself a worthy descendant by one's accomplishments.'[7] This appears a bit ambiguous, and we will encounter many such ambiguities in his career, some of which will be clarified by his own intellectual and political advancement later in his life.

Maulana Azad inherited truthfulness and the courage to state the truth from Sheikh Jamaluddin, who outright refused to declare Emperor Akbar the Imam-i-Adil (the Just Leader). Most of the ulema had signed the mahzar (declaration) of 1579 in the capital of Fatehpur Sikri. When it was sent to Delhi for the consent of the ulema here. Sheikh Jamaluddin reacted, saying, 'Why should we fakirs and people living in seclusion be troubled?' referring to the greater austerity of the Delhi sheikhs and their careful distance from the glamour and lure of the court.[8] Azad informs us in *Kahani* that Sheikh Jamaluddin was an acclaimed teacher who made India known for Hadith instruction.[9] Azad's story of his ancestors emphasizes their firm convictions concerning religious authority, their reputation as religious teachers, and their association with the great religious figure of Sheikh Ahmad Sirhindi.[10] Jamaluddin courageously defended this Naqshbandi theologian when he fell out of favour at Jahangir's court.[11] Abdul Qadir Badauni, the writer, defended the orthodox version of Islam during Akbar's rule. It was the ijtihadi and tahqiqi Islam—Islam based on independent reasoning and facts—that advocated independent thinking and reasoning, which was seen as the bane of orthodox Islam.[12] To avoid the complication that would arise from this conflict, Sheikh Jamaluddin decided to move to Mecca along with his disciples because 'the world has changed, the government of the day is now in the grip of duniyasaaz and deenbaaz people'.[13] There is no place left even for the reclusive or gosha nasheen such as him, and Azad explained this:

Daaman us ka to bhala door hai dast-i-junoon
Kyon hai bekar, gareban to mera door nahin[14]

Granted, the hem of his robe is beyond reach,
O hand of frenzy
Why remain idle, my collar is not far

Azad also writes about Jamaluddin's involvement in the Mahdavia controversy in the late fifteenth century that raged during Akbar's time—his observations in *Tazkirah* reflect his own understanding of Islam centuries later. When Syed Muhammad Jaunpuri declared himself the Mahdi, or messianic figure, leading to a huge outcry against him from the ulema, Sheikh Jamaluddin took a firm and categorical position. He wrote a book, says Maulana Azad, where he endeavoured to prove with incontrovertible arguments that the sainthood (vilayet) of Syed Muhammad of Jaunpur was true (haq) but the belief that he was the promised Mahdi (Mahdi al-Mauood) was not sound (batil).[15]

Azad then discusses the other line of ancestry, his father's maternal grandfather, Munawaruddin. Munawaruddin's father came from Herat as part of the entourage of Ahmad Shah Abdali and died fighting the Sikhs. Munawaruddin, at the age of sixteen, ran away from home to study with Shah

Abdul Aziz, a Sufi of the Naqshbandi order, in Delhi. He was, according to Azad, a great scholar who also looked after Azad's father Khairuddin. Abdur Razzaq Malihabadi has written about the stature and erudition of Munawaruddin on behalf of Maulana Azad. However, some scholars, like Mushir ul-Haq, do not agree with Malihabadi's assessment since it was patronised by Azad.[16]

However, despite all these discrepancies in the accounts, what we know is that Azad admired his ancestors. This is also significant in understanding Azad's predilections and choices.

Azad describes Munawaruddin's independence thus: 'In spite of royal contacts, he chose poverty as his way of life, never going to any rich man's house; and he practised enjoining the just and forbidding the evil'.[17] This is one of the many prime aspects of Maulana Azad's life we will discuss later in different contexts of his career.

Munawaruddin, and many other Muslims, felt uneasy with the socio-political developments in and around Delhi—the decline of the Mughals and rise of the East India Company. Many feared that the British would interfere with, and even challenge, their faith and culture through the East India Company. Anticipating the turmoil, they chose hijrat (migration), a well-established practice among educated Muslims all over the world. Even before the events of 1857 came to pass, they decided to leave India and move to Mecca. Munawaruddin moved with his family, which included Azad's father Khairuddin. There is some disagreement regarding the fate of Munawaruddin—some reports say that he died in Bhopal while others believe that he travelled to Bombay but died there and did not reach Mecca. In any case, the family, including Khairuddin, managed to reach Mecca.

The whole region of Arabia (it was not yet called Saudi Arabia* when Azad's family arrived there) was part

---

*I am not aware of any other example in today's world where a country is named after the ruling family. It is important to raise this because the Ibn Saud family was

of the Ottoman empire and involved in persistent violent engagements with the Wahhabis and the collaborating Saudi Arabs from the Najd region. The Ottomans were fighting the emerging nexus between Abdul Wahhab and Ibn Saud, which would turn out to be the most toxic collaboration in the history of Islam.

From the early nineteenth century onwards, the tussle between the Wahhabis and other Muslims intensified. The Najdi Wahhabis considered Hejaz a territory to be conquered, subjugated, and corrected, as it was in control of the Ottomans, being technically a Dar al-Harb (a territory of war). On the contrary, it was Najd (or rather the southern parts of it) which, in the early years of Islam, was the abode of the anti-prophet Musaylimah,* and was thus accursed territory that could in no way figure as Dar al Hijra (a place of refuge), as the Wahhabites claimed.[18] Even the Prophet himself believed Najd to be one of the cursed regions of Arabia and also believed that this region will one day raise a calamitous challenge to Islam. It was as this ideological battle was raging that Khairuddin, Azad's father, reached Hejaz in Arabia.

Khairuddin saw the Wahhabis in action, practising and preaching a version of Islam that he saw as a perversion of his faith. His contempt for Wahhabism was intense and anything remotely connected to it was anathema to him. This not only impacted his life but also informed Azad's in significant ways as we shall see.

---

in league with Abdul Wahhab, who despised those who venerated the Prophet and his family. And he did that by flaunting his version of Islam (Wahhabism) in which the veneration of an individual or family was forbidden.

*Musaylimah's real name was Maslamah ibn Habib. He belonged to the tribe of Banu Hanifa, one of the largest tribes of Arabia that inhabited the region of Najd. Musaylimah declared himself a prophet and had a considerable number of followers. He questioned several Quranic teachings and practices like selecting Kaaba as direction of prayer, prescribing three daily prayers, and much more. Muslim historians allege that he was a skilled magician who dazzled the crowd with miracles.

Muhammad Ibn Abdul Wahhab, the founder of Wahhabism, was born in 1703 in the central Arabian region of Najd. We know little about his early life but he 'emerged from an emptiness that was not only physical and economic but social, intellectual, and spiritual'.[19] He belonged to a family of scholars in the small oasis town of Uyayna. He had extremist religious tendencies as a young man, which both his father and brother Suleiman warned the world about. Suleiman even wrote a book, *Divine Thunderbolts*, opposing him and his philosophy. Abdul Wahhab condemned all mystical practices associated with Sufism as deviations from the true path of Islam. This antipathy towards mystic Islam was one of the major reasons for Khairuddin's dislike of Wahhabism. Wahhab travelled around in the Islamic world from Basra, Baghdad, Damascus, through Iran and India, with a plan to be a merchant. He returned to Najd around 1737–40 with a group of African slaves and a clear set of beliefs and the ambition to put them to practice immediately. He publicly gave a call for his version of Islam and was joined by some younger members of his family. Even though he hailed from one of the most backward regions of the Islamic lands, he appealed to the Muslim world far and wide—from the Balkans and Turkey, the ancient cities of Syria, and the culturally rich Iran and Central Asia, and of course to an intellectually aware India—to follow his vision of Islam, which he claimed was the authentic and original one. He ended up calling for a revolt against the Ottoman caliphate and even wrote a book called *Kitab al-Tawhid* (*The Book of Monotheism*). His book, and his philosophy in general, was inspired by the controversial Islamic thinker, writer, and activist Ibn Taymiyyah (1263–1328).* His

*Ibn Taymiyyah's full name was Taqi ad-Din Ahmad ibn Taymiyyah. It is unusual in that it is derived from a female ancestor as opposed to a male one, which was

Islam 'was puritanical, vigorous, simple. Its message was straightforward: a return to classical Islam.'[20]

Wahhab's call for revolt was a reaction to Ottoman misrule and weaknesses, and its perceived laxity in the practices of Islam according to him. He has been called a reformer, a man who hated taqlid or inherited traditions. This may be one of the reasons why Khairuddin hated him. But we need to explore the reform Wahhab believed in. In his view, merely deriding taqlid was not enough. Wahhab also hated the cultural diversities that Islam had acquired over the centuries as it expanded into different cultural and linguistic areas. He still perceived Islam as a narrow pristine faith of the Arabic-speaking tribal groups of the seventh and eighth centuries. Elsewhere I have described this as frozen Islam, an Islam with no dynamism or scope for change. To quote Wilfred C. Smith, 'It rejected the corruption and laxity of the contemporary decline. It rejected too the accommodations and cultural richness of the medieval empire. It rejected the introvert warmth and other-worldly piety of the mystic way. It rejected also the alien intellectualism not only of philosophy but of theology. It rejected all dissensions, even the now well-established Shi'ah.'[21] Truly, in the spirit of Islam, it began with negation and rejection of everything. It finally accepted only the Book and the Sunnah, the body of traditional social and legal customs in the Islamic tradition. Everything else was merely an unnecessary accretion that had crept in due to the influence of 'other' religions and cultures, which needed to be weeded out.

---

the custom at that time as it still is. Taymiyyah was a woman, famous for her scholarship and piety and the name Ibn Taymiyyah was used by many of her male descendants. He belonged to the Hanbali school of jurisprudence founded by Ahmad ibn Hanbal, a polarizing figure in his own lifetime. Ibn Taymiyyah's iconoclastic views on widely accepted Sunni doctrines such as the veneration of saints and visiting to their tomb-shrines made him unpopular with the majority of orthodox religious scholars of the time, under whose orders he was imprisoned several times. Maulana Azad himself was influenced to some extent by his views. Taymiyyah greatly impacted Wahhabi and Salafi Islamic ideology.

At first, the passionate Abdul Wahhab enjoyed the support of the ruler of his hometown. However, his views soon proved too controversial. When Wahhab ordered the public execution of a woman for adultery, leaders in neighbouring towns and key trade partners of 'Uyayna were appalled and alarmed. This was not Islam as the townspeople of Uyayna had known and practised their faith. They pressured their ruler to kill the radical theologian, but he chose to exile Ibn Abd al-Wahhab instead.'[22] The decision to exile him cost Islam quite dearly. The barbaric practice of chopping off the hands of a thief or stoning of women accused of adultery or such crimes were pre-Islamic Arab tribal practices which outraged most people even in those times. This is the Islam he finally peddled in collaboration with the Ibn Saud family. The Saudi regime today, and some Islamic countries that are under their influence, continue to use these barbaric punishments in the name of Islam. They have been used so widely and for so long that even calling them un-Islamic seems incongruous.

Abdul Wahhab and his version of Islam had precedents, chiefly in the form of the Khawarij of the seventh century.* Nor were they completely novel in the broader stream of world history. At the time Wahhab began recruiting followers, the burning of 'witches' had come to an end in Britain and Massachusetts, USA, only some decades ago and was still practised widely in the Catholic Inquisition in Peru and Mexico as well as Spain. The burning of books, too, was so widespread as to not even be noticed.[23]

The Najd region is known for producing early factionalists in Islam, particularly the Khawarij, who were overtly pious but baying for blood from within. Many leaders of the Khawarij came from the Banu Tamim, a powerful Najd tribe, of which Ibn Abdul Wahhab, born more than 1,000 years later after

---

*The Khawarij were an early faction of Islam in the seventh century. They were the supporters of Ali, the fourth caliph, but later turned against him and assassinated him in 661 CE.

the Khawarij, was a member. As noted by the commentator Kerim Fenari, the Banu Tamim came late to Islam. They first demanded a public debate with Prophet Muhammad, and there is a Hadith indicating they asked to be paid to convert to Islam.[24]

The exiled young theologian with dangerous ideas did not have to wander far. Wahhab was welcomed by the ruler of the nearby oasis of al-Diriyah, Ibn Saud. Modern Saudis date the founding of their state to this historic meeting in 1744–45, when the two men agreed that the reformed* Islam preached by Ibn Abdul Wahhab would be observed by the Saudi ruler and his followers. The Diriyah Agreement set out the basic tenets of the movement that would come to be called Wahhabism.[25]

The Wahhabis refused to accept the dynamism of Islam over the past few centuries, and its spread to diverse cultural and geographical regions. For the Wahhabis, the faith of the Prophet was frozen in time while, in reality, Islam had acquired diverse features and practices. The Wahhabis sought to draw a line around the seventh century after the revelation of the Quran, and to ban all subsequent developments as 'pernicious innovation'. There was, for instance, widespread veneration of saints and holy men in the Arab world, from the companions of Prophet Muhammad to the humblest of local holy men, each with his own shrine or sacred tree.[26] Abdul Wahhab chopped down sacred trees and shattered the tombs of holy men with his own hands, which horrified the Sunni Muslim society. Not just saint worship, he detested all aspects of mystic Islam. Islamic mysticism takes many forms, from the kind practised by mendicant ascetics to the famous whirling dervishes. 'Sufis use a wide range of techniques, from fasting

*It was clear from what followed from the mid-eighteenth century that it was not really a reformed Islam that the combine followed but a poorly deformed faith. It was an innovation and the poor imagination of its proponents that continues to torment Islam and its followers to this day.

to chanting and dancing to self-immolation, to reach the ecstasy of mystical union with the Creator.'[27] The Wahhabis were up in arms against the Ottoman empire, whose religious and social life was steeped in Sufism.

Maulana Khairuddin's deep dislike of the Wahhabis grew from his close proximity to the late nineteenth-century struggle between the Ottomans and the Wahhabi–Saudi partnership. He saw to it that his son, Azad, even as a child, stayed away from Wahhabi influence and strictly monitored the choice of his teachers at home, interrogating them about their faith. Any hint of Wahhabi linkage or sympathy would result in the interviewee being immediately rejected. Azad wrote in one of his letters in *Ghubar-i-Khatir* that 'I was educated in an atmosphere circumscribed by conservatism and conformity and had no opening for any outside wind. The teachers, apart from father, who taught me had been selected by father after making sure that they were true to the ideas and beliefs that he himself held and his test was so strongly rigid that hardly a few could pass.'[28]

Azad had some disagreements with his father and one of them was the linking of the Waliullahis with the Wahhabis.* During the late nineteenth century, the followers of Shah Waliullah from Delhi were mistaken for Wahhabis and their visit to Mecca invited protests from many Indians—chief among them Azad's father. The ulemas of Mecca convinced Khairuddin to write a detailed book explaining the truth about the Indian Wahhabis. The book, *Najm-al-Mubin fil Rajm-al-Shyatin*, ran into ten volumes, of which only two were published. Azad says that other volumes could not be published because of his father's travels.[29] Khairuddin also

*This link with the Wahhabis was not really very far-fetched, as there were many similarities between them. Both the groups believed that Islam had acquired some extraneous features due to its exposure to different religious and cultural practices. They wanted Islam to go back to its pristine purity. The Waliullahis talked of ijtihad (independent reasoning), not to open up Islam to modern, rational influences, but to question many of the 'newer' inherited beliefs.

wrote a book on the advice of the shaykh al-Islam of Turkey to prove that forefathers of the Prophet Muhammad were unitarians (muvahhid). In this book he took pains to prove that Abu Talib, the father of Ali and one of the uncles of the Prophet, was a Muslim.[30] The question of Abu Talib's faith has always been an issue between the Sunnis and the Shias, particularly because Muhammad was brought up by Abu Talib after the death of his father. Abu Talib is denigrated by the Wahhabbi Sunnis because he played a key role in Prophet Muhammad's life, from childhood to adulthood and even during his prophethood, often saving him from his enemies, mostly from the rivals of the Prophet's Banu Hashim tribe, one of the tribes of the Quraysh clans.

Khairuddin's prejudice against the Wahhabis continued even after he came back to India. His father's hostility towards the Wahhabis created for Azad the image of a Wahhabi as a monster, a kafir who condemned the Prophet, a one-eyed ugly man with a mutilated forehead who struck terror in him.[31] Within the family, Wahhabis were called mosquitoes or rats. These were early lessons for Azad where he learnt that blind antipathy towards anything, even if it was towards something as undesirable as Wahhabism, needed to be shunned. Azad tells a story about a man who had come to meet his father. When Azad asked his father who the man was, he responded curtly, 'The Wahhabbi'. Khairuddin had become furious when he came to know that the man held Wahhabi leanings and treated him shabbily. Despite Khairuddin's oppressive conduct, Azad picked up the courage to question his father and ask if this man had a black face. His father told him that the man had a black heart dotted with innumerable black and sinful spots.[32] Azad did not like this vilification and did not agree with the contempt hurled at the man for his Wahhabi beliefs. The issue proved to be a sore point between father and son. It was not that Azad had any love for the Wahhabis, but he disliked the idea of irrational hate for anything. Later in life, when Azad understood the history of Islam independently from his father, he freed himself from such prejudices, including the blinding hatred for Wahhabis.

MAULANA KHAIRUDDIN: A FORMATIVE INFLUENCE ON AZAD

Maulana Khairuddin, as pointed out before, was a formidable Arabic and Islamic scholar with a gigantic reputation in the Islamic world. Khairuddin married into the family of his teacher Sheikh Muhammad Zahir Watri, thus Azad's father was an Indian while his mother, Aliya, was an Arab.* As Hejaz was part of the Turkish empire, Khairuddin became a Turkish national and completed his education in Mecca. Azad was born there in 1888. He lived in Mecca till the age of nine or ten with his family—parents, three sisters, and a brother. During these years, Khairuddin visited Constantinople and stayed there for about two years. The sultan of Turkey gave him a pension, which is usually given to learned people.

Khairuddin was a reputed scholar and a Sufi of the Qadariya and Naqshbandi order. He was a man of immense personal piety. He would go to his room every evening at eleven, have a glass of milk, and then take some time to pray by name for all those who had sought his help or who treated him well. He never missed this prayer. Azad had faith in the effectiveness of his father's prayers in relieving the difficulties of his beseechers.[33] Though Khairuddin was known for his uncompromising antipathy towards Wahhabism, he never had any issues with other faiths and always stayed remarkably unprejudiced.

*There is no disagreement among scholars that his wife belonged the family of the famous Arab scholar Sheikh Muhammad Zahir Watri. But it's unclear whether she was his niece or daughter. Azad himself has given two views in two books. Azad's early biographer Mahadev Desai says that she was Sheikh Watri's daughter while Abdur Razzaq Malihabadi calls a the niece. However, all of them agree that she belonged to the great scholarly Watri family.

Khairuddin got his early education in Delhi* under the tutelage of Mufti Sadruddin, who was a remarkable authority on the Hadith. Sadruddin also performed the Dastar Bandi (turban tying) ceremony for Khairuddin that is done on the completion of the course. Mufti Sadruddin wrote poetry under the takhallus 'Azurda' and was closely involved with the teaching and administration at the famous Delhi College. As a member of the managing committee, 'he helped in the selection of competent teachers. In 1842 it was he who suggested the names of Ghalib, Imam Baksh Sahbai, and Momin as possible candidates for the post of a Persian teacher, and it was Sahbai who eventually got the job.'[34] (Ghalib felt insulted and went away as no one came to receive him at the gate of the college when he arrived for the interview.)

Khairuddin could cultivate relationships with the important people of his time due to the influential position of his grandfather Munawaruddin, who had access to the Mughal court. He used to participate in literary gatherings at the diwankhana of Mufti Sadruddin and Azad writes that he may have encountered the reformer and educationist Sir Syed Ahmad Khan at one such gathering.[35] He tells us that both Khairuddin and Sir Syed Ahmad Khan later nostalgically recollected these enjoyable literary gatherings, now a thing of the past.† However, Azad also wrote that his father had serious misgivings about Syed Ahmad and did not appreciate his son being influenced by Syed Ahmad's worldview, as we find out later.

Azad devotes a section in his *Kahani* to his father's love for books; boxes of them accompanied him on his travels. His love for books, Azad writes, was a passion that 'we are

*The family returned either in 1895 or 1898, the dates are not confirmed.

†However, it looks highly improbable that his father and Syed Ahmad could have ever met again. Khairuddin came back to India around 1896–97 and Syed Ahmad died in 1898. Khairuddin was not very favourably disposed towards Syed Ahmad Khan, as Azad repeatedly points out, so their meeting seems quite improbable, p. 159.

unable to express in words. Nothing among all the gifts of the world could unsettle him as much as the existence of a book, a book of his taste and liking.'[36] One of Khairuddin abiding passions was purchasing books wherever he was. He was familiar with all the big book shops in Hejaz, Iraq, Syria, Egypt, Constantinople, and Hindustan. He had longish stays of over one or even two years in Constantinople and Egypt, only because of his love for books.[37]

With no technology to easily copy books, whatever one needed from the library had to be copied by hand. Khairuddin got special permission from the Ottoman government to get books of his choice copied at the expense of the state. 'He copied many books himself in the libraries of Egypt, spending all his money in purchasing books of his choice or getting them copied in the libraries.'[38]

Azad goes on to say that his father was not concerned about the content of the books alone but also its form. Even if he had a certain book, he would buy the new edition of the same book, even if it were expensive. During the late nineteenth century, Calcutta was known for the best English-style book binding. Khairuddin would send his unbound books from Mecca to Calcutta to get this special binding done.[39] Unlike most of the scholars and ulema, Azad says, 'my father never faced any financial crunch, though he spent most of it on the purchase and upkeep of books.'[40]

However, Azad tells us with a heavy heart that most of this precious collection of his father's books did not survive. He had left his collection of books in thirty trunks back in Hejaz, and they were not looked after well. 'They were attacked by the biggest enemies of knowledge—the termites, destroying most of them.'[41]

Khairuddin was very fond of the good things in life. He used to buy nice things for himself and also received gifts from his admirers from all over the country. 'He had a trunk full of rare Kashmiri shawls, carpets, and rugs, exclusive clothes from Dhaka and Murshidabad and beautiful ivory and sandal wood products, which were all kept packed in trunks. But after the death of my father, I did not find any of this stuff, it was all vandalized and taken away. It did not hurt me very much. But I was pained at the loss of books, which were all stolen and sold in the streets of Bombay.'[42]

Maulana Azad shares in his *Kahani* the beginnings of his own love for books. It all began when one Maulvi Ziya ur Rahman Nami opened a book shop next to the mosque where Azad used to pray. This shop soon became one of his favourite places to spend time in. He writes 'I could find here books of Persian, Arabic, and Urdu which were not available at ordinary bookshops. I used to read all sorts of books there and buy whichever I could afford to purchase.'[43] This was a period when Azad's interest in Urdu literature had just begun and the book shop introduced him to the writings of Mohammad Husain Azad, one of the most important intellectual figures of nineteenth-century Delhi.*

'My father,' Azad wrote, 'did not just inspire me to read books but also taught me the way to read a book. He always insisted that I should take notes while reading any book.... Once you write what you read, [it] becomes etched in your memory forever.'[44] This habit stayed with Azad even while he was trying once to memorize the Quran.

Besides his love for books, there are some other important traits of his father which Azad records in his memoirs and most of these stayed with him. Khairuddin was frank and outspoken when it came to speaking the truth and did not respect

---

*Mohammad Husain Azad (1827–1910) was born into a Persian immigrant family. His father Maulvi Muhammad Baqar was also a prominent face of the city who founded a newspaper called *Delhi Urdu Akhbar*, known to be the first Urdu newspaper published from Delhi. The British hanged him after 1857 on mere suspicion that he was a supporter of the sepoys and did not save the life of Principal Taylor of Delhi College. Muhammad Husain Azad's most important and well-known work is *Aab-i-Hayat*, which is a history of Urdu poetry from Wali Daccani to the times of Zauq and Ghalib.

someone only due to his stature as a rich man. He taught his children, '[Be] proud before the rich, humble before the poor; this is true etiquette'. Azad says that his father represented the old Islamic outlook and maintained manners and customs that resulted from 'family inheritance and restrained temperament', habits which have now disappeared.[45]

Most of the traits he admired in his father can be seen in Azad's own life and behaviour. 'He never did anything that would bring him dishonour, never bowed before anyone, neither the rich nor the great, neither the public nor the government.'[46] Even when Azad entered public life, he remained dignified in his dealings with senior leaders within the Congress, many of whom were obsequious. He had immense respect for Mahatma Gandhi but did not accept all his beliefs. As Mujeeb points out, Azad not only 'declared openly that non-violence was for him a matter of policy, not creed,' he also 'smoked freely and continuously in Mahatma Gandhi's presence, in spite of it being known that Mahatma Gandhi was strongly opposed to such indulgence.'[47] He became embarrassed when people recognized him in a tram in Calcutta, which he had to board because his car broke down.[48] This is unimaginable in today's public life.

Another noticeable trait he inherited from his father and cultivated all his life was his father's remarkable memory. 'My father's memory,' he wrote, 'belonged to the ajaibat-e-rozgar (rarest of the rare).'* He rarely remembered what vegetable was cooked with meat during the day but would recall with precision the book he read fifty years ago, including its subject, title, and even the cover. He never consulted any written text while teaching us. Azad says that his father would sometimes ask them to bring a particular book, ask them to open it

*Even Maulana Azad's paternal grandfather, Sheikh Mohammad Hadi, had a remarkable memory. He is known to have memorized all the course books and his teachers often said that if someday we lose all the books, Hadi would rewrite them from his remarkable memory. Azad, *Ghubar-i-Khatir: Sallies of the Mind*, 2003, p. 49.

to a particular page just to highlight a specific issue.[49] This remarkable inheritance proved extremely useful to Azad in his later life. At the age of fifty-three, when he was writing *Ghubar-i-Khatir* in Ahmednagar Fort prison, he claimed he remembered every word of the lessons he learnt forty years ago. In 1922, he told Malihabadi the way he had organized his phenomenal memory, which can be attributed to both his hereditary inheritance and his training as a child:

> I...have made compartments in my brain, hundreds of compartments. One compartment for law, one for international politics, another one for history, one for mathematics, and one for military science. I accumulate information in an orderly and systematic fashion, like a discriminating, accomplished storekeeper, in separate compartments. Whenever information is required at any particular time I open the appropriate compartment and keep the others locked.[50]

Azad, who had this enormous recall as well, was always several lessons ahead of his classmates, including his elder brother. His teachers were both irritated and surprised at Azad's capability to remember and thus had to give him separate lessons.

Azad was impressed by and carried forward another outstanding attribute of his father's—his capacity to sway audiences while preaching. Khairuddin famously attracted large crowds to his gatherings where he would speak on a particular surah of the Quran in his weekly discourse—once the number went beyond 30,000 in Calcutta Maidan. Azad wrote thus about this ability of his father in *Kahani*:

> What makes the sermon effective is not sermon craft. It becomes vitalized by human emotion, coming from the heart. Unquestionably, in one particular aspect, his heart was emotionally overwhelmed to a remarkable degree, namely in passionate love of the Prophet. This

was the emotion central to all his intellectual and practical interests, the essential element in all his discussions, and the spirit animating all his thought, and imagination.[51]

Azad had the same magical effect when he spoke but lacked the religious fervour of his father. Azad was more of a poet and artist. Moreover, he was deeply involved in matters of public life and the anti-colonial struggle, which took him beyond Islamic theological concerns. He often used Islam as the inspiration to fight against oppression and injustice for those who were involved in the battle against imperialism.

Another habit of his father's that Maulana Azad cherished and followed throughout his life was that of rising early in the morning. In *Ghubar-i-Khatir*, he says he would take his first cup of tea at 3.30 or 4 a.m. which was again part of the strict regimen enforced by his father, so as to not lose the most productive time of day. Khairuddin was always up in the last hour of the night (3 a.m. to 4 a.m.) and kept up with this habit even when he was sick. 'All this affected me when I was just ten or eleven. I started resisting childhood sleep, got up while it was still dark, and began work on my lesson under the lamp light.'[52] He continues 'My father tried to dissuade me from this practice apprehending its adverse impact on my health but I had developed such fondness for early morning that whenever I was late I remained disturbed the whole day.'[53]

He inherited so much from his erudite father yet had serious reservations about the reverence with which others regarded his father. Azad passed through an emotional and mental crisis at the age of twelve. He had no one, inside the house or outside, to share his agonies with. The gulf between him and his father kept increasing and there was no way to bridge this growing distance. The time had come for Azad to break the traditional chains of taqlid, which had kept him bound.

EARLY DISSENT AND DISAGREEMENT

Maulana Azad had much to celebrate in his father's life and a lot to learn as well, which he acknowledged with pride in *Tazkirah* as well as *Kahani*. However, he was aware of the claustrophobic atmosphere in the house, which was under the strict surveillance of his father. His formal education was based on Dars-i-Nizami, the curriculum used in many Islamic schools, with some modifications under the tutelage of Khairuddin. Azad came to Calcutta with his father in 1898 and a year later his mother died. After this the home was ruled ruthlessly by Khairuddin, where Azad was devoid of any emotional support:

> My late father's awesomeness overshadowed his affection. Because, on the whole, his public life consisted of influence on the masses, regard, and respect, and there was no mother at home, naturally even to us in the house, that influence seemed dominant and we were mentally so overawed that his very voice made us tremble...our hearts trembled at the very suspicion of his anger or displeasure.[54]

Not many people, wrote Azad, can even imagine how strict and authoritarian his father was during their childhood. 'Our world,' he wrote, 'study, sport, and fun, everything was limited to the confines of the house.... He had serious issues with our education and had serious misgivings about most of the ulema around, while there was constant fear that we may get exposed to Wahhabi Islam. His standards were so high that hardly any teacher could live up to them.' Most of his elders, including his father, Azad writes, 'were so rigid and unbending that even the slightest departure was infidelity or hypocrisy in their view.... My mind was overburdened by that stagnant sense of crucifixion. I was educated in an atmosphere circumscribed by conservatism and conformity and had no opening for any outside wind.'[55] Azad laments his disconnect with the outside world and the revolutionary changes of the time which did not reach the family, confined as they were within the four walls of the house. He had access only to the family elders and relatives and of course to all the devotees and disciples of his father. These disciples and devotees 'would either kiss my [Azad] hands and feet and stand before me with folded hands or retrogressively recede and respectfully sit at a distance from me.'[56]

English education was out of the question, but he could have had contact with the outside world if he had been sent to a traditional madrassa. His father, however, did not allow even this relaxation. Khairuddin's own public and academic commitments were too many so he did not have the time to engage with his children. However, according to Azad, he provided equal opportunity to the girls in the family to receive the same education as the boys and made sure that they all studied together. This only stopped when Azad and his brothers started going out for lessons but his sisters continued their education at home.

> We stepped out only on Friday with our father and were allowed to relax and play in the hall adjacent to the mosque when Maulana Khairuddin began his Friday discourse. It was only once or twice in a year that we got a chance to go out into the city with Hafiz Waliullah.[57]

His father's domineering presence meant that Azad had to rebel and question everything he had learned to revere and respect as a child. Khairuddin was a strict disciplinarian, so, to have such a father as your teacher is always a tricky proposition. Azad was not allowed access to any school or madrassa, not even the much sought after Calcutta Madrassa*,

---

*Calcutta Madrassa was the earliest of the state-managed institutions during British rule. It was founded by Governor-General Warren Hastings in October 1780. It produced scholars adequately trained in Persian, Arabic, and Muslim Law (Fiqh)

a theological school founded under British auspices. Thus, his education remained the responsibility of his father, who taught him personally or carefully chose the teachers. He had no peer group; most of his friends were decades older to him; and he was never exposed to any other school of thought other than what his father wished. This was indeed a very unusual childhood which was bound to result in an unusual adulthood.

Yes, something unusual did happen as Azad informs us: '[B]y 1902 when I entered [my] fifteenth year I had already completed the Nizamia syllabus...according to the old belief, education is not perfect till you teach what you have learnt. Therefore, I was assigned a group of students at the time of [my] passing out ceremony itself.'[58] This was indeed the beginning of an extraordinary intellectual and public life. Azad writes that by the age of fifteen many doubts began to prick his conscience. He had begun to feel that 'there must be something beyond the noises I heard around me and that the world of knowledge and truth was more extensive than what I saw before me. These pinpricks grew more with advance of age so that within a few years all the walls of faith and thought given by family and environment shook violently and collapsed.'[59] Azad was himself surprised at this dissent because his education had not been contradictory to his father's beliefs so as to cause any conflict on that count.

Even before Azad made any mention of his disagreement, his father was suspicious of his intelligence. Azad explains in *Kahani* about Maulana Khairuddin's attitude and fear of exceptionally bright children. 'Too much intelligence many times becomes reason for waywardness. I fear his intelligence.'[60] In this context, writes Azad, 'my father used to narrate stories of people who, due to being too bright,

---

for services in lower posts in government offices and courts. It followed the Dars-i-Nizamiyah of Firangi Mahal, Lucknow.

frittered away their attention…and finally lost both—the faith as well as the world.'[61]

In one episode from his life, Khairuddin talked to Azad about a remarkable man—Abdur Rahim 'Dahri' Gorakhpuri (c. 1785–1853)*. Abdur Rahim was an extraordinary rationalist of nineteenth-century India. He was born around 1785 in Gorakhpur in the erstwhile United Provinces. His father, the weaver Musahib Ali, was a great admirer of the Persian language and wanted his son to learn it in addition to Arabic. As a young boy, Rahim fell from horseback and injured his left hand. This meant that he could not take up the family profession of weaving and it allowed him to continue his education. By the time he turned fifteen, Abdur Rahim had mastered Persian and acquired proficiency in Arabic. His father then placed him under the tutorship of a spiritual guide in Tandah, near Gorakhpur, where Rahim stayed for three years.

In 1804 he moved to Lucknow for higher education. In the intellectual atmosphere of Lucknow, Abdur Rahim underwent a transformation. He started writing poetry. He was disgusted with the frequent religious bickering between the Shia and Sunni sects. After spending a year in Lucknow, he proceeded to Delhi where he studied the Islamic texts under the guidance of Shah Abdul Aziz and his brother Mullah Rafiuddin, two leading Islamic theologians of the time. One of his fellow scholars was Sayyid Ahmad of Rai Bareli, a prominent Wahhabi of nineteenth-century India. In Delhi, Abdur Rahim also studied the classical treatises on philosophy and science that were then available in Arabic and Persian languages and acquired some proficiency in Oriental indigenous medicine. Khairuddin once told Azad that Abdur Rahim, even as a student, raised such difficult questions and objections in class that Shah Abdul Aziz had to concede many times. Aziz strongly

---

*Some of the details about him are available here: http://en.banglapedia.org/index.php?title=Rahim, Abdur. Also see A. F. Salahuddin Ahmed, *Social Ideas and Social Change in Bengal 1818-1835*, Calcutta: Riddhi, 1976, p. 164.

believed that Rahim's inquisitiveness, and thus his intelligence, betrayed the beginnings of atheistic thought (dahariyat). In 1810, Abdur Rahim left Delhi for Calcutta and took up a job at the newly established Fort William College as a teacher, learnt English and Latin, and soon became, what was then seen as, an apostate and atheist.

In his early life, however, Abdur Rahim had been a devout Muslim and zealously performed the religious rituals and practices laid down by the sharia. But in the cosmopolitan environment of Delhi, and particularly after reading the sacred books of different religions and the treatises on various schools of philosophy, his mind was freed from religious dogma. Completely shedding his former religious beliefs and prejudices, he became a freethinker and a rationalist. According to Abdur Rahim, the idea of God or a Supreme Being was the innovation of the imams (religious leaders). He believed in the law of nature and in his opinion the sun was the source of all creation.

In Calcutta he seemed to be quite at home because the cosmopolitan metropolis drew all kinds of people with all kinds of ideas and provided a safe haven for both conformists and heretics. For quite a few years in Calcutta, after his employment with the British government, Abdur Rahim stayed in the house of Tipu Sultan's son, Sultan Shukrullah, in Tollygunge and tutored the prince's two sons. In this house, poets and lovers of literature assembled periodically and Abdur Rahim became the focal point of a lively intellectual circle.

In his personal life, Abdur Rahim was a simple and kind-hearted gentleman. He never married. A lover of nature and animals, he considered the killing of birds and animals unlawful and thought it improper to pluck flowers or tear away the branches of trees, for he believed that trees and plants have life. He found pleasure in seeing birds fly in the sky and sometimes purchased them from hunters to set them free.

Abdur Rahim's exemplary life is a testament to the fact

that it is ultimately inconsequential whether he was a dahri or not. Azad is obviously sympathetic to Abdur Rahim. He even goes on to question those who dubbed him an atheist just for questioning long-held beliefs and emphasizing rational thought. Azad even invokes Badauni of the Mughal emperor Akbar's court, who dubbed Abul Fazl*, 'Faizi', and many others 'dahri' just because they didn't share his idea of Islam. This narration foregrounds Azad's own struggles with his father's authoritarian outlook.[62]

Rahim spent the last days of his life in seclusion, devoting his time to studying and teaching in a tent pitched in a park. He died on 29 December 1853. Azad includes a small section on Abdur Rahim in his *Kahani* calling it 'a strange celebrity before 1857' where he openly defies his father's position and defends Abdur Rahim as a bright and rational thinker who should not be called a dahri—this even as Khairuddin told this story to Azad to make him wary of turning out like Abdur Rahim. According to Azad, Rahim was among those few Indians before 1857 who appreciated the progress that had been made in expanding knowledge.[63] Azad, despite his father's discomfort with anyone too intelligent, admired Abdur Rahim's talent and skills as a scholar and a man of erudition. We see this in his writings in *Tarjuman al-Quran* and when he held the responsibility of a minister for education, science, and culture in post-Independence India.

Indeed, Azad's disenchantment with his father and his beliefs began very early in his life. He disliked the very sight of the people who came and kissed his father's hands in veneration and blindly followed anything which was uttered by him. They began doing the same with him whenever they saw Azad in the house. Azad writes in *Ghubar-i-Khatir* about these unbearable experiences thus:

*Abul Fazl was one of the most important figures of Akbar's court, included among his nine jewels. He was the son of Sheikh Mubarak, another well-known noble of the period. Fazl is well-known as the author of *Ain-i-Akbari*.

I was born in a family proud of its reputation for knowledge and nobility. Thus, what political leaders get today in the form of reverence of the crowd, I got the same from the religious devotees without any desire or even effort. Even before I developed any consciousness people kissed my hands and feet thinking that I was the son of their *peer* (religious preceptor) and stood before me with folded hands. This inherited leadership and reverence is a testing time for the young minds. Invariably, the arrogance turns their head and they are afflicted by the disease of racial pride and an inborn vanity, dispositions that cause disaster for the hereditary rich. Quite possible I too may have been thus influenced but, as Urfi has pointed out, it is not too easy to sit in judgement on one's own faults:

> Khwahi keh aibha-e-tu roshan shaved tura
> Yakdam munafiqana nasheen dar kameen-e-khwesh[64]
>
> If you want to detect your own faults,
> Sit like an opponent in your own den

It was at this time in this life that the reformist and educationist Sir Syed Ahmad Khan's writings stirred Azad's mind, generating huge intellectual and religious discomfort, and raising innumerable questions. He questioned the ulema of the time and 'subjected [the] Quran to rational criticism and rejected all that was opposed to logic and nature'.[65] Syed Ahmad challenged long-held beliefs and notions of the Islamic school of thought and rebelled against the established orthodoxy, writing:

> Now with great humbleness I ask: of the different religious books which exist today and are used for teaching, which of them discusses Western philosophy or modern scientific matters using principles of religion? From where should I seek confirmation or rejection of the motion of the each, or about its nearness to the sun?

> Thus, it is a thousand times better not to read these books than to read them. Yes, if the Musalman be a true warrior and thinks his religion right, then let him come fearlessly to the battleground and do unto Western knowledge and modern research what his forefathers did to Greek philosophy. Then only shall the religious books be of any use. Mere parroting will not do.[66]

Azad admired Syed Ahmad's open and aggressive rejection of taqlid and his defence of Islam on rational grounds. Azad used the term mujtahid-i-mutlaq (the absolute interpreter) for Syed Ahmad Khan indicating the intellectual debt that he owed him. He described himself at that stage of his religious development as mujtahid fil-mazhab (interpreter with a juristic school).[67]

Azad was conscious of his father's antipathy towards Sir Syed and his interpretation of Islam. He accessed Sir Syed's writings clandestinely. 'It is difficult for me,' writes Azad, 'to explain now my dimaghi sarshari (mental imbalance) and qalbi makhmoori (inebriation of the heart) of those times. I used to worship Sir Syed like an idol. It is strange that a human being never gives up on following tradition forever, though the most precious gift I got from Sir Syed in those times was giving up on tradition (tark-i-taqlid).'

However, Khairuddin confronted Azad, having observed that his son was going through some intellectual discomfort. Azad writes quite movingly about this encounter with his father. One day his father stopped him and, patting him affectionately, asked, 'What is the matter, what ails you? Why are you so sad and mute? Why do you get lost? Why don't you open up?'[68] Azad did not answer but when his father insisted, tears trickled down his face and with a choked voice he mumbled, 'I am not on the wrong path. Nor am I a Wahhabi or a Nechari.* I am not a rebel against my family

---

*Nechari is derived from nature, the critics of Sir Syed used to call him and his followers Necharis, meaning those who believe in the worship of nature.

as you consider me to be. I seek peace from wherever I find it.' Khairuddin asked him 'Who gives you peace?'

'Sir Syed Ahmad Khan's works', Azad answered. With this, Azad had made a clear declaration to his father that he would not like to succeed him as pir; his brother was more suitable for the job and could carry on the family tradition. This dissenting attitude annoyed his father and was the beginning of a break between the two.[69]

His dissent took an extreme turn soon after Khairuddin's death in 1908. This year took Azad on a trip to several West Asian countries and to France.* This visit exposed him to a much wider world that led to the widening of his intellectual horizons. He also found some of his tastes changing, including his indulgences, some of which were not really Islamic or even morally upright, as Ian Douglas comments.[70] Douglas speaks about Azad's sexual indulgences, which Azad confessed in his letter to Sulaiman Nadwi. However, V. N. Datta has a more practical and sympathetic take on the matter: 'His foreign tour had opened a new world to him. Being young he had natural sexual urges which needed an outlet, but to blow this out of proportion, as Douglas has done, is to misunderstand Azad and the changes he was undergoing in personality and outlook.'[71]

Sulaiman Nadwi wrote a letter to Azad, lamenting that Azad hardly had any trace of his father's Islam left in him and even called his claims to be a votary of Islam pretentious. In a very private letter, Azad, with all his dignity, which reflected his nobility of mind, confessed with frankness his failings as a human being. To the charge that he was addicted to drinking alcohol, Azad said that drinking was a minor affair compared

*There are several discrepancies in the dates of his travel to so many countries. Azad's father died in August 1908 when Azad was in Calcutta. Elsewhere he says that he got information about his father's death when he was in Paris. Azad also refers to an affair in Bombay in 1909, so it is indeed difficult to imagine that he spent time in so many countries in 1908.

to the serious misdeeds to which he had been driven by his youthful indiscretions.[72] Azad wrote:

> I am not an abstemious man of saintly life.... I used to drink. Why single out drinking? I did every kind of hateful deed.[73]

Writing to Abdul Majid Daryabadi privately on 26 October 1913, Maulana Sulaiman Nadwi compared Azad to flowers that look pretty but have no fragrance.[74] Reminiscing about his early youth, Azad stated that whatever he did, he did in extremes; be it virtuous deeds or sinful life, he never held back.[75]

Maulana Azad referred to this again:

> When I opened my eyes, adolescence had already dawned, and every thorn in the wilderness of my world was gay as a flower with the dews of ambition and desire. When I looked at myself, I saw a heart filled with quicksilver instead of blood. When I looked at the world, it seemed as if the morning delusion would have no midday sun to dispel it, and no shadows of failure or despondency would mark its evening. This whole habitation of hope and picture-house of fascination was for me only, for the delight of my eyes and the satisfaction of my heart: every nook and corner, every inch of its expanse lay anxiously in wait for me and my appetites. Whichever way I turned to listen, I heard the same call (to fulfill my heart's desire). Was it the throb of my pleasure-seeking heart that was re-echoed, or was it a melody that life plays on the instruments of our senses to cast on us the spell of youthful heedlessness?....
>
> Heedlessness and inebriation chanted their magic spells, passion filled with the cups, the madness of youth caught me by the hand, and my heart, loving to surrender itself, accepted as its goal the way shown to it by impulses and desires. Common sense and reason

were first disconcerted, but later they also beckoned me to come along. There was no way but this, there was no time but this:

> Do not be offended, O Saki,
> I am young and the world is young with me....[76]

There was also a serious romantic affair, which gave Azad a new vision of life.[77] Azad did not divulge any details about the woman he was involved with. He only tells us that he was a besotted lover who had been spurned and terribly hurt. This happened in Bombay in 1909, when Azad was already a married man. We can only make conjectures about his plans, about whether he actually wanted to marry another woman or just quietly continue with his relationship. Azad confesses that it was the physical aspect of love that inflamed the intensity of his passion.[78] According to him, it is the physical manifestation of love that governs the entire universe.[79]

Azad takes yet another philosophical turn and says in his *Tazkirah* that 'I thank God that this stage (of profane love) was not one where I tarried for long. In a year and five months I became versed in all its usages and conventions, leaving no nook, no corner unseen.... Each traveller (on his way of profane love) has to adopt one of two methods; either the boisterousness and aimless wandering of the 'tuti' (songbird) and the nightingale, or the silent burning of the candle....' It seems Azad went for the second option: 'though in appearance this affair (of profane love) ended tragically, in reality all the joy of victory lay hidden in this defeat....' He acknowledged that he did not 'regret the gaiety, the pleasure-seeking, the indulgence from which in my twenty-first and twenty-second year (the real season of the madness of youth) I squeezed out all that could be got without leaving a drop of juice behind.' It was after this emotional turmoil he went through that Azad wrote about Sarmad in 1910, where he narrates, rather indirectly, his own experience 'and the "lesson" he drew from it, especially regarding the nature and place of human and divine love.'[80]

One thing is clear from his autobiographical confessions—Azad was forthright and did not hide anything he indulged in.

EARLY STINT IN JOURNALISM AND EXPOSURE TO THE ISLAMIC WORLD

The early twentieth century saw the emergence of journalism as a viable and essential career. As people prepared to fight a long and bitter battle against the oppressive colonial regime, it became increasingly clear that now, more than ever, there was a need to reach out to the masses, record the injustices of the British government, and speak truth to power. The emerging nationalism of the time needed voices in all the languages of this diverse country. Newspapers such as *Bande Mataram*, *Kesari*, *Mahratta*, *The People*, *Amrita Bazar Patrika*, *The Tribune*, *The Comrade*, *Hamdard*, and many more were launched. There were also many prominent nationalists whose life was closely intertwined with journalism, like Bal Gangadhar Tilak, Aurobindo Ghosh, Maulana Muhammad Ali, and Mahatma Gandhi. Even Bhagat Singh, who lived a short life of just twenty-three years, began his political career as a columnist for different newspapers in Hindi, Urdu, and Punjabi like *Kirti*, *Milap*, *Pratap*, and many others.

Azad's accomplishment in this field is even more commendable since he achieved this at a very young age. He was a serious columnist, an editor of a monthly, and a poet before he turned fifteen.

Azad's home, due to his father's wide network of friends and murids, was an institution where he met people from varied backgrounds. He writes of one Muhammad Moosa who used to visit his father and had recently set up a press. One day Moosa expressed a desire to launch a paper, purely for commercial purposes, and asked Azad to join in this venture. This was of interest to Azad too, so the two went ahead. Azad had heard of *Misbah al-Sharq*, a paper published in Egypt, so he suggested *Al-Misbah* as their paper's name. The first issue came out on the occasion of Eid ul-Fitr and Azad wrote the lead article on Eid. It also carried articles on topics as varied as 'Newton and the law of gravity', 'Imam Ghazali', and 'Khakani Sherwani'. Azad's article on Eid was later reproduced by several established Urdu papers like the *Paisa Akhbar*, which overwhelmed Azad, who was just twelve years old when this paper came out at the end of 1900. Sadly, *Al-Misbah* didn't last for more than a few months.[81]

Around the same time, Sheikh Abdul Qadir launched *Makhzan* from Lahore, which had created a huge interest among readers and followers of Urdu poetry and prose. Azad had subscribed to it as it was a high-quality magazine of the time.[82] He also published several articles in it which gave him immense pleasure and satisfaction. In May 1902, his first contribution to journalism appeared in *Makhzan*, followed by another on the Persian poet Khaqani in August 1902. One Abdul Ghaffar, who was a bookseller and owner of Mustafai Press in Calcutta, convinced Azad to launch a weekly paper in partnership with him and so *Ahsan ul-Akhbar* was born. This paper had a proper office which allowed them to immerse themselves in serious journalism and follow world politics through many other magazines and papers which were not just in Urdu but also in Arabic, from Egypt, Constantinople, Tunis, and even America. It was here in the office of *Ahsan ul-Akhbar* that Azad got a chance to explore Arabic newspapers and magazines and was properly exposed to the complexities and questions confronting the world of Islam. He also wrote a controversial article on 'Islam and Muharram', that was critical of some of the rituals and practices of Muharram. His life was even threatened by the outraged Shias of the city. It took some time for the matter to die down.

Azad saw *Al-Hilal* and *Al-Muqtataf** of Egypt for the first

---

**Al-Muqtataf* was a monthly popular science magazine published from Beirut and Egypt from 1876 to 1952. Along with *Al-Manar* and *Al-Hilal*, it was one of the time here and also got acquainted with *Al-Manar* and the writings of Rashid Rida. '*Al-Manar* was something new for me,' writes Azad, 'in terms of Arabic literary standards and preciseness of language.'[83] He frankly admitted that 'religious discussions did not have much interest for me [Azad] as my heart and mind were under the spell of Sir Syed's school. However, I came across the genuine samples of Arabic lettering and conciseness of language that impacted my mind and helped me a lot in my future studies of Arabic language and literature.'[84]

He was also exposed to Sheikh Mohd Abduh and his literature and politics at the *Ahsan ul-Akhbar* office. During this time, Azad contributed articles to *Tuhfa-i-Ahmadiya*, published and edited by Maulvi Ahmad Husain Fatehpuri from Calcutta. Earlier, this journal used to come out of Kanpur as *Tuhfa-i-Muhammadiya* and mostly published religious articles. It used to publish polemics against Christian missionaries, because Maulana Muhamad Ali was very of fond of pursuing an anti-missionary agenda. 'Now,' writes Azad, 'I suggested that this magazine should be transformed into an academic and religious one and the responsibility to bring about this change was given to me, which I readily accepted.'[85]

> There used to be a paper called *Khadang-i-Nazar*, which came out from Lucknow and Munshi Naubat Rai Nazar used to bring it out from Noward Ganj. Besides a section on ghazals, it also used to deal with articles on taqlid

Arab world's three most popular journals in the early twentieth century. *Al-Muqtataf* was founded in 1876 by the Arab Christians Yaqub Sarruf (1852–1927) and Faris Nimr (1856–1951) at the Syrian Protestant College (SPC, today American University of Beirut) in Beirut. Both of them graduated with a Bachelor of Arts degree in science and then worked as lecturers. Sarruf, who had made a name for himself as an important science journalist and promoter of modern Arabic literature, was interested predominantly in scientific and literary topics. Nimr, on the other hand, dedicated himself additionally to current politics. The third publisher Sahin Makariyus (1853–1910) who was also a journalist, was responsible for the printing technology, and he developed this already in the production of the journals *Nasra al-Usbuiya* (1871) and *At-Tabib* (1884–85).

> makhzan and all well-known columnists of the time like Abdul Halim Sharar, Dr Allama Iqbal, Munshi Ahmad Ali, Marhum Kakorvi etc. used to contribute. Both me and my brother wrote for it regularly. After the lapse of a year, the paper added a larger section on Urdu prose and the responsibility to edit the section came on my shoulders. Thus, I began editing and requisitioning articles for it even more seriously. Maulana Shibli wrote to me after reading one of my articles published in the paper on X-rays.[86]

Azad continued to write for various other Urdu papers and magazines, however, we should remember that he was not even fifteen years old at this time. It was at this age that Azad launched *Lisan al-Sidq* (Voice of Truth), a fortnightly paper from Calcutta, which was launched after *Ahsan al-Akhbar* shut down. This paper established him as an editor and a writer of consequence. It seems that Khan Bahadur Muhammad Yusuf provided some financial assistance to launch the paper.[87] The first issue came out on 20 November 1903 and the last one in April–May 1905. It began with sixteen pages and went up to forty-eight and then sixty. Among its thirteen issues, most were published from Harrison Road in Calcutta, but some had to be published from Agra and Bombay, because of Azad's travels. Maulana Shibli was kind enough to recommend *Lisan al-Sidq* as an organ of the *Anjuman-e-Taraqqi-i-Urdu*, which he had founded recently. This helped the paper to have close to 700 paid subscribers, and also attracted established contributors like Munshi Zakaullah, Abdul Halim Sharar, and others.

Lisan al-Sidq was a literary fortnightly which did not cover politics. Azad explained the objectives of the paper in its August–September 1904 issue. It had three main goals—to promote social reforms by rejecting social abuses; popularize literary criticism through book reviews to promote quality of literature; and cultivate taste for literature among its readers. Azad had a firm commitment to literary criticism which he felt did not exist in Urdu literature, what goes 'in the name of "criticism" is to indulge in indiscriminate praise. *Lisan al-Sidq* would change this and live up to its name.'[88] These were all lofty goals, but Azad's main aim was not to entertain readers but to encourage new and existing readers to engage with new ideas and contribute articles on scientific subjects. The issues of *Lisan al-Sidq* show clearly that he was deeply committed to the cause of reforming the Muslim community.

His early journalistic as well as Islamic worldview was impacted by Syed Ahmad, Jamaluddin Afghani, Mohammad Abduh, Altaf Husain Hali, and of course Shibli Nomani. I have discussed enough about Syed Ahmad in different contexts before but not much on Afghani, who influenced Azad's perception of Islamic global politics as well as Islam. He also convinced Azad of the indispensability of modern science and its compatibility with Islam. It will be instructive to explore Afghani a bit more to understand Azad and his worldview in some detail. As we will see in Azad writings, his pan-Islamism and later his nationalism were both influenced by Afghani's writings and politics.

Syed Jamaluddin Afghani is the most fascinating example of an early pro-modernity and pro-science pragmatist. A pioneer of Islamic resurgence, he has been referred to as the Sage of the East.[89] His ideas deeply influenced the Muslim world, particularly his view of Islam as a unifying force against Western imperialism, and this is what impacted Azad in a big way. His early travels to West Asia in 1908 exposed him to the malaise most Muslim nations were going through. Afghani, with his Persian upbringing, was under the spell of Ibn-Sina's rationalist thinking and remained a constant source of worry and discomfort for the orthodox. He was expelled at their behest from Istanbul for pressing for the establishment of a Darul-Funun, a new university, to impart instruction exclusively in modern science.*[90] It is particularly interesting to explore Afghani's views on science and modernity because, in contrast to Sir Syed Ahmad Khan, Afghani did not make a serious attempt to reinterpret Muslim theology. Azad, as we have seen earlier, was enamoured with Syed Ahmad's idea of a new Ilm ul-Kalam, an attempt to understand faith by logical reasoning instead of relying on revealed texts, which Afghani derided in his writings. His central concern was the mobilization of people against Western colonialism, and Islam seemed the most potent rallying force for this purpose. Azad used Islam as an inspiration to devise his own idea of composite nationalism, which has been referred to earlier as well. Afghani's advocacy of modernity was also marked by caution. He never emphasized the Western origins of the elements he borrowed for fear that it might encourage a trend of admiration for the West and feelings of Islamic inferiority and helplessness.[91] These were the seeds of an emerging nationalism, which began as pan-Islamism to mobilize the colonized Muslim world against European imperialism. We see that very distinctly in Azad's career as well.

I shall refer mostly to the three years that Afghani spent in India (1880–82). As a matter of fact, 'he acquired in India his first knowledge of the sciences and mathematics of Europe'.[92] He spent these years delivering lectures and writing a few insightful articles. The most controversial of these was 'Al-Radd ala al-Dahiriyin', or the 'Refutation of Materialists' or, in its original Persian title, 'The Truth about the Neicheri Sect and an Explanation of the Neicheries'. This can however be

*However, Ekmeleddin Ihsanoglu feels that there was not much conflict between religion and science during the first half of the nineteenth century. In the works of several Turkish scholars there is no mention of any religion versus science controversy; on the contrary, one comes across expressions to the effect that in the golden age of Islam, religion was the motivating factor in the progress of science. He even goes to the extent of saying that it is difficult to suppose the existence of anyone who defended the old sciences against physics, chemistry, astronomy, and other branches of modern science.

understood properly only in the context of his other writings. Six of these articles were written for the first issues of the Hyderabad journal *Mu'allim-i-Shafiq*, while five more lectures were published along with these original six in the first edition of the collected articles of Afghani titled *Maqalat-i-Jamaliyyeh*, from Calcutta in 1884.[93] According to Nikki Keddie, the three striking features of Jamaluddin Afghani's writings in India, which make them distinct from his writings elsewhere in the Islamic world, are, firstly, the advocacy of nationalism of a linguistic or territorial variety, meaning the unity of Indian Hindus and Muslims, with little said about the unity of Indian Muslims with Muslims abroad. In Afghani's writings, pan-Islamism is shelved and local nationalistic ideas emphasized instead. Secondly, his emphasis on the benefits of philosophy and modern science. And finally, his attacks on Syed Ahmad Khan as a lackey of the imperialist government. All these three features appear, in one way or another, in Afghani's attempts at reconciling science with Islam in India. When he talks of nationalism of a linguistic variety, he emphasizes the cultivation and teaching of modern science in the local language of the people. He maintains that linguistic ties are more important than religious ties.

As a young journalist, Azad confronted differing views about Islam and engaged with the virtues of cultivating modern science. His early years were also spent in managing these diverse influences, ranging from his father to Sir Syed and Altaf Husain Hali to Jamaluddin Afghani, Mohammad Abduh, Shibli Nomani, and many more. It was not an easy task to cull out what he liked and agreed with from the corpus of immensely profound writings of many of these men.

Azad has written evocatively about Hali and his first meeting with the author of *Hayat-i-Jawaid*, a biography of Sir Syed, which he hugely admired. While Azad appreciated the book, it received mixed reactions, with some criticizing it as a hagiography and not an objective study of the man who caused a split among the educated Muslims in the post-1857 period. It was a phase when Azad was editing *Lisan al-Sidq*, which coincided with his blind imitation of and adherence to the late Sir Syed. Azad writes in *Kahani* that 'I had crossed all limits of my devotion to him and was not ready to tolerate even a word in his criticism.'[94] Azad was aware of all these reactions before he met Hali.

Azad writes in *Kahani* that he decided to travel to Lahore for a break after launching *Lisan ul-Sidq*. Here he attended the annual session of the *Anjuman-i-Himayat-i-Islam* in 1901. Maulana Hali also participated in this session and it was here that he recited his last nazm as well. 'I was introduced to Maulana Hali by Maulana Wahiddudin,' writes Azad, 'whom I knew before as an editor of *Ma'arif*. Pointing towards me he asked Maulana Hali to guess my age. He thought for a while and said you are too young…may be fifteen or sixteen years, to which Maulana Wahiddudin added that he is the editor of *Lisan al-Sidq*. This was a pleasant surprise for Hali who took some time to digest this reality.'[95] Azad writes that 'I was sitting at a distance so Hali called me close and asked me if I was a student. He was in for a surprise again when I said that I finished my studies more than two/three years ago.'[96] After this meeting Hali encouraged Azad as a young scholar and kept in touch through affectionate letters till he died. When *Al-Hilal* came out in 1912, Azad wrote about his disagreements with Sir Syed's debates against Islam as well as his politics. 'As it happens, many people wrote to Hali about my critical writings, but Hali was generous to concede that I am correct now and Sir Syed was right in 1890 in his historical context.' Thus, Azad hinted at his disagreement with the political policies and anti-Congress sentiments held by Sir Syed. Hali never took any offence, and instead agreed with Azad that the times had changed. He even wrote to Azad that he not only agrees with the policies of *Al-Hilal* but expects it to succeed and flourish.[97] Hali wrote *Musaddas:*

The Story in Verse of the Ebb and Tide of Islam in 1879, a text that delves into the psyche of Muslim India. He touched upon several aspects of the complex subject but one sample, the spirit of which permeates through Azad's later political philosophy, is worth quoting:

Yeh pehla sabaq tha kitaab-e-Huda ka
Ke hai saari makhlooq kunba Khuda ka
Vohi dost hai Khaaliq-e-do-sara ka
Khalaiq se hai jis ko rishta vila ka
Yehi hai mohabbat yehi Din-o-imaan
Ke kaam aaye duniya mein insaan ke insaan[98]

Of Allah's Book this first lesson pursue
That all the world is His family, His own
And one who lays claim to His kinship true
Treats all His creatures as kith and as kin
This is the True Din, the faith and the prayer
Humans help humans, in clime foul or fair

What Azad borrowed from poets and writers like Hali reflected heavily in his later writings, including in his seminal work *Tarjuman al-Quran*. All these early influences on Azad helped him to later formulate his idea of nationalism as well because he believed that the basis of the Quran was not theological hatred but humanity and prescribed correct moral relations between human beings in spite of their different religions.[99] However, this young Azad, the author of *Tazkirah* who was averse to treading the beaten path, was not yet mature enough to discover the humanistic import of Quran. More about this in the next chapter.

We also need to look at another important influence on Azad. He met Maulana Shibli Nomani for the first time in 1904 in Bombay, while he was on his way back from Iraq. Maulana Shibli was visiting Bombay from Hyderabad, where he oversaw the scientific and technical education of the state. Though Azad was meeting him for the first time, they had been writing to each other for the last five years. Azad had also read a lot of Shibli's writing and was keen to spend time with him. Shibli stayed in Bombay for a fortnight and Azad met him almost every other day. Shibli was impressed and wanted Azad to move to Hyderabad and take over the editorial responsibilities of *Al-Nadwa*—a new magazine launched in 1904 by Shibli Nomani from Lucknow. Azad is rather generous about himself on many occasions, and here he says that once when he went to meet Maulana Shibli he found two people engaged in an animated discussion with him. When Azad intervened and made a longish comment on the issue, Shibli was so moved by 'my performance that he even said that my brain need[s] to be displayed in an exhibition, it actually belongs to the rarest of the rare categories (ajaibat-i-rozgar).'[100]

Maulana Shibli resigned from his job in Hyderabad and decided to devote the rest of his life to running *Al-Nadwa* from Lucknow. He continued to ask Azad to join the magazine and finally Azad decided to take up the editorship of the paper. He spent close to eight months as an editor but the main attraction for him was the company of Maulana Shibli. Like him, Shibli was also an early riser, and Azad writes:

> I used to go to his room at four in the morning during the December chill and begin our rounds of hot cups of tea and discussion on diverse intellectual concerns....Many times our discussion revolved around Persian poetry... sometimes we went out for a walk up to Qaiser Bagh and even further away and our literary and academic discussion went on. I learnt a lot in his association. After his death, so many diverse talents got buried with him but the worst is that I never got such an erudite company ever again. His passion for knowledge, broad and comprehensive, also vanished with him.[101]

His association with *Al-Nadwa* at the young age of seventeen helped Azad comprehend Islamic history and theology and

European learning and sciences. Shibli himself was an institution and Azad's close association with him for about six months was bound to vitalize his thinking. This association was to be of great benefit to Azad in his future work. *Al-Nadwa* was a journal for the learned elite and Azad's association with it served to build his image as a sound authority on theological issues.[102]

But what drew Azad to Shibli's work in the first place? Let us briefly understand Shibli in the context of the tumultuous late nineteenth century when the spread of new education in India, particularly among Muslims, gave rise to an educated class with a western orientation. They were Muslims but looked at the maulvis condescendingly and found the whole Islamic tradition backward looking. For many of them, the only panacea for worldly progress was westernization. This alarmed many people and Shibli was one of them. Shibli saw the lack of coordination between religious and secular education and the expanding rift in the Indian Muslim community. He was one of those scholars who put forward the idea that, in order to provide a remedy to this malaise, there should be institutions where both types of education could be imparted side by side.[103] Shibli taught in Sir Syed's Aligarh College for several years from 1882 and left only after Sir Syed's death in 1898—he continued for so long despite his disagreements with Sir Syed's religious and political views. Here he came into contact with Western thought, learnt English, and even took lessons in French. Syed Ahmad put his library at his disposal and persuaded him to write on history.[104] Both Azad and Shibli were impressed by Sir Syed initially but developed a critical attitude later. This was likely one of the common factors which brought them together.

At Aligarh, Shibli was a popular teacher who successfully created among many students an attitude that life is to be lived with dignity and prestige using one's own moral and spiritual resources. Unlike Sir Syed, in theology he was neither a radical nor a rationalist, but he certainly aimed at reviving the rationalizing dialectic of classical Muslim theology. Shibli's theology represented a shift from that of Sir Syed Ahmad Khan's, in that it was not negative or dismissive or overly critical of Islam.[105] Being a theologian, he saw the necessity of some continuities but still believed that Islam should come to terms with modern scientific developments and thinking. However, even this balanced attitude, or an attempt to take both religion and scientific thinking along, did not deter many an ulema from dubbing him a freethinker. Even the institution Nadwatul Ulama, in whose founding he was instrumental in 1893–94, was taken over by the dominant Deobandi ulema. Many secular subjects, which Shibli had initially wanted to be a part of the curriculum, never found a place in the syllabus of the Nadwa.[106] The courses of instruction at Nadwa did not show any radical change from the conventional Muslim studies taught at Farangi Mahal and Deoband. English was included, but for many years 'the English education at Nadwa did not go beyond a,b,c.'[107] The Nadwa was conceived as a middle-of-the-road institution between 'the extremes of Aligarh's secularism and Deoband's rigid conservatism' but, as Aziz Ahmad observed, in no time 'its scholars and their works became almost indistinguishable from those of Deoband.'[108] The orthodox sections became restive and Shibli had to leave Nadwa in 1913. Azad, nevertheless, remained indebted to Shibli. As mentioned before, he never found such enlightened and erudite company ever again. Shibli's rationalism and clarity of expression attracted him to Azad and vice versa. This influence is reflected very distinctly in his *Tarjuman al-Quran*, which again did not find approval among the orthodox quarters of the Muslim ulema.

As we have seen before, Azad pursued many passions against his father's wishes. One major passion was music, which he had to pursue clandestinely as a child. Because of the joylessness at home, music alone brought real consolation to Azad and created in him a body of feelings strong enough to resist the disintegrating influences of the excessive restrictions imposed on him.

Later, while he was in prison in Ahmednagar Fort, Azad wrote in detail about it and also about the history of music in India and the West. We will discuss this in the chapter on *Ghubar-i-Khatir*, however we may refer to some early and interesting episodes related to this passion. Azad wrote that he could never imagine life without music. Though his love for music began at a very early age, its pursuit was nearly impossible in a home controlled by his authoritarian father. Azad learnt music from Masita Khan, a frequent visitor to the family home, since Khan wished to become Khairuddin's disciple. Azad managed to convince him to be his teacher, even though Khan was initially scared, knowing full well of Maulana Khairuddin's antipathy towards music. Azad used to go to somebody's house daily to learn music for some years. He played the flute and sitar and practised these musical instruments for four years. Years later, he recalled his childhood memories of listening to the muezzin Sheikh Hasan's lyrical azaan in the Haram Sharif that moved him deeply. Thus, from childhood, music remained inseparable from him all his life.

He wrote further in *Ghubar-i-Khatir* that 'if you want to deprive me of all the comforts of life, deprive me of this one thing and your purpose will be served. Here in the prison what I miss the most is a radio set.' Lamenting the loss, he quoted an Urdu couplet:

> Lazzat-e-ma'asiet-e-ishq na pooch
> Khuld mein bhi yeh bala yaad aayi[109]
>
> Question not the pleasure of the sin of love;
> The damn thing could not be forgotten even in paradise.

We have touched upon the crucial and formative influences on Azad's early life. One thing that is clear is that Azad learnt and unlearnt many things by the time he was fifteen. He remained a sceptic all his life—this helped him evolve and formulate his own views about everything he touched, including Islam. Azad was, in many ways, the sum total of the different figures he grew up around. He jousted with his intellectually dominant father at home, revered and questioned Sir Syed Ahmad Khan, gained valuable lessons in anti-colonial solidarity from Syed Jamaluddin Afghani, questioned his beliefs with the writings of Altaf Husain Hali, and found the most erudite company in Maulana Shibli Nomani, among others. Azad turned out to be a freethinker because he did his own thinking, despite being exposed to every school of thought, which produced a vital difference in how he perceived society around him. To him doubt was essential for the progress of intellectual development.[110] This childhood experience and learning stayed with him all his life, and his later works reflect his early exposure to doubt and critical evaluation of everything that he had received as inheritance.

TWO

MAULANA AZAD AND CRITICAL THINKING IN ISLAM

We cannot discuss Maulana Azad in the context of religion alone. Religion was not a separate domain but was interspersed through all aspects of his life—political, social, and cultural. Maulana Azad, as we know, was an Islamic scholar who became a political figure. He was a solitary man, lost in his scholarly concerns, always seeking silence to ponder about religious and philosophical issues. This was a family trait which Azad inherited from his father, an orthodox Sufi who expected Azad to lead a religious life. But Azad was more than that, he was a sensitive intellectual open to diverse influences. His understanding of Islam was eclectic, despite his uncompromising faith in the Quran. This explains the way he read the Book and interpreted it in the light of his wider understanding of the world. His reading of the Quran is sometimes contradictory, and his sole dependence on the Book and Sunnah, again, carries different meanings.

Azad's discomfort began early, 'even before his education had been completed, he became restive under the restrictions imposed on him by the opinion of his family and its large circle of followers.'[1] Writing in *Ghubar-i-Khatir*, in the 1940s, he notes that 'normally people receive religion as family heritage. So did I. But I could not remain satisfied with inherited faith. My thirst was more intense than to be quenched by that alone.'[2] He continues: 'new anxieties and new quests appeared even before I had crossed fifteen years of age; my mind began to show dissatisfaction with the shapes and forms in which the inherited beliefs appeared.' Initially he was shocked to discover the internal sectarian differences within Islam and his mind reeled under the contradictory claims and mutually conflicting edicts. That was followed by the mutual conflict of religion and intellect, so that whatever faith was there in him was lost. Some fundamental questions perturbed him no end and he often found himself in a state where answers were not easy to come by. 'What is truth? Where is truth? Does it really exist or not? And if it is there and is one (for there cannot be more than one truth) why are paths to it different? Not only different but contradictory and conflictual?'[3] And he came to believe that the light of intellect reigned supreme, for it had demolished all the ancient and traditional beliefs that were seen as lofty till now. He was convinced that the path to questioning one's faith always starts with doubt and ends at denial and if you cannot proceed further you are bound to face despair. He quotes Ghalib to make his point:

> Thak thak ke har muqaam pe do chaar reh gaye
> Tera pata na payen to nachaar kya karein![4]
>
> At every stage some people stop, exhausted;
> What can they do if you are not to be found!

Azad agrees that he also underwent a similar phase but did not give up or get trapped in the depths of pessimism. He was convinced that rethinking was ingrained in the critical spirit that had been central to Islam from its inception. The Quran indeed has many references to thought and learning, reflection and reason. The Sacred Text denounces those who do not use their critical faculties in the strongest terms: 'The worst creatures in God's eyes are those who are (wilfully) deaf and dumb, who do not reason' (8:22).[5] Azad reposed his faith in the Book so most of his decisions emanated from his reading of the Quran—he did not care much about the opinion of those ulema that flaunted claimed to be spokespersons of the faith. Azad had even stronger words for some of these ulema when he said that 'the perpetrators of oppression have always availed of the services of the ulema who are more than willing to serve the state.... They are described as worse than snakes and scorpions; while reptiles may occupy the same hole in the ground these men of God can never occupy the same space.'[6] He goes on to make a classic comparison between the tavern and the mosque, saying that one may find 'songs of love' in the tavern but right underneath the arch of the masjid, if the reward is imamat or peshwai, their hands reach for the throat and their bloodthirsty eyes are fixed on the blood of their brother.[7]

He refused to be guided by these ulema-i-duniya parast (ulema devoted to the world) and relied more on the Quran and the Sunnah of the Prophet. He called the time-serving ulema sagan-e-dunya (dog of the world), who in the name of religion have sacrificed truth and perpetuated ignorance and fanaticism.[8] His ideas on this issue converged with those of Jamaluddin Afghani, as well as those of Muhammad Abduh, and Rashid Rida of Egypt, who stringently opposed the ulemas of the time who, they believed, had compromised religion for worldly gain.[9] The difference between him and the others who established their arguments in a similar fashion is that he considered the Quran as the real basis of the faith, and it inspired all his thinking. He did not limit his horizons by accepting traditional interpretations and derived his opinions from other sources, using Quranic text as formal proof.[10] His faith in the Quran and Sunnah is close to the Wahhabi/Salafi understanding of Islam, which we will discuss later in the chapter.

A large number of ulemas disagreed with Azad and his interpretation of Quranic verses, and many of them dubbed him 'ghair-muqallid or non-traditionalist, for he challenged the accepted modes of Islamic thought....'[11] Maulana Azad agreed with his critics on this issue and accepted several times in his writings and speeches that he was against taqlid. He wrote:

> Whatever my circumstances of life, I have always disliked defects and imperfections. Consequently, I have always hated tradition (taqlid). I have never tried to find the footpath of another but have sought out a path for myself and left my footprints for those who come. Owing to Divine Kindness there are many ways for man; the easiest and safest of them is to search for a guide. But I wish to make it quite clear that in all my spiritual distresses I have not been obliged to anyone for guidance...I am under no obligation for guidance to any man's hand or tongue, nor to my family nor to any syllabus of education. All the guidance I have received has been from the Divine Throne.[12]

Azad always wanted Muslims to be their own interpreters of faith, not dependent on the faith peddled by the mullahs, who always pushed their own half-baked and narrow interpretations of Islam. It was, however, an onerous task to break the hierarchy between the believer and the interpreter. Azad could give up on taqlid, question his own scholarly father, and rethink Islam for himself, but expecting the same from a lay believer was a bit too much. Through his questioning, Azad could foresee many of the problems Islam faces today—problems as reflected in the conduct of its adherents that arise today mainly due to a lack of understanding.

Muslims are known as ahle-Kitab, or people of the Book, but can they really comprehend the Book, given that a majority of them can't read Arabic? Most of them ritually pronounce the ayat of the Quran, but are not able to comprehend its meaning. True, in Hinduism too, most of the Sanskrit shlokas go over people's head, but in Islam the issue is quite different. For a religion so completely dependent on one authoritative Book and a set of codified practices, not comprehending the sacred text means a lot in the life of a believer, and this lack of comprehension is quite palpable in most parts of the world today, including South Asia.

Within a few years of its birth, Islam expanded into diverse cultural, linguistic, and geographical worlds and became a major world religion within a short time. However, the vernacularization of Islam remained in abeyance, and instead, the ulema espoused Arabic as the language of Islam, a language spoken by the Prophet and by all those who came after him. The language of the Quran has almost acquired a divine status, even if the majority of believers don't understand it. Today, it is enough to ritually recite the Quran, memorize it (hifz), and acquire social respect as hafiz-i-Quran. The distinction between alim-i-Quran (one who understands Quran) and hafiz-i-Quran (one who memorizes Quran) has gradually blurred over the centuries. Maulana Azad's quest to promote an Islam which has space for critical thinking and is not committed to taqlid is still a dream. Indeed, how can we be critical of something we do not even understand?

Maulana's yearning for a faith that is open to rational and critical thinking began early in his life, almost from his teen years. It was from his father's teachings that these questions took root in Azad's mind. Later, Azad engaged with the Quran, Hadith, and Sunnah on his own.

INEBRIATION WITH SIR SYED'S IDEAS

The nineteenth century colonized world, which included a substantial number of Muslim nations, responded to colonization in varied ways. One of them, which is relevant for us here, was a call for engagement with this new world that stood as a challenge to Islam and its history, science, and civilization. Sir Syed Ahmad and many others in India and elsewhere responded by looking to their own faith, its diverse practices, and the role of rationalism and critical thinking in the pursuit of knowledge as well as in daily life. Azad's fascination with the reformer and educationist Sir Syed began early, despite his father's serious reservations about him, as pointed out before. Fazlur Rehman, well-known for his writings on modernism in Islam, wrote about Sir Syed that he 'was not a keen religious thinker, nor perhaps primarily and deeply religious,' but 'was led by the inner logic of the Muslim intellectual history to justify his cultural progressive attitude theologically.'[13] This is what I believe is relevant today, our problems in the past or even today were not merely theological but more than that. Sir Syed spent most of his energies and time convincing the community that inherited beliefs need to be questioned, debated, and reinterpreted in the changed social and historical context. His position on religion was quite often contradictory, yet his emphasis on the use of reason and critical faculties was always consistent and in consonance with Islamic faith. Here we find a lot of similarities between him and Azad—both stressed critical thinking and ijtihad, which had been shunned for centuries.

Sir Syed was primarily a religious scholar, thus the task of scientific exegesis was of paramount importance to him. In a startling break with tradition, which greatly impressed Azad, he proposed that the Quran be reinterpreted so as to remove all apparent contradictions with physical reality. Since the Quran was the word of God, he argued, and since scientific truths were manifestly correct, any contradiction could only be apparent and not real.[14] For him, Islam, as a natural religion contained no dichotomy between the 'word' and the 'work' of God[15]. He, therefore, suggested interpreting the Quran using the following methodology:

1. A close enquiry be made into the use, meaning, and etymology of Quranic language so as to yield the true meaning of the word and passage in question.
2. The criterion employed to decide whether a given passage needed metaphorical interpretation, and which of the several interpretations ought to be selected. Such truth is arrived at by aqli dalil (rational proof) and demands firm belief.

3. If the apparent meaning of the Scripture conflicts with demonstrable conclusion, it must be interpreted metaphorically. In this, Sir Syed follows Ibn Rushd, the Andalusian polymath and jurist, in his problem of reconciling maaqul (demonstrative truth) with manqul (scriptural truth). Yet he makes it clear that such metaphorical and allegorical interpretation is precisely what the Author of the Scripture intended.[16]

The above methodology was questioned by the detractors of Sir Syed, who saw this as some sort of perversion of Islam. The majority of Muslims in India and even elsewhere had already succumbed to a process of perversion which began from the early centuries of Islam. All nineteenth-century efforts to bring reason and rationalism into the reading and understanding of Islam almost failed due to the sway of taqlid, entrenched in the thinking of the faithful since the eleventh and twelfth centuries. Sir Syed and other nineteenth-century modernists were not promoting anything that was alien to Islam or its history. There was a rationalist tradition central to Islamic civilization. A group of philosophers called Mu'tazilites had argued in the eighth century for free will over fatalism and quoted Quranic verses showing God's displeasure at an inactive mind. As discussed earlier, according to a verse in the Quran, 'the worst of creatures for Allah are those who are (wilfully) deaf and dumb, those who will not reason'.[17] In fact, those who clash with reason are the unbelievers. 'They are people,' a verse bluntly decrees, 'who do not use their intellect.' [18] 'Muhammad,' observed Belgian-born scholar Henri Lammens, 'is not far from considering unbelief as an infirmity of the human mind.'[19] Much as Europe had its Descartes and Kant, Islam had its Farabi, Ibn Sina, and Ibn Rushd. Not only were they rationalists, but intellectually they were of the same calibre as their European peers.[20] Islam, however, failed to institutionalize the thinking of these philosophers and scientists, while in Europe the thinking of

Descartes was institutionalized and built upon over two centuries, both philosophically and mathematically. In Islam, instead, much before Sir Syed and other nineteenth-century modernists, knowledge was split into broadly two categories—the praiseworthy and the blameworthy. The first alluded to Islamic sciences, which were also called sharia sciences, while the latter referred to the foreign sciences which had crept in mainly through Hellenization and also through other cultural and intellectual influences—interestingly, the later Mu'tazila school of rationalism in Islam was partly influenced by ancient Greek philosophy.

The ulema created a hostile distinction between the alien sciences, or sciences of the ancients, and the Islamic sciences. Most of the ulema advised Muslims to keep away from blameworthy knowledge or the alien sciences, which unfortunately contained all that could have kept Islam dynamic and forward looking, therefore bringing an end to irrational thinking in Islam.[21]

Syed Ahmad used some strong words to express his anguish in a letter to Muhsin al-Mulk on 21 January 1870:

> If people do not shun blind adherence, if they do not seek specially that light which can be found in the Quran and the indisputable Hadith, and do not adjust religion and the sciences of today, Islam will become extinct in India.

Azad also expressed in strong words his disappointment with the Muslim community:

> All the miseries of the Muslims are due to their negligence and due to the fact that they have turned from this divine source of guidance, and thought they needed to look upon it only in regard to religious rituals, like roza and namaz. They did not realize its importance in all aspects, educational, cultural, and political. The more they turned away from the Quran, the faster the world slipped away from them. Whichever direction

they took they were misled and they fell into the depths of darkness.[22]

The hostility Sir Syed encountered during his lifetime was mainly due to this perverted inheritance, which had already closed the possibility of critical thinking and use of reason in Islam. Even Afghani, who disagreed with Sir Syed's politics, agreed with him on this issue. Here is a longish passage from the scholar Ziauddin Sardar, where he briefly outlines the tragic lack of criticality in Muslim thinking:

> While it is important to explore the reasons why Muslims have developed an aversion to criticism and critical thought, it is also necessary to do something about it. The absence of a critical spirit as well as philosophers, thinkers, writers, and activists who constantly challenge received wisdom and take issue with orthodoxy, over many centuries, has allowed the advent and dominance of a singular interpretation of Islam. It has also contributed to an atmosphere of intolerance and allowed extremism and obscurantism to become intrinsic in Muslim societies. Much of what goes under the rubric of 'religious thought' or 'culture' in Muslim societies is a non-chemical sedative. Islam has thus been reduced to a set of pieties, rendering Muslim societies incapable of generating new and original ideas. Indeed, one can argue that Muslims no longer have a model of living genially with Otherness, accommodating difference, or adjusting to rapid and accelerating change.[23]

Sardar is unflinching in his criticism and points to the distressing state of Islam and of Muslims globally. Sir Syed had to confront the forces of this closed world of Islam in the nineteenth century to push for his idea of modernism.

Sir Syed's views opened new ways of interpreting Islam. The impact of Syed Ahmad Khan's writings on Azad was transformative; it resulted in his repudiation of his family's traditional orthodoxy and a complete refocusing of his ideas on Islam.[24] Sir Syed also changed Azad's approach to knowledge. 'His writings,' Azad writes in *Kahani*, 'not only made me aware of modern knowledge but I got totally enamoured of them. My beliefs and thought processes now were going through a storm. My life was not just moving but galloping at a pace. Everything old looked cheap and distasteful. Modern knowledge for me is all due to Sir Syed; for my heart and mind anything associated with his name became almost divine.'[25] In this period, Azad collected anything which was accessible on modern science in Urdu, of course through translations, mostly from Delhi and Lahore.

One major source of such texts was the Aligarh Scientific Society, led by Sir Syed, which was a pioneer in producing textbooks on modern science and mathematics, mostly through translations. Azad also mentions reading Lord Bacon's autobiography in Urdu, a book on political economy, and several books on mathematics, physics, and astronomy, which were mostly translated by Maulvi Zakaullah* of Delhi. Zakaullah truly represented the prevalent ethos of nineteenth-century Delhi. He 'looks upon diversity as a condition of progress, and the Islamic ethical ideal broadly akin to the ethical ideal of other faiths.'[26] There were also other amazing people who made a deep impression on the young Azad.

As pointed out above, Azad read a lot on science translated by Maulvi Zakaullah, who represents the efflorescence of 'new learning' in nineteenth-century Delhi. Zakaullah wrote extensively on the knowledge systems of the East, particularly in Islam, and their role in the cross-civilizational progress of modern science. He firmly believed that knowledge cannot

*Munshi or Maulvi Zakaullah was a mathematician by training, who was one of the favourite students of Master Ramchandra, the famed teacher and science enthusiast of the mid-nineteenth century India at Delhi College. Zakaullah also wrote several volumes on the history of India and translated many books on mathematics, geometry, algebra, and even moral science. He also authored a book on history of mathematics and also a textbook on physics.

be grounded in any particular religion or culture, and is in fact universal. Zakaullah was a favourite student of Master Ramchandra, the celebrated science and mathematics teacher at Delhi College in the 1840s and 1850s. As someone deeply rooted in the traditional culture of Delhi, he revered it in part, but was simultaneously convinced of the possibility of a bright future if modern knowledge was systematically cultivated. His position is sufficiently explicit in the following lines:

> I believe that it is ignorance to dub the ancient sciences or the Eastern sciences as irrelevant. And this ignorance is further compounded if the modern Western sciences are not preferred over the ancient or Eastern sciences.... The truth is that the light of Eastern sciences is surrounded by an ever-increasing darkness. But, being our own, this light gives us pleasure and its darkness is soothing.... Comparatively darkness around the light of Western sciences is much less. Yet it dazzles our eyes and it is so alien, that we are unable to see anything else. We need to be accustomed to this light. Once this happens, we will be able to witness the splendours of nature and the miracles of human ingenuity.'[27]

Zakaullah was convinced that Muslims can rightfully pursue modern science as they have contributed to its progress in its early stages. On an emotional note he once turned to Muslim rule in Spain when Cordova emerged as a centre of light and learning and said: 'We are asking back from Europe today some payment for the debt you owe to us on account of what we did for you in the Middle Ages. Students from Oxford and Cambridge used to go to Spain to learn from us science and mathematics; now we come to you instead.'[28]

Another remarkable man of the nineteenth century, whom Azad had the great fortune to not only read but also meet in Delhi was Nazir Ahmad, a remarkable educationist, novelist, and modernist. Nazir Ahmad had just published his *Al-Huquq wa Al-Faraiz, The Rights and the Duties*, a copy of which he offered to Azad but told him that he doesn't expect or a favourable review; but he thought the book was important, and so, if Azad felt convinced after reading it, he should write about it.[29] Azad did write a review of the book and published it in the newspaper *Vakil* of Amritsar.

Nazir Ahmad was born in Bijnor and studied Persian and Arabic since his father wanted him to be a maulvi. Ahmad, however, had different plans. He came to Delhi, joined Delhi College with the help of Mufti Sadruddin Azurda in 1845; incidentally, Azurda was also a teacher and a patron of Azad's father Maulana Khairuddin. Here Nazir Ahmad became one of the favourite students of Master Ramchandra and also a classmate of Munshi Zakaullah. The world of science reverberated through the corridors of 'Dilli Kalij', and that stirred him more than anything else. Suddenly, his beliefs were rudely shaken and his religious universe was confronted by scientific and philosophical discussions, the questioning of inherited knowledge, and the critical scrutiny of existing texts.[30] This outlook remained with him all his life, we see that in his regular advice to his son 'to be studious and not end up as a delinquent or a religious bigot.'[31] Though he was not really grounded in Western-oriented traditions, nonetheless, he wished that Muslim societies were purified of their medieval fantasies and reborn under the discipline of natural science. In his view, the core issue was never the rejection or repudiation of traditional values, but their harmonization with the challenges of a modern society. Given his unflinching faith in humanistic ethics, he longed for the formulation of a doctrine that would conform to Islam's rational and tolerant spirit. As in other matters, he sketched his own ideal and went against the existing theological trend by advocating ijtihad in matters of faith and the use of intellect or reason in both temporal and spiritual matters.[32]

These names do not come up very often anymore, but if we were to observe this period closely we will find their imprint on everything from literature, history, and science to politics to education. They were remarkable human beings who represented the true, pluralist, and diverse India that we are on the brink of losing today.

Soon Azad began his engagement with the Mu'tazila school of philosophy which had thrived during the early Abbasid centuries of Islam. Mu'tazila, as discussed earlier, was a radical school of rationalist philosophers of the eighth and ninth centuries. It was declared a state doctrine by the Abbasid caliphs, al-Mamun and al-Mutassim, and more than ten centuries after its birth, Mu'tazilism played a key role in shaping the ideas of Muslim reformers of the colonial era. It even inspired Hindu social reformers and modernizers like Rammohan Roy, whose *Tuhfat-ul-Muvahidin* is replete with Mu'tazila influences. Reacting against the Jabriyah orthodoxy of that period, the Mu'tazila sought a reconciliation of faith with reason.* This synthesis of Muslim theology with Greek logic gave birth to a theological science, called ilm-ul-Kalam, which was to form the basis of Muslim scholasticism and dominate Islamic thinking for centuries to come.[33] Syed Ahmad grappled with the same fundamental questions that Muslims of the early Middle Ages had faced in their encounter with Greek philosophy:

> Today we are in a need of a modern ilm-i-Kalam, by which we should refute the doctrines of modern science

---

*Aydin Sayili, a historian of science of Turkish origin and the author of the famous *The Observatory in Islam and Its Place in the General History of the Observatory* (1988), refers in detail to this failed reconciliation between Islam and Greek philosophy which surfaced as a battle between the Mu'tazilas and the Asharites, ending finally in the defeat of the former. In Christian Europe a reconciliation between Greek philosophy and religion was achieved, but not so in Islamic civilization. Clergymen were the obvious candidates to digest Greek learning. So they did in Christendom, but not in Islam, where awail sciences (present-day European sciences) were either ignored or actively opposed by orthodox theologians, despite the interest displayed by the Abbasid caliphs.

and undermine their foundation, or show that they are in conformity with the articles of Islamic faith. When I am endeavouring to introduce these sciences among the Muslims then it is my duty to defend the religion of Islam and to reveal its original bright face.[34]

Syed Ahmad's influence brought about a radical shift in Azad's inherited Islam. It emancipated him from the fetters of his family's orthodoxy, particularly his father's. Syed Ahmad unravelled Islam for him but now Azad wanted to move away from Islam itself, with a belief that all religions add to strife in the social life and do not bring about harmony as they claim to. He passed through a period of mental anguish when he gave up namaz.[35] He also abandoned celebrating Eid. Several philosophical questions cropped up in his mind and the answers to them were not easy to find. He continued his quest for further enquiry into the purpose of life, raising questions like, 'What is life and its meaning? The beginning and end of it? How to apprehend reality and truth? How do we determine that the method of finding Truth is valid?'[36]

After his father's death in 1908, writes Azad in his *Tazkirah*, he became open to lust and desire—which he never specifies in great detail. Azad describes this phase of his life, which he says lasted for seventeen months, in general terms:

> Intoxication filled the cups. Youth's frenzy took me by the hand. The yielding heart imagined that the path shown by desire and lust led to the destination. Though at first taken by surprise, wisdom and awareness too nodded in assent, that this was indeed the right path, and the right time to enjoy life.... Wherever I cast my eyes, I found a city populated by love adoration...each idol ravishing one's heart and reason, so beautiful that one felt compelled to offer it one's head; each sight of the loved one like a flash of lightening, consuming one's self-respect and self-control...each glance annihilating one's resistance.

> Every corner in which I sought refuge turned into a prison-house for my reason and sanity.... It is better to confess openly.... There is no licence and no heresy which I was not fated to experience.

Three main questions dominated Azad's mind:

1. Firstly, does God exist, and if so, what is the evidence of his wisdom and power in Creation?
2. Secondly, if reality is one, why are there different religions professed in the world by various communities and why are there differences in the world among communities concerning beliefs, traditions, religious practices, and laws, etc.? and
3. Thirdly, if religions promote peace and tranquillity, why does it lead to religious controversies and sectarian intolerance between Christians and Jews, Muslims and Hindus, and Shias and Sunnis?[37]

Azad was puzzled by the fact that so many religions lay claim to the truth but also say that Truth is one. His discomfort is palpable in the writings of this period of inner turmoil, where he is not able to overcome the inner conflict and is unable to decide whether to be a believer or a non-believer. Azad had to observe certain outward religious forms when his father was alive but inwardly he decried all forms of religion.[38] He wrote thus about his state of mind:

> My outward appearance was that of a man who wanted to reconcile religion with reason and intellectual discussion but within I had renounced all beliefs and in practice was a sinner. This was the final stage of my despair.[39]

Azad goes back to this issue again in one of his letters in *Ghubar-i-Khatir*, when he says that the faith he had lost was imitation and what he found was verified and authentic, reiterating his point with a Persian couplet from Urfi:

Raahe ke Khizr daasht z'sarchashma door bood
Lab tashnagi z'raah-e-digar barda emmaa

The path that the guide Khizr could show was far
from the source,
My thirst drove me to destination by another path.

Continuing the argument, Azad reiterated that as long as we remain blindfolded by inherited beliefs and conformist faith, we cannot find true faith. The moment the blindfold falls we begin to see clearly that the true path was neither far nor lost, only our own blindness had misled us in the midst of light.[40] Azad came to realize now 'that what was always believed to be religion was merely a picture of our superstitions and misapprehensions, not religion.'[41] Azad attempted to define true faith when he said that 'one is your ancestral religion; you pin faith on it because it has been your family tradition. Another is geographical religion, which you follow as it has become the mainstream in the area where you live. A third variety is religion of census; you get Islam entered in the religion column and the matter ends. Ritualism is another form of religion; there is a structure of rites and rituals which you continue to follow and become part of. But, apart from all these, there is an essential religion which, for the sake of identification, has to be described as essential religion and it is this path that is lost.'[42]

JAMALUDDIN AFGHANI AND PAN-ISLAMIC ANTI-IMPERIALISM

It is now widely recognized that the pages of *Al-Hilal* and *Al-Balagh* are saturated with the ideas and revolutionary fervour of Sheikh Jamaluddin Afghani, a peripatetic pan-Islamist and anti-imperialist. He was also one of those modernists of Islam who tried to redefine faith in response to the changing times. We can see the spirit of Afghani in the writings of Azad and in his *Tarjuman* as well. One can imagine the influence of Afghani, Abduh, and Rashid Rida* by the fact that the first issue of *Al-Hilal*, dated 13 July 1912, carried in its inaugural issue photos of all three.

Afghani was not very different from Syed Ahmad Khan in stressing the benefits of philosophy and science. This was probably one reason why Azad was impressed by both, though they disliked each other, or at least Afghani did because Syed Ahmad did not make his views about him public. In his Calcutta lecture titled 'On Teaching and Learning', Afghani emphasized the importance of modern science and philosophy. He was passionate in his desire to convince nineteenth-century conservatives to embrace modern science and philosophy. Although he hoped for a modernized Islam, he strongly emphasized the need to avoid identification with the West. Syed Ahmad, on the other hand, had resolved this contradiction. He had no hesitation in openly conceding the superiority of modern Western civilization and the need to borrow and learn from its advancements in knowledge. Despite his opposition to the West, Afghani went on to say that all great empires had been supported by science, up to and including the European conquerors of his time. 'Ignorance is always subjugated by science, which is the basis of advanced technology in all fields.'[43] According to him, it was not the French or the English who had colonized the non-European world, but rather the greatness and power of science. In his lecture at Calcutta, Afghani discussed the medieval philosopher's concept of philosophy as the organizing soul of the sciences: 'The science that has the position of a comprehensive soul and

---

*Rashid Rida was born in a village near Tripoli in 1865. He was initially under the influence of Abduh, who was also involved in a modernist movement. Later, after Abduh's death, he moved away from his influence and went closer to the Wahhabi/Salafi ideology. He founded a paper called *Al-Manar* that made a huge impact in the late nineteenth and early twentieth centuries. Even Maulana Azad was inspired by his writings. The Lebanese British historian Albert Hourani believed that Rida belonged to the last generation of traditionally trained Islamic scholars.

the rank of a preserving force is the science of falsafa or philosophy, because its subject is universal.... It applies each of the sciences in its proper place.'[44] He was critical of the Indian ulema, who, he said, were still busy reading and teaching *Sadra* and *Shams-i-Bazegha*, a seventeenth-century Indian text by Mulla Mahmud Jaunpuri.* They 'vaingloriously call themselves sages, and despite this they cannot distinguish their left hand from their right hand, and they do not ask: "Who are we and what is right and proper for us?" They never ask the causes of electricity, the steam boat, and railroads.'[45]

In today's context, the most serious criticism of the ulema is expressed in Afghani's shock when he found that the ulema had divided science into Muslim science and European science and thus forbidden the teaching of some of the useful sciences. For him all 'those who forbid science and knowledge in the belief that they are safeguarding the Islamic religion are really the enemies of that religion.' The names 'rational' and 'revealed' sciences were also used by the ulema, emphasizing a methodological distinction between the so-called Muslim sciences and the non-Muslim sciences. For while the awail sciences or the present-day European sciences were the products of the human mind, the Islamic sciences were based on revealed truth, i.e., they had sprung out of Islam religion or were closely connected with it. According to Montgomery, 'a distinction 'was made by the conservative clerics between 'native' and 'foreign' learning, and this allowed sides to be drawn over the conflict between traditional allegiances to a purer (and more parochial) Islam versus the new hopes for a more international Islam. Greek knowledge was perceived by all to be a tool for the latter. It was seen by the orthodox clerics as a threat to 'Islamic science', whose grouping of studies (law, philosophy, rhetoric) were deeply grounded in the Quran.'[46]

---

*Mulla Mahmud Jaunpuri was a mathematician and astronomer during Mughal emperor Shah Jahan's time.

Afghani, however, was convinced that the Islamic religion was the closest of all religions to science and knowledge and there was no incompatibility between them. Hence, he did not find the need, like Syed Ahmad, to reinterpret Islam to make it compatible with the requirements of modern science. For him the culprits were the leaders of Islam—the maulvis, who needed a radical change in their attitude towards not only science, but the world in general, which had made rapid strides in the past few hundred years. The minds of the Muslim logicians in India, according to Afghani, were full of superstition and vanity and there existed no difference between their ideas and the ideas of the masses of the bazaar. He went to the extent of saying that the ulema at this time were like a very narrow wick on top of which is a very small flame that neither lights its surroundings nor gives light to others.[47] His mission was to awaken Muslims from obscurantism and encourage them to embrace Western science and rationalism, which he considered inherent in the Quran.[48]

We can find quite a lot of compatibility in the ideas and visions of Azad and Afghani, particularly in their perception of Islam and the centrality provided to critical thinking or rationality in the faith. Both of them also regretted that Islam had gradually, over the centuries, lost this spirit. Like Afghani, Azad found it fallacious to say that Islam and modern science are contradictory or that the pursuit of science leads to atheism.[49] While delivering the convocation address at the Aligarh Muslim University in 1949, Azad touched on this issue once again. He recalled the serious obstacles faced by the reformers in the nineteenth century, possibly referring here to the several modernist reformers of nineteenth-century Islam, including Syed Ahmad and Afghani, when they began to advocate the cause of modern scientific education. 'The cry of religion,' Azad said, 'supplied the opponents of progress with one of their most potent weapons. The path of religion is not in fact opposed to that of reason and knowledge but unfortunately that has often been represented to be so. The usual cry was that Western education was opposed to the teachings of religion and those who held religion dear must therefore adhere to the old tradition.'[50] Azad explained this phenomenon through history and argued that human thought has had to face this conflict at different times in different countries—Europe went through this struggle in the seventeenth and eighteenth centuries while Eastern countries faced this conflict in the nineteenth century. Like Afghani, he was disgusted with the ulema of the time that were quick to block all progress and reform. He wrote to Muhiuddin Kasuri declaring: 'The ulema are a hopeless lot. To believe that a traditional mind can still give way to regeneration is to believe against the laws of nature. We have no alternative but to ignore the rigid thinking altogether, focusing on the creation of a new mind which requires a radically different variety of literature and apprenticeship.'[51] He firmly believed that 'the courses of study had been narrowed down to the point of no return, not to speak of allowing introduction of modern arts and sciences.'* He was not only critical of the prevalent madrassa system of education that kept away from modern scientific education; he equally castigated the Aligarh College 'for its intellectual sterility'. Reminded of the great centres of learning, like Cordova, Granada, and Baghdad in the history of Islam, he observed the utter impotence and futility of Aligarh in advancing the cause of modern science and philosophy within the Indian Muslim community.[52] Let me quote this longish passage from Azad's article in *Al-Hilal*, where we see him at his sarcastic best. We need to keep in mind that Azad was also critical of the politics of the Aligarh

*In his strident criticism of the ossified system of education, Azad wrote: 'Today madrassas do exist, teachers do teach, students do learn, and there is also a specific curriculum in practice; but in spite of all this, education has been suffering from the backwardness over which we have lamented to the extent of becoming ridiculous.' Abul Kalam Azad, *Al-Hilal*, 29 July 1914.

group, so his acerbic and derisive tenor may be placed in that context as well. He wrote:

> If people recall the name of the Aligarh College, they get an onslaught of asthma. The sentiment that compels its ignorant partisans to hide its defects makes its critics shed the tears of blood. For God's sake tell me about the arrangements made for the dissemination of modern sciences and philosophy at this Islamic centre, at this dome of the Muslim community, at this modern Cordova, at this present-day Granada, at this pale imitation of Cambridge and Oxford? What literary and scientific societies have been organized? How many scholars, in the real sense of the term, are produced? And how many of its ex-students translated works on modern philosophy and sciences or made original contributions to these subjects?[53]

Azad expected Aligarh College to pursue modern sciences and philosophy and expressed regret that it did not do that. He also hoped that the college would adhere to the Islamic spirit, more so because the pursuit of modern science was not perceived by him as an un-Islamic vocation. For him both the tasks could be carried out without compromising the faith or undermining Islam. As a young man, as pointed out earlier, Azad was infatuated with Sir Syed's vision of westernization, however he later found comfort in the company of Sulaiman Nadwi, who himself began alongside Sir Syed but later distanced himself and founded al-Nadwa in Lucknow. Azad was critical of the Aligarh group because they emphasized modern education aimed at mere employment and not education per se. Under Sir Syed's influence he strongly felt that there was no conflict between the Quran and science. He believed that the theory expounded by Darwin agrees with the spirit of the Quran.[54] Moreover, Azad always stood by Sir Syed's fight against imitation and his strong endorsement of ijtihad. The *Al-Hilal* phase in Azad's life reflects this ambivalence in his treatment of issues related to modern scientific education. For example, commenting on a review article by Sulaiman Nadwi, in which he says that Azad 'declared the present ruin of the Muslims to be due to their mental slavery to the philosophy of ancient Greece and modern Europe', Professor Mohammad Habib points out how such arguments only show how even the most progressive of the ulema failed to understand Azad. Habib claims that Azad 'objected to the interpretation of the Quran in terms of Greek thought, but to Greek philosophy, science, art, music, culture…he had no objection whatsoever. Also [Azad] at no stage of his career objected to the complete acceptance of European science in every field.'[55] It is a fact that Azad always had Aligarh and its students in mind when he wrote about modern scientific education in the context of Islam. He found them lacking in true love for knowledge. 'Agnosticism used to be considered the result of the spread of learning. But what shall we say of agnosticism which is now linked to sheer ignorance.' It was this lack of knowledge which prompted Azad to introduce columns on scientific matters in *Al-Hilal*.[56]

Jamaluddin Afghani was engaged in a similar task, just a few decades before Maulana Azad. When Afghani was invited by the modernist Ali Pasha, who was a part of the Tanzimat reforms in the Ottoman empire,* to speak at the newly established Darulfunun-i-Osmani, a new modern university, he saw it as a challenge and an opportunity to raise pertinent issues. Thanks to his Persian background in heterodox philosophy, Afghani was more likely than the Sunni Ottoman ulema to recognize the importance of reason and science.[57] I am not sure that this stereotypical view, true to some extent, is valid anymore. In his first recorded speech at the secular-

*The Tanzimat was a period of modernist reform in Ottoman Turkey between 1839 and 1876. It did not aim at any radical transformation but at the social and political consolidation of the foundations of Ottoman empire. It also aimed at integrating the non-Muslim subjects of the empire into Turkish society.

minded Darulfunun-i Osmani in 1870, Afghani lamented the ignorance bred by madrassas and 'dervish convents' among the Islamic people (milla) and their subjugation by the scientific West:

> My brothers, Arise from the sleep of neglect. Know that the Islamic people were (once) the strongest in rank, the most valuable in worth.... Later these people sank into ease and laziness...some of the Islamic nations came under the domination of other nations. The clothes of abasement were put on them. The glorious milla was humiliated. All these things happened from lack of vigilance, laziness, working too little, and stupidity.... Are we not going to take an example from the civilized nations? Let us cast a glance at the achievement of others. By effort they have achieved the final degree of knowledge and the peak of elevation. For us too all the means are ready, and there remains no obstacle to our progress. Only our laziness, stupidity, and ignorance are obstacles to (our) advance.[58]

Almost ten years later, when Afghani was in India in 1880–82, while continuing with his anti-imperialist stance, he warned the Indian ulema against the rejection of foreign sciences and innovation and urged them not to reject everything that is associated with the West. He said:

> The desire to protect fatherland and nationality (watan wa jins) and the wish to defend religion and co-religionists, that is patriotic zeal, national zeal, and religious zeal are essential and a lot can be accomplished through them, but the Muslims in India have applied the desire to defend religion, or religious zeal in a very bad way. For they have carried zeal, through misuse, to a point where it has become a cause of hatred for knowledge and the sciences, and a reason for aversion toward industries and innovation. They believe they must, out of religious

zeal, hate and abominate what was connected with the opponent's faith, even though these things were sciences and arts.[59]

When Azad spoke and wrote several decades later, we find a similar sentiment in his utterances. As an Islamic scholar, Azad did not see modern science and Islam or even the East and West as incompatible. While speaking at a symposium in 1951, Maulana Azad clearly spelt out the compatibility of East and West:

> The Eastern conception of man's status is not only consistent with the progress of Western science, but in fact offers an intelligible explanation of how scientific progress is possible. If man were merely a developed animal, there would be a limit to his advancement. If, however, he shares in God's infinity, there can be no limit to the progress he can achieve. Science can then march from triumph to triumph and solve many of the riddles which trouble man even to this day.[60]

Azad emphasizes further in his address when he says:

> Science is neutral. Its discoveries can be used equally to heal and to kill. It depends upon the outlook and mentality of the user whether science will be used to create a new heaven on earth or to destroy the world in a common conflagration. If we think of man as only a progressive animal, there is nothing to prevent his using science to further interests based on the passions he shares in common with animals. If, however, we think of him as an emanation of God, he can use science only for the furtherance of God's purpose that is the achievement of peace on earth and goodwill to all men.[61]

Azad refers to Mohammad Abduh, who carried forward the task in Egypt, initiated by Afghani, his guru. He borrowed from Abduh the methods of theology and its presentation in the modern age. Born in a village of the Nile delta, Abduh proved to be one of the greatest thinkers of his age. Abduh's call for a more progressive Islam, paradoxically, considered the first community of Muslims—the Prophet Muhammad and his followers, known in Arabic as the salaf, or forefathers—as a role model.[62] Abduh was thus one of the founders of a new line of reformist thought that came to be called Salafism, a term now associated with Osama bin Laden and the most radical wing of Muslim anti-Western activism. However, it was not so in Abduh's time. By invoking the forefathers of Islam, Abduh was hearkening back to a golden age when Muslims observed their religion 'correctly' and, as a consequence, emerged as the dominant world power. This period of Muslim dominance throughout the Mediterranean and extending deep into South Asia lasted for the first four centuries of Islam. Thereafter, he argued, Islamic thought ossified, mysticism crept in, rationalism waned, and the community fell into a blind observance of the law. Only by stripping Islam of these accretions could the ummah return to the pure and rational practices of the forefathers and recover the dynamism that once made Islam the dominant world civilization.[63] Abduh was inspired by the Mu'tazilites of the earlier centuries of Islam, he criticized some of the established Hadiths, including the ones that promote misogyny, and argued for the emancipation of Muslim women.[64] Turkish scholar Mustafa Akyol talks about the neo-Mu'tazilite trend which grew among the Arab intellectuals in the early twentieth century, where a leading Egyptian scholar and intellectual Ahmad Amin remarked in 1936 that 'the demise of Mu'tazilism was the greatest misfortune to have afflicted Muslims; they have committed a crime against themselves.'[65] In any case, these early reformists and pan-Islamists like Afghani and Abduh were opposed to European colonialism and subjugation of the Muslim lands but they were far from being anti-Western. Abduh, who travelled in Europe, famously said that in Paris he saw 'Islam without Muslims', and on his return to Egypt he saw 'Muslims without Islam'. He felt that all the good things Muslim societies should have were in the West but not in Islamdom.[66]

Azad's early years as a religious thinker can be seen to be coloured with such a pristine vision of Islam's past. He was, as a matter of fact, quite impressed by the Salafi doctrine initiated by Abduh, and of course was impressed by Abduh's fascination with modern science and the West. This was one of the phases of Azad's intense intellectual struggle that began very early in his life, though he didn't stay here for very long—we can call this a phase 'of intense dogmatism, then scepticism, followed by denial and repudiation and then a real rapprochement'.[67]

STANDING UP FOR SARMAD SHAHEED (AND DARA SHUKOH)

Maulana Azad's career as a scholar of Islam began early, and it saw several twists and turns. On many occasions these shifts were quite contradictory and ambiguous. It was during the time when Azad admired Abduh's Salafism that he wrote a major essay defending Sarmad in 1910. At this point, Azad had rejected his father's creed and had found his own. This essay on Sarmad* represents the creed Azad had discovered for himself. Still, there are diverse opinions about Azad's evolution as a thinking scholar. Malikzada Manzoor Ahmad argued in his work on Azad that Azad believed in the unity of all religions, which is reflected in most of his publications like *Al-Hilal* and *Tazkirah*.[68] According to Minault and Troll, editors of Douglas's book on Azad, the essay on Sarmad was

*Sarmad (the takhallus of Mohammad Said) was an Armenian Jew born in Kashan who converted to Islam and came to India as a trader in the seventeenth century. He was a poet and scholar of comparative religions. He arrived in India in 1632 at the age of forty-two, settling in Thatta, the capital and port of Sindh. Here he fell in love with a Hindu Vaishya boy Abhai Chand and was so infatuated that he gave up his business and became a naked fakir.

the precursor to Azad's religious and political ideas, which came to guide his life.[69] Troll reiterated the same argument several years later in a research paper.[70] Thus Malikzada and Troll thought that Azad's love of humanity, his advocacy of a composite culture, and his fight for the freedom of his country, all originated from what he expounded in his essay on Sarmad.[71] M. Mujeeb believed that Azad did not change, instead he was liberal and eclectic from the beginning and remained so all his life.

But I believe that Azad's Sarmad essay was an ephemeral, and yet important, milestone in his intellectual evolution. He was not a systematic thinker but an artist, 'his compartmentalized thinking and pragmatic concerns of the moment were far more urgent for him than constructing a consistent philosophical scheme.'[72] V. N. Datta is right when he says that 'Azad's religious and political ideas never remained static. The difference between Azad and traditional Muslim jurists was that Azad had an open and vibrant mind. He assimilated ideas from whatever quarter they came, while the mullahs clung to religious orthodoxy and were quite oblivious to the changes taking place in contemporary social and political conditions.[73]

This essay was written on the request of his old friend Khwaja Hasan Nizami of Dargah Nizamuddin Auliya, who had planned a shahid nambar, or special issue, of his Urdu periodical *Nizam al-Mashaikh*. The essay is a celebratory account of the two much ignored, if not much maligned, characters in the Islamic history of India—Sarmad and his friend Prince Dara Shukoh. Sarmad's eclectic and Sufi form of Islam was always unpalatable to the empowered mullahs. Dara Shukoh, too, was projected as a heretic in comparison to his brother, the puritan Aurangzeb. It is so pertinent for our times to revisit this essay and locate Maulana Azad's perceptive commentary on early twentieth-century Islam. Despite it having been a few hundred years since both Sarmad and Dara were killed for reneging on their faith, we are still persecuting fellow Muslims and others in the name of blasphemy in South Asia and elsewhere.

Sarmad Shaheed and Dara Shukoh, we may say, were the first victims of heresy/blasphemy laws in South Asia. Even in our current context, these laws form the origins of the blasphemy laws in Pakistan. Sarmad fell in love with a Hindu boy called Abhai Chand in the Sindh region. Azad saw this temporal love as the first stage in the journey towards the ultimate Divine Beloved. Sarmad didn't know, says Azad, that 'he would have to trade in the marketplace of beauty and love instead of silver and gold'.

Sarmad came to Delhi in 1654 and entered the close circle of Dara Shukoh, where he was in the company of saints, sadhus, monks, and priests. Azad calls Dara a dervish who spent most of his time in the company of philosophers and Sufis. He was the author of books like *Majma-ul-Bahrayn* (*Merging of the Two Oceans*) about Islam and Hinduism, and *Sirr-i-Akbar*, a translation of Upanishads and the Bhagwat Gita into Persian. Maulana Azad, according to Syeda Saiyidain Hameed, ranked Dara Shukoh with Sarmad due to his capacity to rise above the narrow dogma of state-oriented religion towards an appreciation of the universal truth in all faiths. In both prince and saint, Azad saw a reflection of what he himself wanted to achieve. Azad also perceived both Sarmad and Dara as victims of the nexus between the state and religion.

Azad explains in his essay that Sarmad was not a great political threat to Aurangzeb and thus puts his execution in the broader history of Islam. Most of what Azad wrote sounds so contemporaneous in the context of Islam and the global political mess around it:

> Throughout the thirteen centuries of Islam the pen of the jurists had been an unsheathed sword and the blood of thousands of truth-loving persons stains their verdicts (fatwa). Whichever angle you study the history of Islam,

countless examples will illustrate how, whenever a ruler came to the point of shedding blood, the pen of mufti and the sword of a General rendered him equal service. This was not confined to the Sufis and the nobles; for those ulema who close to the seers of the mysteries of truth and reality also had to suffer misfortunes from the hands of jurists and in the end obtained deliverance in giving their lives. Sarmad, too was murdered by the same sword.[74]

In India, we are fortunate that frivolous fatwas do not lead to executions, yet they do make some impact on the gullible and expose Islam to avoidable ridicule.

Azad comments on the three reasons for Sarmad's execution. First, he recited only two words—la illaha—of the Kalima, which was a negation of God. Azad believed that as a Sufi and a scholar, Sarmad had reached the stage of denial and not an affirmation of God yet. Approving Sarmad's refusal to recite the full Kalima, Azad writes: 'Why should Sarmad have said, 'It exists', concerning something he was not sure about yet...Sarmad's crime was that he drank the cup in public, while others drank in private.' The second reason was that he moved around naked, which was not socially acceptable. The third was that he disputed the accepted interpretation of meraj (Prophet ascending to heaven). The two lines of his rubai, which were interpreted as heresy by the clerics, are worth sharing:

Mullah says that Mohammad ascended the Heavens
Sarmad says that the Heavens descended to Mohammad

Azad found no reason to see this couplet as heretical at all. On the contrary, he found the ulema deeply seeped in literalism and suffering from a lack of imagination and failing to realize that Sarmad had been elevated in the eyes of Allah. Azad reacts poetically when he says, '...they (the ulema) climbed on the pulpits of their mosques and madrassas and dreamt about the heights to which they could still rise. But Sarmad had reached the pinnacle of love from where the walls of the mosque and the temple are seen standing face to face.'

More than hundred years ago, Maulana Azad could appreciate and applaud Dara Shukoh's eclecticism and Sarmad's free thinking and humanitarianism. Unfortunately, all such possibilities of dissent and critical engagement with Islam are almost closed today. We even see some copycat reactions among other religions, where they also want to be the mirror image of a religion they love to hate. Maulana Azad expressed his disillusionment with the ulema in one of his letters where he declared: 'The ulema are a hopeless lot.... We have no alternative but to ignore the rigid thinking altogether, focussing on the creation of a new mind which requires a radically different variety of literature and apprenticeship.'

TARJUMAN AL-QURAN: HIS MAGNUM OPUS

This is the opportune moment for us to move to the magnum opus of Maulana Azad, *Tarjuman al-Quran*. This was a phase in his life when two of his important journalistc ventures, *Al-Hilal* and *Al-Balagh*, were banned by the British and he was interned near Ranchi in 1916 for being a threat to the British empire. He had not yet joined the Congress to fight against colonial oppression but was still perceived by the British as dangerous. It was during this phase that Azad announced an ambitious plan, in 1915, to publish his Urdu translation of the Quran, called *Tarjuman al-Quran*, followed by *Tafsir al-Bayan*, which was meant to provide interpretations of some significant parts of the Quran, and finally, *Muqaddima-i-Tafsir* to serve as prolegomena to the previous two volumes. He says, 'The three works, as I thought, were to meet the needs of three distinct sets of people interested in the Quran—the translation, the needs of the average reader; the commentary, of those who cared to make a detailed study of the Quran;

and the prolegomena, the needs of the advanced scholar.'[75] Sadly, like few other literary works of Azad, this plan also remained incomplete—he could only manage to publish part of the translation and commentary on Quran.

Circumstances turned this project into a never-ending ordeal. The manuscript was destroyed several times by the British police, first during his confinement in Ranchi between 1916 and 1920, and later when he was arrested during the Non-cooperation Movement in 1921. 'It is distressing to rewrite even a single page of what had already been written and lost forever. To revive enthusiasm for intellectual effort once it is smothered by the ruination of one's achievements is by no means easy. Only those can appraise the agony who themselves have passed through it.'[76] Yet, these shocks did not dampen his spirits. He got back to the project with the same enthusiasm and managed to complete at least part of it. Till he went through this traumatic experience, Azad did not believe that Carlyle, who lost his entire work during the French Revolution, did something extraordinary by rewriting it. 'No greater proof could be adduced to establish the greatness of Carlyle as a man of letters.'

Azad's political profile and engagement had also changed since he started this massive project. His involvement with Congress politics had increased even as there was pressure from those who realized the significance of his project on Quran to go ahead with the publication of *Tarjuman al-Quran*.

But Azad was determined to carry on the task to refurbish the Muslim mind through his *Tarjuman al-Quran*. He realized the significance of his task and also felt concerned that if he left it unattended then 'one never knew after what lapse of time what arrangement was possible to fulfil it'. He began in earnestness, with initial hindrances, but soon got attuned to the new situation, and a feeling crept in as if, he writes, 'the past mishaps of life never had any existence for me.' Soon, writes Azad, 'I felt I was seized with the urge to write that I realized that I could not control the movement of my pen.' He was convinced that Surah al-Fatiha was of primary importance to the understanding of the Quran, so he devoted himself to its study. Despite unfavourable circumstances, Azad, as he writes, 'persisted on, and on the 20th of July 1930, when I was in the District Jail of Meerut, I finished my work.' It was in the preface of this edition that Azad reflectively recorded his trials and tribulations in the pursuit of Islamic learning when he said:

> The subject has engaged my mind seriously over a long period of 27 years. Every chapter of the Quran, every part of it, and indeed every verse and every word of it has obliged me to traverse innumerable valleys and to counter numerous obstacles. I may assert that I have looked into a considerable portion of the vast literature, both published and unpublished, that exists today on the subject; and there is not, I believe, any corner of the Quranic knowledge, and of all that has been written so far on the problems that it raises, which I have left unnoticed. Distinction is, no doubt, usually made between the old and the new learning. But in my search for truth, this distinction has never counted with me. The old, I have received as my heritage; and the new is as familiar to me as the old, and I have delved into both:
>
> I have been in life a libertine and a man of piety too. One by one, I can easily recognize-alike the pious and the libertine.
>
> What my family traditions, my education, and my social environment had offered me in the making of my mind, I was from the very beginning of my life, reluctant to rest content with. The bonds of inherited dependence on the past could not hold me under. The zest of search for truth never forsook me. There is hardly a single conviction in me which has not had to bear the strings of doubt, or a single belief which has not faced the test of denial. I have gulped in poison mixed

with every draught applied to my lips, and have also administered to myself elixir coming forth from every quarter. Whenever I felt thirsty, my parched lips did not resemble the lips of others who were equally thirsty, and when I quenched my thirst, it was not from the same fountain as others did. Whatever I could gather in my search for the Quranic truth during this lengthy period of my ability; and spread over the pages of this volume.[77]

Syed Abdul Latif, eminent scholar and translator of *Tarjuman* into English regarded 'this passage as Maulana's swan song; for the circumstances of his life thereafter, marked by a lengthy period of fierce political struggle in the cause of his country, hardly allowed him the time or opportunity to pursue further Islamic studies of any serious importance or of striking originality.'[78]

There have been commentaries on the Quran before but most of them have failed to take the real message of the Quran to its followers or even to the non-Muslim others. One of the reasons for this could be the lack of critical engagement with the Book, something that could have unravelled the real meaning of the Book's message to a wider audience. Most of the commentaries were almost celebratory in nature, where any critical reading and deciphering of the text was rendered impossible. Maulana Azad was conscious of this tradition that he had inherited and wanted to transcend.

Maulana Azad perceived this degeneration of the Muslim mind decades back, what is happening today in India and elsewhere is just an extension of the malaise that began decades ago. In his *Tarjuman*, Azad emphasized the original spirit of engagement with the Quranic text, which was available to all believers of Islam. He refused to accept the canonized Islam; instead he called for independent reasoning or ijtihad to interpret the faith. His *Tarjuman* is written in this spirit, warning Muslims against reading more than what was intended to be conveyed in the Quran. This sounds prophetic when we examine the contemporary context where Islam is invoked by many to claim what they want the Book to claim.[79]

However, many scholars have found Azad problematic in his reference to mutually contradictory positions, like his profession of Sufistic beliefs along with Ibn Taymiyyah's Shariatic tradition. The *Tarjuman* simultaneously invoked esoteric Sufi traditions as well as the literalist and canonical textuality of the fiqh tradition, and further back, in Azad's desire to equally inhabit the ecstatic world of Sarmad (as in the 1910 essay) as well as the punitive, puritanical world of Sirhindi (as in *Tazkirah*), laid bare its contradictions.[80] Azad seemed to be torn between these two major divisions in Islam and not very sure where he actually belonged. The *Tarjuman* is also replete with such split images of the man, who expresses himself strongly in both. However, 'It must be said, though, that the main thrust of the *Tarjuman* was in the direction of tolerance, magnanimity, ecumenism, and the treatment of religion not as a mandatory and exclusivist ritual but as essentially an inward, aesthetic experience.'[81] It is indeed commendable that Azad initiated this sort of project in the politically volatile climate of the 1920s and 1930s when communally divisive forces were on the rise. The Muslim League was using Islam to polarize the Muslims, doing their utmost to prove that Islam is antithetical to Hinduism to justify the demand for a separate Muslim nation. Azad emphasized the civilizational compact between the Muslims and Hindus of India, and of communities generally, to live a life of togetherness as a nation through this work.

Azad insists that the Quran discourages one from wrangling over variations as long as they stick to the basic ideology. Abdul Latif makes a pertinent point when he says:

> Mawlana Azad's painful observation is that this ideology which was meant to keep mankind together as but one family, has, in the course of history, been disfigured

> by vested interests giving rise to a variety of credal dissensions between man and man. He devotes one full section to the subject of the concept of God to show how the followers of each religion including Islam have interfered with the basic concept of Divine Unity. It is round this primary regret of his that his entire discourse revolves: and he makes a pathetic appeal to one and all to return to the basic ideology. This is the way to peace and harmony among mankind. It is, in fact, a call for religious tolerance and self-purification.[82]

Maulana Azad, in his preface, laid down his plan to explain the Quran and how it had been read and understood over the centuries. He emphasized that Quran was a simple text, which could be comprehended easily by lay believers. 'The first generation of people among whom the Quran appeared were not a sophisticated race, they were simple-minded people and not accomplished in philosophical niceties. They were content to receive a simple thought in its plain simplicity. That was why the Quranic thought, simple as it was, sank easily into their hearts.'[83] The Prophet's companions were quick to grasp the meaning of the verse as soon as they heard it. However, Azad is uncomfortable with the later generation which followed, as they brought in influences from Roman and Iranian civilizations, which were sweeping over the new Arab empire. I am not competent to question Maulana's theological competence and erudition but will surely comment on his ambiguities and also his understanding of history. He seemed to have overlooked the fact that Islam was not confined to the Arab race or Arabic language and culture. It expanded into diverse cultural and linguistic groups, all of whom naturally read the Book differently from the early generation of Arab Muslims. Azad seem to be unhappy at this change in the reading of the Book—when the new generation starts reading the Quran, he says:

> Translations from the Greek literature gave them new literary tastes and initiated them into the art of dialectics. Zest for novelty and inventiveness in approach to everything came to be ever on the increase, with the result that the simplicity of the Quranic manner gradually lost its charm for them. Slowly, step by step, a stage was reached when everything Quranic was attempted to be given an artificial mould. Since the Quranic thought could not fit into any such mould, serious complications in thought arose, with every attempt at resolving them ending in more intricate complications.[84]

One can understand the diversity of interpretations but I do not think that this should be seen as un-Islamic or against the spirit of Islam. The Prophet himself reiterated that God has given us the Book and the brains to comprehend it. And the brains were as diverse as the believers themselves, constituting varied cultures, languages, and historical contexts. They read, commented, and practised the Quran as they understood it. Despite the simplicity of Quranic language, Arabic was not the mother tongue for a majority of the believers. They may have faltered many times in getting to the real meaning of a particular verse, which of course led to ambiguities in many of the commentaries of the Book. Azad was in a much better position. Arabic was his mother tongue, he also spent few early years speaking that language alone, and of course he was the son of a scholar of Islam, who also spent several decades in the Arab world. Thus, I find this criticism of the lay believers or even Islamic scholars in general a bit harsh. Actually, the real problem began very early, when the Quran, the word of God for the believers, was declared to be the ultimate panacea for every malaise. The ulema took control and declared themselves the God-appointed interlocutors between Him and the lay believers. All possibilities of independent thinking or ijtihad were closed. In such a situation, reformers of nineteenth-century Islam in India and elsewhere were confronted with an uphill task. The tradition or taqlid had firmly trapped the believers. Maulana Azad, while writing his *Tarjuman*, had such a community and Islam to engage with.

However, Azad is categorical in placing the majority of the blame on the diverse believers who complicated the reading of the simple Quranic text. He says in his introduction:

> The Quran is so simple to understand and yet we do not feel happy until we evaluate its worth by fanciful standards of our own making, standards so distasteful to the purposes of the Quran. That is the picture which today confronts us at every turn.[85]

For Azad, any commentator on the Quran needed to have some taste and accomplishment in literature, and 'for various reasons this taste steadily grew weaker among our commentators, resulting in inept approaches to the Quranic word or to the idiom and usage of the language in which the Quran had been delivered'.[86] Any commentator's approach to the various readings of the Quran was impacted by historical changes which he calls 'the atmospheric influence of every preceding age'. This influence for him was as true and significant as it is in the fields of arts and sciences, thus the reading of the Quran was not beyond the changing circumstances in which it was commented upon. The early scholars of Islam remained mostly unaffected by political influence and seldom tolerated compromises in the doctrinal beliefs of Islam, however, such influences do not come about only through political influences. There are many doors for the influence to seep in and once that happens the doors scarcely close thereafter. Thus, for Azad, 'the general character of the minds of men could not remain unaffected'.

According to Azad, the period of enquiry and research in Islamic learning came to an end after the close of the fourth century of the Hijra (tenth or early eleventh century), and thereafter, barring certain exceptions, the tendency to lean on the past for every idea took hold of the mind of the learned. He was critical of taqlid or the inherited tradition from his childhood, disagreeing even with his scholarly father, so as far as he was concerned all such commentators and their commentaries had no originality. Writing about such scholars in the preface to *Tarjuman* he said:

> Everyone who ever attempted to write a commentary of the Quran chose as a matter of course to have before him the work of some predecessor and to follow it blindly in every detail. If, for instance, a commentator of the third century had committed a serious blunder in the understanding of any particular passage in the Quran, it became the bounden duty of those who came after him to reproduce word by word whatever he had written. No one for a moment paused to scrutinize the statement or question it. The result was that gradually few could develop the urge to write fresh commentaries.[87]

Azad goes further about the commentaries, that made the readings of the Quran even worse, which he called 'Tafsir-bir-rai' or commentary which lets the text subserve one's own opinion on any subject, this was something that the companions of the Prophet did not approve of. 'Not that reason and insight were tabooed in Islam. Were it so, all study of the Quranic thought would seem futile; for the Quran openly invites its readers to exercise reason in their approach to it, and ponder on what it states. At every corner of its presentation, it exclaims:

> Do they meditate on the Quran
> Or, are there locks on their minds. (Q:47:24)'[88]

This is so central to the Islam we practise today that there is hardly any possibility of critically understanding the faith or even its history. Besides this, when several schools of theology arose over the centuries, each of them tried to use the Quran to justify their own interpretation or point of view. It also led to sectarianism and 'the verses of the Quran were exploited to uphold, by hook or by crook, their own particular schismatic obsessions'.[89]

All these questions raised by Azad were valid, but his faith in the elders of Islam raises some doubts as well, particularly if we look at the history of those who are venerated as the upholders of the pristine faith. We often glorify the age of Pious Predecessors (salaf-e-saalihiin), which Azad also did, but that age was also marred by internecine conflicts—the fitnah. We can't ignore the fact that it impacted the future of Islamic faith as well as its history. The War of Riddah, the murder of Caliph Osman, the battle of Jamal and of Siffin all took place during the time of the elders. The early phase also saw the murder of Caliph Ali while he was praying in the mosque. All this took place within a few years after the death of the Prophet, even the Shia–Sunni schism occurred in that early phase, which brought about a paradigmatic shift in future Islamic theology as well. Mustafa Akyol is right when he says that 'only a quarter century after the Prophet's time—the age of happiness, as Muslims called it—fellow Muslims were spilling each other's blood. What happened to the idea that all believers were brothers in faith?'[90] We were also told that the founders of dynasties like Umayyads, Abbasids, Fatimids, the Mughals in India, and the Ottomans in Turkey were all guardians of Islamic faith. I am not saying that Azad held any of these views, but it does have a wide acceptance among the believers across the world. Rashid Shaz is right when he says that 'this created serious methodological problems for Muslim historiographers as they considered it their religious obligation to depict the early Muslims as superhumans, nay, rather angels. Had the Muslim historiographers done their job properly it would have been easier for us to realize that each generation of believers had its own strength and weakness and that the purpose of the prophetic mission was to create a society of humans and not of angels.'[91]

Maulana Azad was categorical even about prophets making 'it clear that the prophets are to be regarded as human beings who have a distinct role to play for the benefit of mankind'.[92] However, by the time Azad decided to interpret and translate the Quran for the people, it was already too late and we had a well-entrenched tradition of believers who had been exposed to centuries of misrepresentation of Islam and its history, a tradition that was already canonized.

Maulana, while translating and interpreting the Quran, also emphasized the fact that truth and humanity is ingrained in all faiths. And this is one major criticism of his *Tarjuman* that despite being a Muslim, he believed in 'the truth of all creeds'. This fact is ingrained in the first Surah of the Quran called Surah al-Fatiha, which he explains with immense passion and commitment. The Surah al-Fatiha, being the first chapter of the Quran, has for that reason styled Fatihatul-Kitab or the opening of the book. He begins the chapter on Surah by reproducing the seven phrases of the Surah thus:

Bismillahir Rahmanir Rahim
Alhamdolillahe Rabbil Alamin
Ar Rahmanir Rahim
Malik-i-Yawmiddin
Iyyakanabudu wa Iyyakanastaiin
Ihdenas siratal Mustaqeem
Siratal Lazeena an amta Alayhim
Ghairil Maghzube Alyhim wa lazzalin

In the name of Allah, the Beneficent, the Merciful
Praise be to Allah, Lord of the Worlds
The Beneficent, the Merciful
The Only Owner of the Day of Judgement
Thee alone we worship and Thee alone we ask for help

Show us the Straight Path
The path of those whom thou has favoured
Not the path of those who earn Thy anger
Nor those who go astray

Azad reiterates while explaining the Surah al-Fatiha, where it is categorically stated that 'by calling God Rabbul-Alamin, the Lord of all creation or of all forms of life, the Surah desires him to acknowledge the universal character of divine concern for every individual, group, community, country, and every form of existence.' Azad stresses that the Quran wanted to put 'an end to all notions of exclusiveness which had hitherto prevailed among mankind, assigning divine blessings and favours to one's own community.'[93] Azad foregrounds the significance of Surah al-Fatiha when he says that if a person cannot read the Quran, he may commit the import of these seven lines and he will understand the basic tenets of Islam. He further says that its significance can be measured by several other names it had been given like Umm-ul-Quran (the Core of the Quran), Al-Kafia (The Sufficient), Al-Kanz (the Treasure House), and Asasul Quran (the Basis of the Quran), with each emphasizing a particular aspect of its importance.[94]

Azad explains the seven verses in detail, however, I will try to focus on aspects which are essentially significant today, not only for the believers, but also for their relationship with others. The second verse proclaims that Rab is Rabbil Alamin (Lord of all beings) and not just the Rab or nourisher of the Muslims alone. Do we see this being practised at all? As a matter of fact, this is one of the major lapses we see among most of the believers, who have turned rabidly sectarian and self-righteous in their relationship with non-Muslim others. They have defeated the spirit of this most important Surah of Islam, often witnessed in the form of sectarian hatred and even violence. Azad was also not pleased with the ulema who interpreted the Quran according to Greek philosophy and science with inevitable misunderstandings, a point I have raised earlier as well. His staunch belief that the Quran must be understood as the Prophet and the Companions understood it sounds to me an idealistic expectation.

In this context we need to see what he wrote to a correspondent of *Al-Hilal*:

> You must always keep in view the difference between a religion and the followers of that religion; they are two different things and must be kept apart. Two-thirds of our disappointments are due to the fact that we forget this basic difference. We cannot take a single step towards the truth by starting from those ideas and beliefs, which are actually found in the minds of the followers of any inculcated religion.... Nevertheless there cannot be more than one path of truth. There were (seemingly) only two alternatives for the Quran; it could either affirm the correctness of the followers of all religions or condemn them all. It could not affirm the correctness of the followers of all religions for they were opposed to each other; similarly, it could not condemn all religions, for this would have meant declaring that the world had been always devoid of religious truths and the foundations of man's spiritual culture and improvement would have been overthrown. So the Quran chose a third path and declared: 'All the religions of the world are correct, but their followers have deviated from the truth. All ignorance, opposition, differences of claims, and conflicts of organizations, which we now find, are due to lack of intelligence and defective actions of the followers of religions; in the teachings of religions there is no difference whatsoever.' If these differences between the followers of religions, which are not based on truth, could be removed, then that which is true would be left with every religious group.... This is that 'unity of Truth' (mushtarik haq), the spiritual content of which is found in all the religions of the world.'[95]

What Azad said above is a very noble ideal and I wish it was equally feasible as well. He himself arrived at this conclusion after going through a comparative assessment of different faiths from Judaism and Christianity to Hinduism. In the light of the Quranic notion of God and the Prophet, Azad states that there is no justification whatsoever for imposing one religion on another because the fundamentals of Din (faith) are one and the prophets have taught mankind the worship of the same God.[96] It is thus categorically clear that everyone has the right to follow her or his faith without any compulsion. There is no justification for people belonging to different religious faiths to revile or upbraid each other on the grounds of professing different faiths. If we go back to the early history of Islam, particularly in the midst of the who-is-right-and-who-is-wrong dispute between Ali and Muawiyah, a group of Muslims called the Murji'ites (Postponers), came up with a reconciliatory idea. They argued that it was simply impossible to solve a dispute over righteousness. Only God would have the ultimate knowledge, they insisted, so humans should refrain from decisive arguments about each other. 'Had God willed, He would have made you a single community,' a verse of the Quran declared, quite tellingly. 'Every one of you will return to God and He will inform you regarding the things about which you differed.'[97] Thus Azad was not wrong when he pleaded that people should return to the true spirit of their religious faith, which is forgotten due to ignorance and blind adherence to obsolete customs practised in the name of religion.[98]

Azad saw rububiyat as the basic attribute of God which he interprets to mean 'creation plus preservation plus promotion plus guidance'.[99] In Arabic, rububiyat means nourishing, but, according to Maulana, 'the term is to be conceived here in its widest sense...the term means, "to develop a thing from stage to stage in accordance with its inherent aptitudes, needs and its different aspects of existence, and also in a manner affording the requisite freedom to it to attain its full stature."'

Azad explains the meaning of rububiyat further, saying that 'if a person should feed the hungry or give alms to the indigent, it will be an expression of kindness, benevolence, or favour on his part. But this will not amount to what is styled rububiyat. Rububiyat is a process of tender or careful nourishment providing from moment to moment and from stage to stage all that one needs to gain the fullest possible development. And this process is always to be marked by the touch of tenderness; for no activity which is not actuated by this can claim to be regarded as rububiyat.'[100]

Another important aspect in the context of rububiyat (Divine Benevolence) is the emphasis on humanity, which the Quran stresses repeatedly and Azad brings up in his *Tarjuman*. He says that 'the quality which distinguishes man from the mere animal and which gives him his station in the scale of life is his humanity, which is nothing but a reflection of the qualities or attributes of God.'

The *Tarjuman* and the Quranic interpretation by Maulana Azad raise many fundamental human concerns, which are so apt for our current times. They are relevant for believers but also for all people, because Azad articulates certain basic common ideals that should permeate all religious faiths. For example, he brings in the notion of mercy and forgiveness when he stresses that 'the scope of divine forgiveness as depicted by the Quran is vast and limitless. However serious the sin committed, whatever the nature of one's wickedness, and whatever the period one has lived in sin, the moment one sincerely knocks at the door of mercy, the response is nothing but forgiveness:

> Say! O my servants who have transgressed to your own hurt, despair not of God's mercy; for all sins doth God forgive. Gracious, merciful is He! (Q:39:54)[101]

This attribute of God should be remembered by the believers though Rab—God here is Rabbul Alamin, God of the whole world, and not just of the believers. One also needs to remember that Azad was translating and interpreting Quranic verses during a watershed moment in our history. This humanism and unity stressed by Azad was being disputed on the streets of India by Muslims and Hindus alike. It was a challenge for him to question all those believers and non-believers who were promoting dissensions and differences to bolster their divisive politics in the name of faith. Azad affirms further that by calling God Rabbul Alamin, the Lord of all creation or of all forms of life, the Surah desires him to acknowledge the universal character of divine concern for every individual, group, community, country, and every form of existence. The concept puts an end to all notions of exclusiveness which had hitherto prevailed among mankind assigning divine blessings and favours to one's own community.[102] The emphasis on questioning 'exclusiveness' is remarkable, particularly when 'othering' in the name of faith was rampant. A nation was in the process of being born merely on the exclusivist idea of the two-nation theory. Through his translation and interpretation of the Quran in the 1930s, Azad did attempt to bring in sanity and unity among all—Hindus as well Muslims—through his reading of the Book.

Azad was not just interpreting the Quran for others, he practised it in his life when he reacted to instances of violence unleashed by the Muslims. They reacted violently to the publication of a book from Lahore called *Rangeela Rasool*, by Pandit Chamupati in 1924, that insulted the Prophet. Azad was outraged as well but he was angrier at the violent reaction of fellow Muslims. His reaction can be perceived well from what he said in *Tarjuman* about forgiveness: 'the Quran does not call on man to love his enemies. Such a direction will have no bearing on the reality of life. What the Quran says is that it is good for us to forgive our enemies; for when one learns to forgive his enemies, his mind will divest itself of hate and ill-will, and get purified.'[103] I hope that all those Muslims who outrage and kill in the name of Islam because some cartoons insult their faith or their Prophet should care to read and understand the real intent of the Quran as explained by Azad in his *Tarjuman.* This is the spirit of the Quran which the ardent believers have lost over the centuries, they seem to have appropriated the tasks which Allah or his Book did not assign the believers to carry out. They were asked to be kind and forgiving even to those who disagreed with them and their faith.

Maulana Azad's scholarship was not confined to his own faith. In fact, in his analysis of the concept of God and oneness, he also delves into the beliefs of the Indo-Germanic tribes and those of Ancient Egyptians and Babylonians among others. In the section titled 'Innaka Nabudu Wa Iyyaka Nastain' (Thee alone do we serve, and thee alone do we ask for help), Azad goes into a comparative account of different religions and beliefs. In Surah al-Fatiha, Azad includes a long section dealing with Chinese, Hindu, Zoroastrian, Judaic, Christian, and Greek concepts, which seem designed to show Azad's acquaintance with the views of the followers of other faiths.[104] I am not sure whether Azad wrote this detailed comparative account just for affect, as Douglas seems to suggest. He may have a rudimentary understanding of other religions and may have not grasped properly the anthropological works he cites but his sincerity is not suspect as his other writings, much before *Tarjuman*, reflect this trajectory. Though he was writing a commentary on the Quran yet it was not presented within the narrow confines of his own faith. He set up a broad canvas to locate the place of the Quran, which was described as one of the modern faiths in the midst of ancient religions. He stressed repeatedly that research in the twentieth century had established that the earliest belief that inspired humans was a belief in the unity of God, shorn of all symbolic representation.[105]

He also discusses the love versus fear aspect in Islam and other religions. In Islam, khauf-i-Khuda is a widespread belief among believers. This fear of the Almighty is not confined to Islam alone, many other faiths from Judaism and Christianity to Hinduism also have this concept. The believers are told by a large number of ulema that they have to be mortally scared of the fury of the infuriated God. They have to follow the Quranic path to escape the anger of the Almighty. This may be against the spirit of Quran, as Azad has very lucidly explained in his *Tarjuman*, but the lay believer goes by the preaching of the semi-literate mullah from the neighbourhood mosque. Maulana Azad's assertion that we need to make a distinction between the faith and its believers seems to be untenable. And this is true for most religions but truer and more visibly apparent in the case of Islam.

In Christianity also, Bertrand Russell's critique of religious belief was based on his claim that religion is based on fear, and that fear breeds cruelty. While delivering a lecture *Why I am not a Christian* in 1927, he expressed himself with characteristic clarity: 'Religion is based primarily and mainly upon fear. It is partly the terror of the unknown and partly the wish to feel that you have a kind of elder brother who will stand by you in all your troubles and disputes. Fear is the basis of the whole thing—fear of the mysterious, fear of defeat, fear of death. Fear is the parent of cruelty, and therefore it is no wonder if cruelty and religion have gone hand in hand. It is because fear is at the basis of those two things.'[106] Virtuosity is often confused with being 'God-fearing' even today.

However, in Sufi Islam we have a very deeply ingrained idea of the love and empathy of God. Of course Sufism is not a monolithic faith. I say this not because Islam, including the Quran and Hadith tradition, does not have the notion of love for God as its core belief, as a matter of fact, fear of God has been used as an instrument of control by the so-called custodians of Islam. The Prophet used to pray thus: 'My God, give me thy love and the love of him who loves thee and the love of that action which will bring me nearer to thee and make thy love sweeter than cold water to the thirsty.'[107] It is this dynamic force of love and longing that has inspired so many Persian poets:

> Every moment this love is more endless,
> in every time people are more bewildered in it. (U:9)

> Says Attar, and Hafiz continues:
> The adventure between me and my beloved has no end—
> That which has no beginning cannot have an end.
> How could this love, inspired by God, be adequately described?
> It is greater than a hundred resurrections,
> for the resurrection is a limit, whereas love is unlimited
> Love has got five hundred wings, each of them reaching
> from the Divine Throne to the lowest earth.[108]
> (M:5:2189–90)

Sufi Islam took the idea of the love of God from the Quran and the prophetic tradition but went on to make it manifestly central to its mystical practices. In more traditional Islam the love element receded into the background. It is the awe and fear of Allah that continues to dominate the faith of most of the preachers and the preached. Azad, however, concludes that in the Surah al-Fatiha all the attributes of God are summed up in the three attributes of rububiyat (providence), rahmat (mercy), and adl (justice) and there is here absolutely no reference to terror. In theoretical terms there cannot be any disagreement with Azad's conclusion, because this is how Quranic text can be explained.

We will go into detail about all the aspects of Islam and other faiths that Azad describes and analyses. He identified five leading religious groups into which mankind was divided at the time the Quran was delivered—the Chinese, the Indian, the Magian, the Judaic, and the Christian.

Azad puts Hindu philosophy on a high pedestal. He writes that the Hindu concept of God is a panoramic view of conflicting ideologies. On the one hand, there is its philosophy of the unity of God, and on the other, is its religion as practised. Hindu philosophy presents such deep and intricate problems of spiritual contemplation and raises the human mind to such great heights that we scarcely find a parallel for it in the religious ideologies of the ancient peoples.[109] After a detailed survey he concludes that 'it is these ideals which went ultimately to contribute to the pantheistic view of life presented in the Upanishads and on which were raised the metaphysical systems of Vedantism.'

Azad dwells in detail on Buddhism and its expansion and evolution over the early centuries: '[W]e should not lose sight of the fact that Buddhism appeared at a time when the evils of image-worship had struck deep roots in the soil of India and were a powerful obstacle in the way of a free search for God. Buddha wished to clear this path and therefore concentrated all his attention on the problem of good life.' Buddha could achieve all this only by denying what existed for centuries and thus began his fight against Brahminism which later degenerated into extremism. However, we know that despite Buddha's explicit position on the concept of God, his followers 'when found the seat vacant, they hastened to install Buddha himself in that seat. Then began the process of the multiplicity of image worship; so much so, that today more than a half of the world is peopled by these images.'[110]

Tarjuman continues with the survey of other religions like the Magism in Iran, Zoroaster and his followers, and of course the Judaic concept of God. Azad specifically touches upon the parallels between the teachings of Zoroaster and the Vedic faith of the Indo-Aryans.

There is much more which one can find in the *Tarjuman*

in terms of comparative religious account but I want to discuss a few more pertinent aspects of Surah al-Fatiha. The Surah concludes with Divine Guidance or hidayat (Ihdanas Sirat Al Mustaqim-Sirat Al Ladhina An 'amta Alaihim; Ghairil Maghdubi 'Alaihim Waladdallin), which means 'Guide us to the straight path, the path of those to whom thou hast been gracious; not of those who have incurred Thy displeasure, nor of those who have gone astray.' This is an appeal to the followers to be on Sirat Al-Mustaqim or the straight path, where God specifies different types of guidance or hidayat which the Quran refers to. Azad writes that the Quran points out that even as the rububiyat of God has provided each object with a form and inward and outward talents and assigned to it an appropriate role in existence, so also, it has endowed it with the gift of self-direction or hidayat.

> He said, 'Our Lord is He who hath given to everything its form and then guideth it aright'. (Q:20:50)[111]

Hidayat is also not just one, but of three kinds. One is hidayat of instincts—this is innate in animal life. It serves as its inspiration. Next to instinct is the hidayat of senses which is higher in rank than the former. This provides us with the talent of seeing, hearing, tasting, feeling, and smelling by means of which we gather a knowledge of the external world of relations. And now comes the vital hidayat, which makes a distinction between the common man and the lower animal. This third hidayat is the hidayat of reason. It is this third variety of directive force provided in man which opens up for him an endless vista of progress and marks him as the consummation to which all creation on earth has moved.[112]

Even in the formative centuries of Islam there are episodes that reflect upon the centrality of reason in Islam: the clash between the ahl al-ray and ahl al-hadis, or the People of Reason and the People of Tradition. What is this faculty of reason in man? I think this is one of the most significant questions that confronts a large number of believers who seem to be oblivious/unaware of this faculty, which is the most precious one and distinguishes man from lower animal—it occupies centrality in the Quran a Book, which is the basis of a believer's faith. The *Tarjuman* continues it says that 'just as the human form is the finest expression of life in its outward or physical aspect, the quality of reason in man is the noblest of the inward forces at work in him. The quality of perception which lies hidden in plant life and which expresses itself in instincts and senses in animal life reaches its perfection in human life and comes to be styled reason.'[113] The Quran laid down many principles for Muslims to follow and human reason and the Prophet himself were the two examples to be followed. Imam Abu Hanifa, whom the majority of Muslims in India follow, was a sympathizer of the Postponers' school, so his thinking was firmly based on the Quran and human reason and a little less on the example of the Prophet:

> He felt apparently that local conditions differed, and that even if Medina was through force of circumstances the city of Mohammad, yet it was a desert town and therefore you could not possibly expect a desert law to apply to city life, when it came to matters of universal import...(hence) Abu Hanifa relied on his threefold cord of Koran, qiyas, and Ra'i, with occasional use for istihsan, and scarcely any for Hadith.[114]

The flexibility and the need for adaptability are conspicuous in the words of Imam Abu Hanifa. Both the above features have unfortunately disappeared from the belief and practices of the majority of the Hanafites over the centuries. This was one of the major challenges before Maulana Azad, who strived hard to restore some of these distinctive features of Islam, which was, according to M. N. Roy, a modernist movement of its time.[115]

I will conclude this section on the *Tarjuman* with the universal message that Azad deciphers in the Quran: 'the message of these prophets was one and the same and was not meant for any particular clime or country or people. It had a universal application for mankind as a whole and wherever they lived.'[116] Azad was inspired by Syed Ahmad Khan in many ways, as we have seen earlier, despite his later disagreements with his political position. Here, Syed Ahmad, referring to the Muslims, raises a similar point when he says: 'God sent his prophets for their moral improvement. It is absurd to believe that the prophets appeared only in Arabia and Palestine to reform a handful of Arabs and Jews, and that God condemned the peoples of Africa, America, and Asia to ignorance.'[117] He went further and said that whoever followed God's prophets achieved salvation, and it was immaterial whether the prophet was from China, America, Mongolia, Africa, India, or Iran, or if he preached God's message to savages or civilized men.[118] In this way, Syed Ahmad tried to broaden the world view of the nineteenth-century Indian Muslim, and in the process conveyed an important message in eclecticism to the future.

Azad continues and says that the Quran is categorical in emphasizing that there is no corner of the world where this universal message was not delivered. The Quran adds that numerous were the messengers who thus delivered the message in the past, though only a few of them are mentioned by name.[119]

> And yet how many prophets sent We among those of old. (Q:43:6)
> We never chastised until We had first sent an apostle. (Q:17:15)
> And we have already sent apostles before thee: Of some We have told thee, and of others We have told thee nothing. (Q:40:78)

Azad stresses that whatever the clime and time the prophets belonged to, the message was the same. It has therefore addressed itself to humanity in one and the same fashion. All prophets descended on earth to convey the message of unity of mankind and bind them together through love and affection. Azad gives the Quranic argument when he says:

> God has given you all but one form—the human form, and welded you into one community. But you have divided yourselves into so-called races and have kept yourselves aloof from one another on the basis of this distinction, and have carved out accordingly different homelands. You have divided yourselves into countless so-called nations, each running at the throat of every other.[120]

Azad also attempts to understand and explain the difference between the real meaning and manifestation of religion. One is that which is the result of a deliberate deviation from the common basic message effected by its followers. For instance, one religion prescribes a particular form of worship; another a different form. A difference of this nature is not a difference touching the basic character of religion, but a difference touching its outward manifestation.[121] Azad points out that the teaching of a religion is two-fold—and here he is not just talking about Islam alone—one constitutes its spirit; the other its outward manifestation. Maulana Azad emphasizes the core aspect of any religion when he says that the essential purpose of religion is the progress and well-being of humanity. He goes on to point out the reasons for circumstantial differences when he says that the intellectual and social aptitudes have varied from time to time and from country to country necessitating variations in Sharia and Minhaj. This interpretation of Azad makes it clear that Islam as a faith is no monolith, it is practised in diverse ways though the tenets remain the same. No one interpretation can be imposed on all believers across varied cultures and habitations.

Azad also comments on the reactions when the Prophet gave up his practice of turning toward Jerusalem in prayer and chose to turn toward Kaaba in Mecca instead, the change was displeasing to the Jews and Christians. That proved how great an importance was given to the outward form. But the Quran made a different approach where outward form did not remain the basis of religion, instead the only thing that mattered was devotion to God and righteous living.[122] The Quran makes it clear what really contributes to a good life in the religious sense of the term. Religion does not lie in merely turning to the east or the west. The Quran presents the essential elements which enter into the composition of religion in the following words:

> Righteousness is not that you turn your faces (in prayer) towards the east or the west; but righteousness is this, that one believeth in God, in the Last Day, in the angels, in the Books and in the Prophets, and the love of God giveth of his wealth to his kindred and to the orphans and to the needy and to the way-farer, and to those who ask and to effect the freedom of the slave, and observeth prayer and payeth the poor-one and is of those who are faithful to their engagements when they have engaged in them, and endureth with fortitude poverty, distress, and moments of peril-these are they who are true in their faith and these are they who are truly righteous. (Q:2:177)

Azad observes that this verse has been there in the Quran for the last 1,300, nevertheless, the world is yet to grasp its basic objective, and it certainly is not the fault of the Quran. The Quran, says Azad, refers to different religious dispensations, from Moses and Jesus to the Prophet of Islam, the Chapter on Ma'ida (chapter 5) of the Book proceeds to state:

> To each among you have We prescribed a law and an open way. If God had so willed, He would have made you all of one pattern; but He would test you by what

> He hath given to each. Be emulous then, in good deeds. (Q:5:48)

Azad continues to comment that in the period the Quran was delivered, the followers of the prevailing faiths took the outward form of religion for religion itself and ritual was the main aspect of faith. However, the spirit of faith was something superior to it, and that alone was din or religion, and was not an exclusive heritage of any single group of people. On the other hand, it was the common heritage of all mankind, and knew no change. Actions and customs are but secondary to it. They have changed and are liable to change from time to time and vary from country to country under the exigencies of time and circumstances.[123]

We should be aware of the fact that Azad was writing all this when he was in the middle of a battle against the formation of a nation in the name of Islam. There was a concerted campaign to divide the country in the name of religion and this was being done by communalists of all hues—Hindus as well as Muslims. It was in the middle of this communal hatred that Azad was translating and interpreting the Quran to convey the message of unity of mankind, which cannot be torn apart due to religious sectarianism. He continued further:

> Dispersed as you are under different climes, you have in the course of history, developed different colours. This has furnished you a further excuse for mutual dislike. You have also developed different tongues or languages. Even this is made an argument for mutual isolation. And then you have created classes among yourselves—of the rich and the poor, the master and the servant, the touchables and the untouchables, the strong and the weak, the high and the low, and so on.[124]

The spirit behind the above lines is direct and clear, it conveys the objective that Azad had in mind—his aim to unite people across all sorts of dissentions and differences. He could discern the message of unity of mankind in the Book which eluded most of its commentators and most of the adherents for centuries. Azad stresses the need for tolerance, even for those who have opposed the Quranic message. He cites the well-known verse of the Quran:

> Revile not those whom they call on beside God, lest they, in their ignorance despitefully revile Him. We have fashioned the nature of man that they like the deeds they do. After all, they shall return to their Lord, and He will declare to them what their actions have been. (Q:6:108)

Azad's critics saw the *Tarjuman* as a Congress version of the Quran, an interpretation that suited the political needs of the party. They do not realize that Azad had espoused a similar faith from a very young age; his *Al-Hilal* and *Al-Balagh* are replete with such eclectic and relaxed readings of Islam. His *Tarjuman* was surely not an original work but was certainly a high-quality scholarly reading of the Quran. It was unfortunate that Azad remained pre-occupied with his public life, and got little time to even complete the *Tarjuman*; however, a lot of the discussions are relevant and worth reading even now. There are diverse opinions which explain the reasons for Azad's reluctance to complete the *Tarjuman*.

It could be that he thought that that the Muslim community had been won over by the Muslim League's propaganda and had no interest in reading what he writes. He was also preoccupied with political activities and any time he had left he spent in reading rather than writing. V. N. Datta also writes that 'a noted Indian scholar who was close to Azad and who does not wish to be quoted told this writer that Azad was compelled by financial difficulties to write his books and that he was a lazy person by nature who derived great pleasure from extensive reading. This is not an unusual attitude on the part of a scholar.'[125]

It is clear from a close reading of his life and works that Azad's understanding of the world as well as of religion was dynamic, and it evolved over a period of time. He inherited Islam from his father Maulana Khairuddin, but he did not find that path worth pursuing. His contempt for taqlid left him without faith for a few years till he discovered one for himself, which was open to criticism and conceded due place to reason as directed by the Quran and Hadith or prophetic tradition. It is sometimes puzzling to see that Azad espoused the Islamic ideals of Ibn Taymiyyah while also having great admiration for the Mu'tazilites. Both these Islamic worldviews differed with each other fundamentally while Azad could get along with both of them comfortably, something that seems so unbelievable. However, this is again a reflection on Azad's unprejudiced view of the past as well as present, which includes his Islamic theological past as well.

I remember hearing about conversation Azad had with the legendary poet late Anand Mohan Zutshi Gulzar Dehlvi, who had a huge corpus of stories about Urdu culture and Sufism. He was himself a great murid of Khwaja Nizamuddin Auliya and Amir Khusrau, and once he was requested by Hasan Nizami, Sajjada Nashin of Nizamuddin dargah, if he could facilitate inviting Maulana Azad for a programme on Jashn-i-Khusrau. Gulzar, who had access to Azad and had invited him for several such jashns on Ghalib, Daagh, and Momin etc., expressed apprehension because Azad, according to Gulzar, was a Wahhabi, a follower of Ibn Taymiyyah, who may not like to be part of a Sufi get-together. However, Gulzar did raise it with Maulana, who not only came and spoke eloquently about Khusrau and his espousal of composite culture, but even stayed for a few hours when he agreed to be there for forty minutes. He quoted Ibn Taymiyyah approvingly when needed but showed abroad-mindedness and openness to other religious traditions that are very different.[126] The faith he espoused was based on the rejection of dogma, rituals, and taqlid, and he remained committed to his version of Islam which was not narrow or sectarian. He left enough space for critical imagination and rational thinking and always derided dogma and superstitious behaviour.

THREE

AZAD, ISLAM, AND NATIONALISM

Before we begin to discuss the above three together, let me digress, if one may call it digression at all, and talk about the birth and evolution of modern-day nationalism. It is well established now that the modern concept of nationalism is one of the by-products of the politics of democratization in Europe. The word 'nationalism' first appeared at the end of the nineteenth century and was used to describe groups of right-wing ideologists in France and Italy who were keen to brandish the national flag against foreigners, liberals, and socialists and in favour of that aggressive expansion of their own state, which was to become characteristic of such movements.[1]

This is so close to what we are witnessing in India today. We got rid of European colonization using the ideological tools developed by them, however, the same liberating ideology has become a bane for us. Our nationalism today needs an enemy, and even a fellow citizen can be demonized to keep the country perpetually on the boil. Gandhi saw this in 1925 when he raised a fundamental question, while speaking in Calcutta: 'Is hatred essential for nationalism? You may not love, but must you also "hate?"'[2]

Even before nineteenth-century German and Italian unifications that concretized the idea of territorial nationalism, it was the French and American revolutions in the late eighteenth century that challenged the might of empires. The Americans got rid of the British empire and 'the French defenestrated their own king.... After a few years of floundering as a collection of colonies united only by their determination to be rid of British rule, the Americans inaugurated a new idea of nationhood born of a unified people with common political and economic interests, under a system combining democracy with capitalism. Modern-day nationalism was born.'[3] It was the beginning of what followed in Europe in the nineteenth century with the emergence of the first proper modern nationalist figures like Count Cavour, Garibaldi, and Mazzini in Italy and the iconic nationalist, the Prussian Chancellor Bismarck. They developed a feeling of love for 'their native land and soil, the traditional cultural heritage from their parents, and allegiance to the established authorities ruling their homelands, and converted them into a newly defined loyalty to a nation-state.'[4] This was also the period when the song 'Deutschland Uber Alles' (Germany above all others) replaced rival compositions to become the actual national anthem of Germany.[5] In India we find a similar race to anoint a particular one over all others, with some rabid ones even challenging the national anthem.

We see the use and misuse of history in defining a certain brand of nationalism, which is not a recent phenomenon, even Maulana Azad coped with this malaise in the 1920s and 1930s. Eric J. Hobsbawm, the British thinker and historian, makes a connection in his book, *Nations and Nationalism since 1780*, between history and nationalism and explains how history is reconstructed in a way that suits the ideology of nationalism and is essential to its construction.[6] Hobsbawm compares the role of history to nationalism with that of the poppy to the heroin addict.[7] This explains why in India today the past has become more relevant than the present or the future. Most of the political battles are fought to reclaim an imagined past, and to set right imagined historical wrongs, while the present seems to be perpetually in abeyance. This is one explanation for 'why history in India has become the arena of struggle between the secular nationalists and those endorsing varieties of religious or pseudo-nationalisms'.[8] Even anti-colonial nationalisms, like in India, which aimed to rid their nations of oppressive colonial regimes, used religion as a divisive tool to weaken inclusive nationalism. The demand from some Muslim leaders during the freedom struggle for the creation of Pakistan as a homeland for India's Muslims rested on the then novel proposition that Muslims were a 'nation' entitled to their own territorial homeland in India.[9] Religious nationalisms, both Muslim and Hindu, remained on the fringes of the freedom struggle. The former eventually divided the country while the latter kept weakening it from within. Romila Thapar explains it succinctly when she says that 'what we take to be nationalism can be a positive force if it calls for the unification of communities', as was being done by Gandhi, Maulana Azad, Nehru, Patel, and others, 'but equally it can be a divisive and therefore negative force if it underlines exclusive rights for one community on the basis of a single identifying factor'.

Hannah Arendt, the German American political theorist, said about America in 1973: 'This country is united neither by heritage, nor by memory, nor by soil, nor by language, nor by origin from the same...these citizens are united only by one thing—and that is a lot. That is, you become a citizen of United States by simple consent of the Constitution.'[10] Many of us invoke the Constitution of India to definre our national identity but a large section barely pays respect to the values enshrined in the Constitution. The economist Pranab Bardhan cites a speech by Barack Obama from 2009 where he says, 'One of the great strengths of the United States is...we do not consider ourselves a Christian nation, [but] a nation of citizens who are bound by ideals and a set of values' as enshrined in the Constitution.[11] The Hindu supremacists today need to take a cue or two from the voices above and shun the path being followed by Erdoğan in Turkey. 'We've seen a very severe example of negative nationalism in the case of Germany in the 1930s when the Nazis propagated the idea of the purity of the Aryan race and the origin of European Aryans....'[12] Azad was aware of the dangers involved: 'Nationalism, in its simplest form, has existed for ages. But the collective belief and ideas that the term brings to mind are the product of the new era of European civilization. It started as a defence for human rights and liberty, but has, today, become its greatest threat.'[13]

All those aware of the dangerous implications of this variety of nationalism fought a relentless battle to keep India free from it. Maulana Azad was in the vanguard of the struggle to keep India united within the broad framework of inclusive nationalism.

He expanded on these ideas in detail as a youngish man of thirty-five when he presided over the Congress session in 1923. He talked of the natural laws that govern society, which are obscured for us due to our emotional biases; he stressed the importance of surmounting all differences of views and opinions to collectively strive for independence. He spoke about the amazing uniformity of laws of social life—quoting Omar Khayyam he said, 'Life is the same story, repeated over and over again, with new names and new characters.'

Maulana Azad, as we know, was an Islamic scholar who was committed to his faith and its future. He was also a strong believer of pan-Islamic solidarity. His antipathy towards British colonial occupation was not confined to the fate of India alone—'Azad's concept of nationalism included not only the Muslims of the Indian subcontinent but embraced Muslims all over the world.'[14] This was when Azad was more concerned about pan-Islamic solidarity against the colonial regime, and not as worried about Hindu-Muslim unity. Thus, while articulating his anti-British strategy he stressed on the unity of the Muslim world to take this battle forward. Discussing the problems of 'self-reliance' and 'self-awareness' among the Muslims, Azad maintained that

> Hindus can, like other nations, revive their self-awareness and national consciousness on the basis of secular nationalism, but it is indeed not possible for

> Muslims. Their nationality is not inspired by the racial or geographical exclusivity; it transcends all man-made barriers—Europe may be inspired by the concept of 'nation' and 'homeland', Muslims can seek inspiration for self-awareness only from God and Islam.[15]

He moved away from an exclusivist vision based on geography very early on. Even his *Al-Hilal*, which was focused on Muslims and their future, stressed the inclusivist idea of Indian nationalism. We may go through a short account of this early phase, which will explain Azad's drifting away from the exclusivist phase to a more inclusive ideal of nationalism.

When Azad was editing *Lisan al-Sidq* from Calcutta (1903–1905), his press was at 14 Tara Chand Dutta Street—at the crossroad of Hindu and Muslim settlements in the city. This area was geographically situated between Bow Bazaar and College Street, which was the stronghold of the Bengali Hindu elite and nationalists. Machua, close to Tara Chand Dutta Street, was home to Bengali Muslims, Egyptians, Punjabis, Peshawaris, and Marwaris. When the Swadeshi Movement started, it became an active centre of mobilization with regular meetings at street corners.

It was here that Azad was truly exposed to the revolutionary fervour through groups like the Jugantar and Anushilan that shaped his political world view. After the partition of Bengal, the revolutionaries in the state gained strength and reorganized themselves into several groups. The Jugantar and Anushilan Samiti were militant Hindu groups who were wary of Muslims, particularly after the partition of Bengal. It was difficult for Azad to gain entry to these groups and also earn the confidence of the other group members. His principal contact among the extremists was Shyam Sunder Chakravarti, an associate of Aurobindo Ghose. He met Aurobindo himself two or three times. He also made an acquaintance with several revolutionaries who were surprised to find that he was prepared to join the movement. Azad mentions in his memoirs that he actually joined a revolutionary group, possibly one of the Jugantar cells which were not, like the Anushilan Samiti, actively anti-Muslim.[16]

Azad was also in close contact with Obaidullah Sindhi and Maulana Mahmudul Hasan who were jailed in Malta. There is also evidence of his involvement in the Reshmi Rumaal Conspiracy, or the Silk Letter Movement (1913–1920), which was organized by Deobandi leaders in India to gain independence from the British by forming an alliance with the Ottoman empire, the emirate of Afghanistan, and the German empire.* There are government records that also establish his links with the revolutionaries Sufi Amba Prasad† and Ajit Singh‡ of Punjab.

In 1908 Azad travelled through West Asia and met anti-colonial nationalists in Iraq, Turkey, and Egypt.[17] In Egypt he kept company with Mustafa Kamil Pasha, the leader of the national party, Al Hizb al-Watani, and was impressed by his preference for territorial rather than Islamic nationalism. Kamil's policy of zero tolerance of British imperialism helped Azad formulate his own anti-imperialist political agenda.[18] Azad was impressed by the Egyptian nationalists under Mustafa Kamil

*This plot was uncovered by the Punjab CID with the capture of letters written by various leaders to each other. The letters were written on silk cloth hence why it was called Silk Letter Conspiracy.

†Sufi Amba Prasad (1858–1917) was originally from Moradabad, UP, who travelled as a revolutionary to different parts of India as well as Iran. He was closely involved with agrarian unrest in Punjab in 1907. He began his nationalist activities as a journalist in Moradabad, writing against colonial oppression. He was also the editor of *Peshwa*, where he often wrote sarcastic editorials. He later fled India to Iran where he was involved in pan-Islamic mobilization against imperialism. He was in touch with Raja Mahendra Pratap, Har Dayal, and Maulana Barkatullah. Sufi Amba Prasad also worked closely with the Berlin Committee of nationalists. He died in Iran and is buried there.

‡Sardar Ajit Singh (1881–1947) belonged to the early revolutionary group called the Ghadr party. He was also a peasant leader of Punjab and fought relentlessly for their rights. He also formed the Bharat Mata Society. Ajit Singh was the uncle of iconic revolutionary Shaheed Bhagat Singh. He spent most of his life in exile, mobilizing support for the freedom struggle in Europe and North America.

for their advocacy of greater cooperation between Muslims and non-Muslims. For Azad, 'the idea of solidarity based on human as against strictly religious ties, was deeply compelling'.[19] In his readings, he found that Arab Muslim nationalists took it for granted that their non-Muslim compatriots would be involved with them in struggle.[20] He could see, during his travels, how the intellectuals and Islamic scholars in Egypt and Syria fused Islamic concepts and nationalism together into a single, unified discourse.[21] Afghani, as I said before, wanted harmony to prevait between compatriot of different religions in countries like Egypt and India. Abduh stood for similar political ideals. In short, the whole spirit that Azad had imbibed from his Indian and Arab heritage was of a common cause against the alien ruler.[22] These Arab, Iranian, and Turkish revolutionaries expressed surprise at the indifference of the Indian Muslims to nationalist demands. In their view, Indian Muslims should have been in the vanguard of the national liberation movement. They could not comprehend why many Muslims in India had instead become camp-followers of the British.[23] This was obviously a reference to the emergence of the Muslim League and its claims of representing all Indian Muslims as well as its comprador character. Azad thus returned more convinced than ever that Indian Muslims must be mobilized in the struggle for liberation.[24]

All this helped Azad to counter the faith-based nationalism of the Muslim League and its own narrow understanding of nationalism. He also understood all those majoritarian nationalists better who merely pretended to question separatist Muslim nationalism. Maulana Azad saw himself as a Muslim, but more than that he declared himself a proud Indian and part of the indivisible unity called Indian nationality. It was a precious part of his being which he was not prepared to surrender at any cost. Azad declared in 1921 that 'the need of the hour is that the seven crore Muslims living in India should establish such close ties and develop such fellow feeling with the twenty-two crore Hindus, that they may henceforth be reckoned as one single nation and country, as inseparable parts of one combined and indivisible whole.'[25] He wanted Hindus and Muslims to be part of one homogenous group which he called Ummat-i-Wahida (one nation).*

Maulana Azad was no doubt an Islamic scholar and began his public life espousing the cause of Muslims, which is reflected in his early writings in *Lisan al-Sidq* and *Al-Hilal*. However, even in 1912, Azad was clear about the indispensability of Hindu–Muslim unity and wrote in *Al–Hilal* about the fear that the colonial government and the League were spreading. This article was quite explicit about Azad's commitment to independence and the role Muslims should play—he wanted them to be a part of the freedom struggle. Maulana Azad wrote this mainly in response to the growing influence of the Muslim League and to dissuade Muslims from getting carried away by communal politics. He was pretty harsh when he prompted them to join the battle against colonialism. He began by saying that 'it is certain that a day will come when a political revolution will sweep India. The fetters of subjugation, with which she has tied down her feet, will be severed by the strong winds of liberty, and all that has to be done will be done. Suppose at that time a history of India is written, do you know what it will

*Aijaz Ahmad, in one of his papers on Azad, says that no adequate translation of the term Ummat-i-Wahida is really possible. Azad later took to translating it simply as muttahida qaumiyat, with the emphasis falling both on nationalism and on ittehad, meaning 'unity'. But that is something of an interpolation. The translation of ummah as nation is of course in keeping with the exigencies of the modern nation state, but 'people'—even in the generic sense of 'human species'—would be closer to the etymological root; in the strictly religious discourse of Islam, meanwhile, the term connotes a sense of 'community', mainly of shared belief, as in Ummat-e-Rasul, i.e., community of the faithful held together by a shared belief in the Prophethood of Muhammad. Wahida, meanwhile, carries the literal sense of 'united', but Azad cites the case of a treaty between Muslims and non-Muslims, concluded by the Prophet of Islam, as the basis of his conception. The 'unity' implied in the term, then, has the sense of an 'alliance'. Aijaz Ahmad, *Lineages of the Present: Political Essays*, New Delhi: Tulika Books, 1996, p. 135.

record about seven crore people of India?' He goes on to answer the question: 'history shall record that they were a pitiable and bewitched people.... They were led by nose by their master, who made them dance to their tunes.... They neither used their brains nor raised their voices.... Theirs was an inert existence, like a tree which depends on the wind for making the slightest movement.'[26] This was surely a serious indictment of the community, and also a grave comment on the politics of the early twentieth century.

Azad had a highly exalted idea about Islam, where Muslims were the chosen ones of God who were sent into this world 'to liberate God's creatures from tyranny and bondage. They were sent to break the chains of slavery, not to put them on their own feet!' He interpreted Quranic verses to convince the believers that struggle against tyranny is their political as well as religious duty. They need to give up scepticism and inaction. There is a lot of self-righteousness in what Azad writes, and this is not a surprise to me. Most Islamic scholars, even the likes of Azad, could not escape this weakness, maybe it was intrinsic in the spirit of Quranic text, which none were able to transcend. We can see this clearly when Azad says that 'they were Muslims and, therefore, it was their duty to do in India all that which ultimately the others did. They were Muslims, therefore, the flag of India's independence and progress should have been in their hands.... The power of Islam is such that others, by acknowledging its greatness, attain physical and spiritual salvation.'[27] Let me quote a longish passage from this article, some of the issues raised here are relevant even now:

> We are not demanding self-government at this moment so that the question whether or not the country is capable of managing its own affairs may, once again, be raked up. The objective is to keep it as an ideal before us and to gradually strive to attain it. For heaven's sake get rid of the fear of the Hindu majority. This was a Satanic

> suspicion created in the minds of the Muslims. Power is not only a numbers game, it depends on something else also. The important factor is the real strength of the nation which is the result of its moral values and character, its unity, and to use the Islamic terminology, the will of God and good deeds.[28]

Azad was aware of the fault lines between the two communities which were being used by the British as well as the Muslim League to polarize the people. Unfortunately, the same fault lines continue to be exploited today by those who unabashedly promote hatred and fear of each other. Ayesha Jalal was somewhat off the mark when she observed that 'a false dichotomy between good "secular nationalism" and bad "religious communalism" in statist historiography has long bedevilled our understanding of late nineteenth and early twentieth century anti-colonialism.... Hindus and Muslims in India were trying in this period to contribute to an emerging discourse on the Indian nation.'[29] This can be true only if you decide to see Indians as Hindus and Muslims, which the communal groups were doing. The Muslim League and the Hindu communal groups did not contribute to the emerging discourse on the Indian nation but corroded it from within by helping the British and dividing the nation between these two religions. Maulana Azad was one of those leaders who began as a spokesperson of the Muslim cause but soon merged his sectarian identity into a larger Indian one. He remained a proud Muslim and an equally proud Indian. He believed that since Islam came to the subcontinent almost eleven centuries ago, its claim on the soil of India was as legitimate as that of Hinduism.

> Everything bears the stamp of our joint endeavour. Our languages were different, but we grew to use a common language. Our manners and customs were dissimilar, but they produced a new synthesis. Our old dress may be

> seen only in ancient pictures.... No fantasy or artificial scheming to separate and divide can break this unity.[30]

There were also leaders like Bipin Chandra Pal who, despite being the proponents of faith-based nationalism, did not conceive an idea of an India truncated on divisive terms. He could admit his partiality towards his own Hindu culture and civilization, but he affirmed respect and tolerance for natural differences. He saw his own religion and civilization merely as part of the larger world when he wrote:

> Even as advocates of Hindu culture and Hindu civilization, we cannot, therefore, consistently with the teachings of Hinduism itself, refuse to admit that our culture and civilization represent only a part of universal human culture and civilization, and at their best, have so far rendered only a few notes of that universal humanity which includes all the different races and cultures of the world.[31]

Bipin Chandra Pal also articulated the cultural basis of our nationalism, we can call it an early rudimentary idea of composite nationalism, which appears so different from the exclusivist cultural nationalism being hoisted today. He pointed out that:

> Under the Moslems we had, whether Hindus or Mahommedans, one common government, but that did not destroy the integrity of Hindu culture. We took many things from our Mahommedan neighbours, and gave them also something of our own, but this interchange of ideas and institutions did not destroy our special character or our special culture. And that special character and culture is the very soul and essence of what we now understand as Nationalism.[32]

This is quite an explicit statement on a shared and universal idea of humanity from someone who was known as one of the ideologues of Hindu nationalism. It also questions the persistent campaign that the Muslims and Hindus were waging against each other. Azad was deeply moved and shaken by the communal violence that occurred at Chauri Chaura and the lack of trust between the Hindus and Muslims. He was elected the youngest president of the Congress party in 1923, in the midst of this awful divide between the communities. His address was to reaffirm his own faith as well as that of others in the strength and need for togetherness to wage the fight against the colonial government. He began with a long introduction, touching upon several national, international, as well as philosophical questions, then went on to say:

> I have taken so much time in describing our superstructure that the question of the foundation, i.e. Hindu–Muslim unity still needs to be considered. Without this foundation, our freedom and all the factors of our country's life and progress will remain a dream. Without it, once again, we cannot create, within ourselves, the primary principles of humanism. Today, if an angel were to descend from the heaven and declare from the top of the Qutub Minar that India will get Swaraj within twenty-four hours, provided she relinquishes Hindu–Muslim unity, I will relinquish Swaraj rather than give up Hindu–Muslim unity. Delay in the attainment of Swaraj will be a loss to India, but if our unity is lost, it will be a loss for entire mankind.[33]

Azad's vision of composite nationalism was shaken immensely during those years, which is reflected further in his address when he said that four years ago the world had great expectations from India, and everyone waited for India's freedom as the historic mass movement for independence began. But, sadly, according to Azad, the story took a different turn; it was now a story of shamelessness and bloodshed. He continued:

> Instead of Swaraj and Khilafat, slogans of shuddhi are being raised. 'Save the Hindus from Muslims', says one group, 'Save Islam from Hinduism', says another. When the order of the day is 'Protect Hindus' and 'Protect Muslims', who cares about the nation? The press and platform are busy fanning bigotry and obscurantism, while a duped and ignorant public is shedding blood on the streets.[34]

The bitterness of the 1920s haunted Azad as was evident in his 1923 address as Congress president. He concluded with an emotive appeal that 'we can either achieve the greatest possible success or the most dismal failure. This is a time of trial for our patriots, our determination, and our courage. Come, let us overcome every obstacle and devote ourselves to building our common destiny.'[35]

The 1920s witnessed intense communal discord, both Hindu and Muslim communalists were busy fanning divisive politics. After the Lahore session in 1929 leading to the passage of the Purna Swaraj Resolution, Gandhi was planning another mass movement based on civil disobedience. Though many leaders like M. A. Ansari wanted to resolve the communal issues first, Gandhi felt that these questions could be resolved only when there was a mass political action launched in view of the Lahore Congress's mandate for Purna Swaraj. The newly constituted Congress Working Committee, which included Maulana Azad amongst others, had begun preparations for the movement. In its meeting on 2 January 1931, the CWC passed several resolutions including the plan to observe Purna Swaraj Day on 26 January 1930. The resolution said:

> In order to carry the message of Purna Swaraj—complete independence—to the remotest village in India, the Committee appoints Sunday the 26th January 1930, as the day of celebration when the declaration to be hereafter

> issued by the Working Committee will be read to the meeting in the provincial language and the members present at the meeting will be invited to signify by show of hands their assent to the declaration.[36]

Gandhi began the movement by launching the satyagraha with his band of seventy-eight trained satyagrahis on 12 March 1930 with a march from Sabarmati to Dandi to break the Salt Act. Maulana Azad led the Congress satyagrahis at the Dharasana Salt Works along with Sarojini Naidu. He delivered fiery speeches traveling all over India. While speaking in Delhi in a meeting held at Queen's Park on 6 August 1930, he pointed out that 'the success in defying the Salt Act was really unparalleled. The Salt Act was not only defied but it was trampled under feet.... The foreign cloth boycott had proved so effective that England was keenly feeling its effect and it was therefore all news about the economic conditions in England effectively being censored.'[37] He concluded the speech with an emotive warning that 'a country which is ready to die cannot be kept in bondage by any country and shall surely win the fight.'[38] The British government was now looking for an opportunity to silence Azad's voice and they did that by arresting him on 21 August 1930 for a speech delivered in Meerut on 7 August 1930. He was arrested in Calcutta and taken to Meerut by Dehradun Express, where he was asked to disembark at Garh Mukteshwar and taken to Meerut in a lorry.[39]

A large number of Muslims participated in the Purna Swaraj Movement with the support of the Jamiat ul-Ulema-i-Hind, Ahrar Party of the Punjab, the Khudai Khidmatgars of the NWFP, and several nationalist Muslim groups who enthusiastically participated in the movement.[40] Maulana Azad did refer to this participation when he said that 'it was an irony of fate that those Musalmans who were from the fountain of modern learning had not joined the movement. But the members of the Jamiat, who were scholars of the Arabic on older lines, had thrown themselves whole-heartedly into the fray.'[41]

Almost a decade later, Azad took this idea of Hindu–Muslim participation forward in his famous Congress presidential address in Ramgarh in 1940, when he referred to the several centuries of Muslim presence in India, and how these 'years of common history have enriched India with our common achievements. Our languages, our poetry, our literature, our culture, our art, our dress, our manners and customs, the innumerable happenings of our daily life, everything bears the stamp of our joint endeavour.' Soon after independence, Azad delivered a convocation address at Patna University in 1947 and cautioned people to be wary of nationalism saying, 'We have to keep in mind that the nationalism propagated in nineteenth-century Europe is all shattered and the world is sick of the bounds of narrow nationalism. It is anxious to break those shackles. Instead of small cooped up nationalities the world wants to build super nationalism. Obviously, there is no room for narrow-mindedness in this modern age. We shall find a secure place in the comity of nations only if we are international minded and tolerant.'[42] Azad could see the consequences of faith-based aggressive nationalism, which divided the country and killed millions in the name of religion. Addressing the students at Aligarh Muslim University in 1949, Azad reiterated his commitment to indivisible nationalism saying that 'I have no doubt in my mind that if you can imbibe this spirit of progressive nationalism, which is the motto of our secular democratic State, there will be no position in any field of life that will be beyond your reach.'[43]

ISLAM AND NATIONALISM (WATANIYAT)

We cannot fully comprehend the notion of Maulana Azad's composite or indivisible nationalism without understanding the founts of his inspiration. And the foundational spirit here was his deep and critical reading of Quran and its history. He attempted to reinterpret Islamic theology itself in such a way as to make it compatible with the religiously composite, politically secular trajectory of India, which found its most extended statement in the unfinished *Tarjuman al-Quran* in the 1930s.[44] However, we need to explore in detail the notion of nationalism within Islam at a global level before we delve into Azad's brand of nationalism further. Azad, who travelled to other parts of the Islamic world and confronted issues of identity quite early in his life, was aware that Islam is wary of territorial nationalism. Islam is a faith beyond geographical boundaries, it claims to unite the ummah across national or even cultural borders. Many Islamic scholars have dealt with the issue in India as well as elsewhere, even Azad's contemporaries debated and discussed the question in detail. Maulana Azad, being a scholar himself and not just a run-of-the-mill politician, got deep into the notion of nationalism and identity within Islam and attempted to articulate an understanding specific to the Indian context. The context is essential, because pan-Islamic discourse of the late nineteenth century tends to blur that necessary distinction. Even pan-Islamists, like Jamaluddin Afghani, shifted their focus away from pan-Islamism while they were in India and emphasized cooperation with non-Muslim others to form a composite nationality.

The notion of composite nationalism, which Azad espoused, can be traced back to the early history of Islam. There is the oft-cited example of the Prophet of Islam who formed the first nation of the early believers in Medina. He signed a covenant to form a United Front, which included the Quraysh, the Ansars, and the Jews, and which brought them together as one nation against their common enemy. Stressing on the possibility of composite nationalism, Maulana Azad argued:

> First of all, I would use a word of our own language then one of another language. Actually, I wish to say that the Hindus and Muslims must unite in a manner that they together form one 'Qaum' and one nation. Now I shall address the Muslims in particular and remind them that after the Quran it is the Prophet whose voice is the most authentic and he had said that he extended the hands of friendship to all those who lived in the vicinity of Medina and declared that we should be 'Umma Vahidah', one people. 'Umma' means 'Qaum' and 'Vahidah' means one.[45]

Azad explained the Quranic idea of jihad in many of his speeches and writings as a potent tool of Congress's anti-colonial politics. The Indian national struggle was a jihad because the British were waging a war to exterminate Muslims. 'If Muslims had any spark of faith left in them, they would befriend snakes and scorpions rather than make peace with the British government. Referring to the Prophet's constitution at Medina in which Muslims and non-Muslims were described as one nation, Azad asked Muslims to perform their religious duty by uniting with Hindus.[46] In the context of India and its fast spreading communal discourse in the midst of the Muslim League's rhetoric of Islamic exclusivism, the pertinent issue was: if Muslims cannot form a nation with non-Muslims, if Islam does not permit it and if Islam does not have the flexibility to form in any condition a composite nationalism on the basis of race and region, then how was it that the Prophet formed a composite ummah with the Jews? And how did the Jews and Muslims become one ummah according to the covenant of the Prophet as against other aqwam?[47] The followers of Islam all over the world are one community and not one nation, Maulana Hussain Ahmad Madani argued, because what is common to them is the spiritual content of the Quran, not its advice about worldly conduct.[48] Maulana Hussain Ahmad Madani and the Deoband seminary countered the League's exclusivism through such strong insights from the early history of Islam. It is essential to discuss the strategies devised by the Deoband seminary and its most credible face during the 1930s.

The Darul Uloom Deoband and its founders and promoters from the late nineteenth century onwards represented a different brand of politics from what it is known for today. It was not known for issuing frivolous fatwas on trivial matters as it often does now. Instead it was committed to a sort of pan-Islamic thinking, which was closely aligned with its anti-imperialist sentiment. This pan-Islamism spoke of all subjugated nationalities, many of which professed Islam. It was this pan-Islamism that made the Khilafat issue a tool into the hands of Muslims, and even Gandhi, to fight the colonial government. For Maulanas Madani and Azad, this was not a communal issue at all and thus they dissociated from the cause once the Turks, under Mustafa Kemal Atatürk's leadership, decided to do away with the Khilafat institution. Maulana Azad issued a statement supporting Atatürk, which the Kemalist government distributed in the form of leaflets.[49]

Maulana Husain Ahmad Madani was also a mentor of Jamiat-i-Ulema, an organization founded in the early twentieth century, which openly questioned the Muslim League and Jinnah on their two-nation theory. The Jamiat and Darul Uloom were regressive in their social and religious vision and are much worse now, however they provided a firm nationalist footing to those who were fighting the League. Maulana Azad firmed up his vision of composite nationalism with the support of the Darul Uloom and Jamiat's widespread network among a large number of Muslims, particularly the ajlaf or pasmanda (poor) sections of its society. Maulana Husain Ahmad Madani's campaign against the idea of a separate homeland for Muslims was relentless, despite increasing vilification by the League and its leaders. He even had an intense debate on the issue of composite nationalism with Allama Iqbal, who almost derided Maulana Madani for his formulations. The debate between Maulana Madani and Allama Iqbal began with the usage of the word 'qaum' by Maulana Madani in his definition of composite nationalism. He also defined a nation and nationalism territorially, conceiving of a nation bound by territorial limits. Iqbal had problems with both the positions and engaged Madani philologically to explain the meaning of qaum as per the Arabic usage and also its use in the Quran. Iqbal also questioned Maulana Madani on visualizing Islam within territorial limits, as Islam was a global religion, which can't be reduced to territorial constraints. Iqbal was also critical of narrow nationalism and its evils, as they surfaced in Europe, which led to wars and bloodshed. This is also how Rabindranath Tagore perceived nationalism two decades before Iqbal and saw humanity as one, without narrow racial, linguistic, religious, or cultural chauvinisms. Iqbal valourized Islam as a universal faith devoid of constricted nationalist territorial barriers, but if we go by this logic then it is difficult to explain the existence of fifty plus Islam majority nations in the world—many of them at war with each other.[50] It is also interesting to see how Maulana Madani goes deep into Arabic grammar and philology to counter the serious charges levelled by Iqbal regarding the meaning of qaum and millat, even equating him with Abu Lahab—the inveterate enemy of the Prophet. Maulana Madani clarified that he did not give the definition of millat but of qaum and the two are used differently in scriptures. Millat denotes deen or shariat whereas qaum means any group of men or women. He further remarked in one of his speeches:

> The word qaum is used for any group which has characteristics of comprehensiveness or togetherness or commonality; it may be of religion, country, race, language, vocation, colour, or any other material or non-material quality. For example, the Arab nation, Ajam nation,

> Egyptian nation, Pakhtoon nation, Persian speaking nation, or expressions like Syed, Sheikh, cobbler, black, white, Sufi, worldly nation etc. In Arabic language and Islamic scriptures this kind of usage is quite frequent.
>
> The term 'Indian nation' has a similar usage. Currently in foreign countries all inhabitants of India are treated as one Indian nation, no matter if they be Urdu-speaking or Bangla-speaking, black or white, Hindu or Muslim, Parsee or Sikh. The word Indian denotes each of them.... Equal and brotherly treatment is a different matter altogether although the distinction can be seen in scriptures as well. I had not used it in the context of Islamic teachings or ideology.[51]

In his campaign for composite nationalism, Maulana Madani went beyond religion and culture to define Indian nationhood when he said:

> We the people of India have one thing in common and that is Indian-hood which survives all differences of religion and culture as our common humanity is not affected by differences of caste, attributes, colour, and size. Similarly, our religious and cultural differences are no bar to our common nationhood. As compatriots we are all Indians.[52]

The debate could not be resolved or continued as Iqbal died in 1938. However, the exchange between the two important ideologues did help to debunk the two-nation theory and its false premises. It is strange that the two contemporaries, Azad and Iqbal, with common intellectual pursuits, did not engage with each other. They spoke and wrote on common subjects, like nationalism and identity, but did not comment on or critique each other.

A few years before this debate with Maulana Madani, Iqbal had delivered the presidential address at the Muslim League session in Allahabad on 29 December 1930. He delved deep into the question of identity and nationality, which may be clearer if we read parts of the address:

> The units of Indian society are not territorial as in European countries. India is a continent of human groups belonging to different races, speaking different languages, and professing different religions.... The principle of European democracy cannot be applied to India without recognizing the fact of communal groups.... The Muslim demand for the creation of a Muslim India within India is, therefore, perfectly justified.... The...repudiated Lucknow Pact...originated in a false view of Indian nationalism.... No Muslim politician should be sensitive to the taunt embodied in that propaganda word 'communalism'.... We are 70 (sic) millions and far more homogenous than any other people in India. Indeed, the Muslims of India are the only Indian people who can truly be described as a nation in the modern sense of the word. The Hindus, though ahead of us in almost all respects, have not yet been able to achieve the kind of homogeneity which is necessary for a nation, and which Islam has given you as a free gift.... One lesson I have learnt from the history of Muslims. At critical moments in their history, it is Islam that has saved Muslims and not vice versa. If today you focus your vision on Islam and seek inspiration from the ever-vitalizing idea embodied in it, you will be only reassembling your scattered forces, regaining your lost integrity, and thereby saving yourself from total destruction.... I am opposed to nationalism as it is understood in Europe...because I see in it the germs of atheistic materialism which I look upon as the greatest danger to modern humanity.[53]

His exposure to Europe and its social, religious, and political developments had a serious impact on his perception of India and Islam. Most of these articulations for Muslim nationalism were made in the 1930s, a decade that saw a radical shift from the possibilities of a shared nationhood to separatist nationalism and also the hardening of attitudes within the Muslim League leadership. Iqbal was almost on the same track as those Hindu nationalists who saw majority Hindu religion in India and nationality as interchangeable when he wrote to Jawaharlal Nehru saying:

> In countries with a Muslim majority, nationalism and Islam are practically identical, but in countries where Muslims are in the minority, their demand for self-determination as cultural unification is completely justified.[54]

I cited this longish passage above from his address to raise some foundational weaknesses in the address, particularly coming from an erudite philosopher and poet turned politician like Iqbal. He talked of the homogeneity of the 70 million Muslims of India, which is hardly corroborated by facts. It is difficult to believe that a man of his stature was not aware of the doctrinal differences within the Muslims in India and elsewhere. The Muslims were diverse on cultural and linguistic as well as on so many other counts. The Muslims in India were split into many caste-like groups, unlike other Muslim nations, and were also broadly categorized as ajlaf and ashraf (backward and forward/elite groups within Islam). Iqbal was right in asserting that modern nationalism was a European ideal, but did we accept it without necessary changes to make it our Indian context? He called it dangerous because it is atheistic, yet our nationalism was mostly inspired by religion, including his own definition of nationalism where he used 'Islamic nationalism' as a valid category, which for him was non-territorial.

There are many contradictions and conflicts in Iqbal's politics of nation and nationalism. Sometimes Islam takes precedence over everything else while at times India as a nation is supreme. In one of his last poetic works called *Zarb-i-Kalim*, there are two poems and in one of them, called 'Gila' (Complaint), he wallows in the travails of India, expressing his indignation. This was published in 1936, just two years before Iqbal died, when he was an ardent supporter of Islamic nationalism. He says:

> Who knows the fate of India which is still but a
> Bright jewel in some other crown;
> The peasant is like a corpse exhumed from its grave,
> Its shroud still buried underground!
> The body and the soul are alike mortgaged to others
> Neither the house nor the house-owner remains.
> You have reconciled to the slavery of the West;
> My grudge is against you, not against the West.[55]

This ambiguity in Iqbal's philosophy and politics continues to he misused and misinterpreted even today by Islamist ideologues in Pakistan who just see the side of him that is convenient and useful in defining Islam-centric nationalism.[56] K. G. Saiyadain wondered: 'is it fair to say that a poet who writes with such a pain-racked pen about the conflicts which disfigure our national life, is devoid of the sentiment of patriotism?'[57] However, all these ambiguities seem to be lost in the current global rage for stoking raw nationalism to sway public opinion.

Coming back to Maulana Azad, we find a huge distance between him, Maulana Madani, and Allama Iqbal in their interpretation of nationalism. And we know well that all three were inspired by their faith, by the same book, which moved them to perceive nation and nationalism so differently. Azad and Madani spoke the language of the common people and Madani actually worked with a large number of poor and low-ranking Muslims. A large segment of these Muslims ultimately decided to stay in India, despite the persistent fear mongering of the League and temptation of brighter prospects in Pakistan. It was a victory for all those who believed in composite nationalism that such large number of Muslims decided to choose India as their homeland over the Islamic nation of Pakistan. Maulana Azad lost the battle for a united India but he did succeed in convincing many Muslims that their future was not safe with the League and its sectarian politics. The substantial Muslim population in present-day western Uttar Pradesh, in districts like Saharanpur, Muzaffarnagar, Meerut, Bijnor, Muradabad, and Rampur etc. is because their ancestors decided to stay (the Muslim population is around 26 per cent today in these towns, though the overall percentage of Muslims in Uttar Pradesh is at 19 per cent).[58] They could muster the courage to do this despite the fact that these districts were adjacent to the worst affected border state of Punjab. Most of these Muslims were from the backward and artisanal classes and did not share much with the core support base of the League, which constituted landlords, professional classes, and the businessmen. The latter were the sections which succumbed to the fear mongering unleashed by Jinnah and the League—obviously they had much to lose while the poor had no such worries. The Muslims in western Uttar Pradesh did not leave their home for an alien land with an uncertain future.

Maulana Azad went through an early pan-Islamist phase which was in large part inspired by Afghani. Azad's pan-Islamist views and unflinching anti-colonialism proved to be strategic for him as the Khilafat issue was brewing at the same time as the Non-cooperation Movement of Mahatma Gandhi, and he brought the two together in his attack on imperialism. Ever since Azad became a public figure with the publication of *Al-Hilal*, pan-Islam remained a significant plank of his religious-political formulations. This was partly the result of Azad's conviction that in order to maintain cohesion in the community, it was necessary that the Khalifa was looked upon with reverence and clear allegiance, not only spiritually but also politically.[59] However, we can see a shift in his politics after the Khilafat issue became irrelevant and he felt no need for pan-Islamic unity to push any such cause. Azad realized that the time had come to move to a more integrative politics, where Hindus and Muslims together form a cohesive group to fight for an independent India.

Even Afghani decided to give up pan-Islamism while he was in India during the three years in the 1880s. He knew that India's non-Muslim majority population can also be harnessed for his anti-imperialist project. This was a smart move. He realized the need for composite nationalism several decades before Madani, Azad, or any other leader in India did. In Egypt, Afghani reminded the Egyptians of their pre-Islamic heritage to bring the Muslims and Christians together and in India he lauded the discoveries of science and mathematics by the Hindus of the Classical Age. Addressing a largely Muslim audience in Calcutta in 1882, he pointed to the young students around and expressed his joy, saying:

> Certainly, I must be happy to see such offspring of India, since they are the offshoots of that India that was the cradle of humanity. Human values spread out from India to the whole world. These youth are from the very land where the meridian circle was first determined. They are from the same realm that first understood the zodiac. ...Thus we can say that the Indians were the inventors of arithmetic and geometry. ...the Code Romain, the mother of all western codes, was taken from the four Vedas and the Shastras. Greeks were the pupils of the Indians in literary ideas, limpid poetry, and lofty thoughts. (The Indians) reached the highest level in philosophic thought.
>
> The soil of India is the same soil; the air of India is the same air; and these youths who are present here are fruits of the same earth and climate.[60]

This was the syncretic cultural nationalism espoused by Afghani in the late nineteenth century, which is different from the sanitized cultural nationalism of the Hindu nationalists a century later.* He saw linguistic ties as being stronger than religious ties. In his own words:

> A single people with one language in the course of a thousand years changes its religion two or three times without its nationality, which consists of unity of language, being destroyed. One may say that the ties and the unity that arises from the unity of language have more influence than religious ties in most affairs of the world.†

This position of Afghani was reinforced by the creation of Bangladesh, when the division of India on the basis of the two-nation theory floundered within twenty-five years of its creation. The Bengali language and culture trumped so-called Islamic nationalism, which proved so ephemeral.

The whole idea of composite nationalism that Azad espoused was entrenched in linguistic, cultural, and social togetherness, which took precedence over religious identity. He saw diversity and pluralism as our strength.

Maulana Azad wrote an insightful and interesting article for *Al-Hilal* in 1927 on 'Islam and Nationalism', which is even more relevant when seen in lifht of the protests against the Citizenship Amendment Act, 2019. In this article Azad attempted to explain who an Indian is and how a national

---

*Cultural nationalism is in vogue with a particular genre of scholars and politicians these days and involves the careful sifting of intellectual and cultural icons and ideas. Jamaluddin Afghani's formulation of cultural nationalism came close to what the Bengali Bhadralok intelligentsia, such as P. C. Ray and Benoy Kumar Sarkar, found suitable a decade later in their attempt to articulate the emerging nationalist aspirations.

†The creation of Bangladesh in 1971 is an example of the prioritization of language and culture by the people over their religious identity. Afghani, *Maqalat-i-Jamaliyyeh*, pp. 75–87, cited in Keddie, *An Islamic Response to Imperialism*.

identity is formed. He also attempted to make a distinction between patriotism and nationalism. Today we find that the distinction between the two seems to be blurred. However, let me mark the difference in a few sentences. While patriotism means affection for one's country and willingness to defend it, nationalism is a more extreme, unforgiving form of allegiance to one's country. The main shortcoming of nationalism is that it can blind people. Love for one's country is imperative and necessary, but if this love becomes more important than Constitutional values or democratic ideals, it is misplaced.[61]

Azad begins by saying that man develops a natural affinity for the place where he lives for a period of time and this affinity is based on multiple factors—one of the most important factors, Azad points out, is affinites with the place of habitation. As man has his kith and kin at the place where he is born and brought up, according to Azad, the place's every nook and corner becomes associated with affections and memory.[62] According to Azad, after racial affiliation, man feels a kinship with his place of nativity, and gradually, its hold becomes firmer.

On patriotism, Azad says that it is a maturing of one's allegiance to the 'city-state'. As civilization progresses and expands, man's contacts become more extensive and the concept of city-state also starts to widen. Now, instead of his place of birth and habitat, man starts to regard the entire area as his native land, gradually the scope widens and soon the concept of patriotism encompasses an entire country.[63] While writing this Azad is not alluding to any religion, he is talking of a human being who goes through this process and acquires a special connect with the region and the country. This is patriotism for Azad, which no religion can question, including Islam.

Moving to the next stage, Azad says that the consciousness of place and habitat creates a unit more common and extensive than race. It includes different tribes and races and unifies them. 'Nationalism' follows 'patriotism' as the next stage of social consciousness. It connotes a wider scope of human relations, and encompassing all the earlier orbits, creates a higher order of unity.[64]

Azad moves to the final stage, where this process of evolution reaches maturity and completion, which is the stage of humanism and universalism. At this stage man realizes that the boundaries and relative affiliations of human associations and areas that he had created were not actual and natural. True relationship is only one, the entire earth is man's native land, mankind one family, and all human beings are brothers. At this stage the voyage of man's collective affiliations terminates, and, in place of the unity of race, unity of place, and unity of nationality, the only and perfect unity, the unity of the human race, created by God Almighty, manifests itself.[65] Continuing further on the subject, Azad says that to begin with, the piece of land where he (man) was born meant everything to him. After birth, the four walls of the home became his universe. He looked at other creatures, and, before long, recognized the different species and the nature of each one of them. He looked at the sky, and, after thousands of years, realized that the sun has a social system and the earth is one of its members.[66]

In a 1927 article, Azad, like Gurudev Tagore, concludes that humanism is the ultimate destination of any human being. Most of the nationalisms in circulation, particularly in Europe, are xenophobic and aggressive. Tagore could see the dangers in the early twentieth century itself and travelled around to dispel advice and warn people of the consequences of such narrow perceptions of nationalism. It was Tagore who dared to question nationalism and propose a humanist vision, castigating the parochial and the bigoted[67]:

> India has never had a real sense of nationalism. Even though from childhood I had been taught that idolatry of the Nation is almost better than reverence for God— and humanity, I believe I have outgrown that teaching,

> and it is my conviction that my countrymen will truly gain their India by fighting against the education which teaches them that a country is greater than the ideals of humanity.[68]

When Tagore was talking of humanism as the ultimate objective in the early twentieth century, Azad was still entrapped in his Islamic identity and concern. He grappled with the question theoretically as well as practically by debating in his early writings and later upholding the Khilafat cause along with the Gandhian Non-cooperation Movement. The futility of the Khilafat cause dawned on him, like on many others, after the Turks uprooted the Khilafat institution and established a modern dictatorship under Kemal Atatürk. He was one with Gandhi in using the Khilafat cause to strengthen the nationalist struggle by maximizing the Muslim participation and building composite nationalism. However, the failure of both led to widespread frustration and outbreaks of violence all over India. Most of the Khilafat leaders like Maulana Abdul Bari, Hakim Ajmal Khan, Ali brothers, and Maulana Azad were shocked by the development but reacted differently. Azad 'did not betray any emotion nor was he mortified by the development in Turkey. To Azad, Khilafat as an issue of political mobilization was no longer relevant since he had already embarked on the course of integrative politics, even more so after he became the president of the Congress in September 1923.'[69]

As he often did, Azad used Islam and its early history to make his point about humanism. When Islam was born in the seventh century, the world was still in the throes of tribal patriotism. Arab society was a conglomeration of tribes, and each tribe was confined to its racial nationalism and refused to accept a wider domain. Azad acknowledges that the ruinous passions of pride and boast, of contempt and disdain for mankind, and of conquest and domination over one another were deeply and strongly entrenched in these tribes.[70]

Maulana Azad was an Islamic scholar and journalist by the time he turned fifteen. Not only did he break away from his father's rigid faith and come up with his own understanding of Islam, he tried his hand at journalism and editing—experiences that helped him launch his formal journalistic career with *Al-Hilal* in 1912.

Photo courtesy: Husnara Salim

Maulana Azad (left), pictured here with Netaji Subhas Chandra Bose (right). Throughout Azad's political career, he was routinely mocked by the Muslim League for being a showboy of the Indian National Congress since his politics posed a major threat to their idea of a Muslim nation.

Photo courtesy: Husnara Salim

Sarojini Naidu, Sardar Patel, Netaji Subhas Chandra Bose, and Jawaharlal Nehru with Maulana Azad after a meeting with Mahatma Gandhi at Segaon. Before Independence, the Congress leaders' primary role in the freedom struggle was twofold—fighting the colonial government and confronting Muslim and Hindu communalists.

Photo courtesy: Nehru Memorial Museum and Library

Maulana Azad (centre), pictured here with Sarojini Naidu (far right). After Gandhi's defiance of the Salt Act, in May 1930, Azad and Naidu led the Congress satyagrahis' march at Dharasana Salt Works.

Photo courtesy: Husnara Salim

The essays in Maulana Azad's epistolary work, *Ghubar-i-Khatir*, introduce us to the versatility of Azad. In some of the letters he is a philosopher, another one turns him into a connoisseur of tea as well as its expert taster and historian. During the course of the essays, Azad is by turns an expert ornithologist, horticulturalist, music lover, and musician.

Photo courtesy: Husnara Salim

Maulana Azad loved his solitude and seldom opened up in public, particularly about his personal life. A reticent man, he was unwilling to write about himself. Whenever he did so, it was under strong inducements and pressure from others, which, due to his courteous nature, he could not always resist.

Photo courtesy: Husnara Salim

Maulana Azad (second from the right), with Rajkumari Amrit Kaur, Edwina Mountbatten, and Louis Mountbatten (L–R), watching Mahatma Gandhi's last rites at the banks of the Yamuna, 31 January 1948. Inspired by Gandhi, Azad joined the nationalist movement in the 1920s—though he had been writing about nationalism in *Al-Hilal* since the 1910s—and became one of the strongest voices supporting composite nationalism.

Photo courtesy: Husnara Salim

Maulana Azad with Jawaharlal Nehru and Sardar Patel at the reception hosted by Dr Rajendra Prasad on 27 January 1950. For Gandhi, Azad, Nehru, Patel, and others, nationalism was a positive force that called for the unification of communities.

Photo courtesy: Nehru Memorial Museum and Library

Jawaharlal Nehru inaugurating the National Art Theatre Fund in the Parliament on 22 February 1952, with Maulana Azad and Humayun Kabir. The best-known work from Azad, *India Wins Freedom*, was not penned by him—it was dictated by Azad to the novelist and politician Humayun Kabir.

Photo courtesy: Nehru Memorial Museum and Library

Maulana Azad and Jawaharlal Nehru at the inauguration of the new Council for Scientific and Industrial Research (CSIR) building in New Delhi on 10 January 1953. As education minister, Azad was well aware that expanding the network of diverse research labs will expedite the process of national reconstruction.

Photo courtesy: Nehru Memorial Museum and Library

Maulana Azad inaugurating a two-day conference of education ministers in New Delhi on 9 September 1956. Nehru believed Azad was 'a bridge between the cultures of the East and the West, as the man who magnificently spanned in his person the gulf between the past and the future'.

Photo courtesy: Nehru Memorial Museum and Library

Azad referred to this early history to remind the Muslims and others in twentieth-century India that nationalism cannot be defined in terms of narrow tribal identities. It has to be open and inclusive and have no place for sectarian loyalties. Unfortunately, we have learnt nothing from the experiences and observations of scholars and freedom fighters like Azad. We often indulge in hideous exclusivism in defining national identity and do that in the name of nationalism and national interest.

Maulana Azad further says that belief in the enclosures of family, tribe, race, place, and its bigotry is conveyed in Arabic by a word which can be translated as chauvinism. Chauvinism was based first on Arabism, i.e., the superiority of the Arabs over non-Arabs and then, among the Arabs themselves, each tribe was steeped in the pride of its own racial superiority.[71] Azad invoked this early history of Islam by to reflect upon the divisive political developments in the 1920s and the challenges of building a collaborative Hindu-Muslim front to confront British imperialism. He could see the same chauvinism endangering the possibility of composite nationalism. Azad was convinced that recurring communal riots would not only hamper good relations between the two communities but also impede the formation of a united nationhood.[72] In his presidential address at the Congress session in 1923, Azad reiterated the need for a united nationhood thus:

> The need of the hour is a single and united nationhood. As we all are aware that so long shouting of slogans such as 'malechcha' and 'kafir' would rent the air, it is impossible that we can build a culture of tolerance and brotherhood, without which the unity can't exist.[73]

Azad was so deeply concerned about Hindu-Muslim unity that he wrote several letters to Gandhi, urging him to call for a special session of the Congress to resolve Hindu–Muslim issues. For him nationalism and patriotism were possible only if all Indians presented a united front. His efforts bore fruit when the Congress Working Committee was convened in Calcutta on 4 July 1926 and decided to form a permanent publicity bureau to develop sound 'national life'. This meeting authorized Motilal Nehru, Sarojini Naidu, and Maulana Azad to take the necessary steps to organize such a bureau[74] with a view to counter communal conflicts and differences among the masses.

Coming back to Azad's article on Islam and nationalism we need to keep in mind that this was written in 1927 in the midst of huge divisive turmoil. Shuddhi and Sangathan movements of the Arya Samaj and Tableegh and Tanzeem movements of the radical Muslim groups were creating social and political fissures. Three caricatures of Prophet Muhammad came out in the 1920s but the most damning was *Rangeela Rasool* by Pandit Chamupati, published by Mahashay Rajpal in Lahore in May 1924. The *Rangeela Rasool* controversy cast a pall of gloom over the political climate of the country. The Muslim reaction was intense and violent, particularly in Punjab. The intensity of feelings had already claimed the life of Shraddhanand, an Arya Samaj leader.[75] Azad was disgusted with the book but was also disturbed at the violent reaction of the Muslims. As he put it, 'It is distressing that such behaviour is against the values of patience, restrain, and self-respect of the community. Instead, all this has given way to narrow-mindedness and ill behaviour. And all this is being described as sacrifices of the Fidayan-i-Rasool.'[76]

Reacting with restraint to all the provocations around him, Azad said in his 1927 article that 'The whole mankind belongs to one race, one family, one kinship. If, in fact, there is no difference of race for all race is one race, nor is there a difference of place, for we all inhabit the same earth, why is one group separated from the other? Why do members of one family and kinship live with one another like aliens?'[77] Azad continued to stress that 'the truth of the matter is that the entire human race stands on the same footing and at the same rank. Providence does not bestow superiority on any individual, save the one who proves himself worthy of distinction and superiority by virtue of his own deeds and efforts,

> Jo barh kar utha le hath mein, meena usika hai.[78]

> One who picks it up by extending his hand, the
> goblet is his.

Maulana Azad was up against a huge challenge from communalists of all hues who were doing their utmost to unleash the fissiparous forces to polarize the people. He attempted to see the issue as a serious human concern, beyond any divide. It is sad that 'nationalism' continues to pester us as one of the most contentious political and social problems.

He was arrested on 21 December 1921 in Calcutta but he refused to be part of the court proceedings. One of the most foundational documents that will let us understand Azad's idea of belonging or nationalism is a document he drafted as his address to the presiding judge in 1921 in Calcutta. The document was subsequently published in Urdu under the title *Qawl-i-Faisal* or *Final Verdict*. It will be worthwhile to quote a few passages from this iconic piece of writing. He was scathing in his critique of the colonial government when he said:

> I believe that liberty is the birthright of every nation and individual. No man, nor any man-made bureaucracy, possesses the right to enslave human beings. Howsoever attractive the names that we may coin for slavery, slavery will remain slavery all the same. It is imposed on man by man against the will of God. Therefore, I refuse to accept the present Government as a rightful government, and consequently think it to be a national, religious, and human duty to relieve my country and nation of their servitude....[79]

He did not mince words in calling out the colonial regime as a tyrannical institution which has no moral or human basis to exist. Going beyond the religious divide he continued:

> Why is it that this has become an article of my faith as well as that of millions of my countrymen? Let me make it clear that this is my faith simply because I am an Indian; because I am a Muslim; because I am a man. It is my belief that liberty is the natural and God-given gift of man. No man and no bureaucracy consisting of men has the right to make slaves of the servants of God. However attractive be the euphemism invented for subjugation and slavery, still slavery is slavery.[80]

He goes back to his faith and the responsibilities of a true believer when he says:

> I am a Muslim and by virtue of being one, this has become my religious duty. Islam never accepts as valid a sovereignty which is personal, or is constituted of a bureaucracy, or a handful of paid executives. Islam constitutes a perfected system of freedom and democracy. It has been revealed to recover for the human race the liberty which has been snatched away from it. Monarchs, foreign dominations, selfish religious pontiffs, and power brokers, all had misappropriated this liberty of man.... All men are equal and their fundamental rights are on a par. Only he is greater than others whose deeds are the most righteous of all.[81]

Maulana Azad was conscious of the ground realities and knew well that Muslims must be weaned away not only from the British colonial government and the sops it offered but also from the fear-mongering of the Muslim League. He continued in *Qaul-i-Faisal:*

> I confess that it is the moral decadence of Muslims and their renouncing the real Islamic life, which is responsible

for this fallen state. While I am writing these lines, I know that there are still many Muslims in India who pay homage to this very tyranny. But the failure of man to live up to the spirit of certain tenets cannot belie the intrinsic truth of those principles. The tenets of Islam are preserved in its scriptures. Under no circumstances is it permissible for Muslims to enjoy life at the expense of freedom. A true Muslim had to either immolate himself or to live as a free man; no third course is open for him in Islam.[82]

Azad, as a young man, made some fundamental assertions when he stressed that 'Continuously in the last twelve years, I have been training my community and my country to demand its rights and liberty. I was only eighteen years old when I started speaking and writing on this theme.' He proclaims with a lot of passion that he has dedicated his 'entire existence to it, and have sacrificed the best years of my life, i.e., the whole of my youth, to my love for this ideal.' Azad called it a 'national ideal', and for its pursuit he invited all Indians to join hands. We can see this as his early commitment to the idea of inclusive nationalism.

Writing in *Al-Hilal* in 1912, Azad was aware of the ongoing divisive strategies of the League as well as the British when he said:

> Indian Muslims followed blindly the policy of the British government. ...(They) broke off all relations with the Hindus who were the real active group in the country.... We were warned that the Hindus were a majority and if we went along with them they would crush us.... The result was that the government which should otherwise have become the target of the Muslims spears was saved, and their own neighbours became their mark instead.[83]

Muhammad Ali Jinnah 'set forth the two-nation theory dichotomizing Hindus and Muslims as two discrete, hostile nations. Muslim nationalism became the hallmark of Jinnah's separatist politics, and he resorted to all sorts of populist arguments and political manoeuvres to win the case for Pakistan in the face of stiff opposition from a host of opponents, among whom the most inveterate opponent was the Indian National Congress, while the final arbiter over the future of India were the British.'[84]

Thus, Maulana Azad and other leaders of the Congress like Gandhi, Patel, and Nehru were confronted with a challenge on two fronts. They had to fight the colonial government for freedom and had to cope with the dangers of the divisive rhetoric used by the Hindu and Muslim communalists. Azad was mocked by the League as a showboy of the Congress party as his ideology was a major threat to their idea of a Muslim nation. The League was aggressively competing to occupy the political and social space on behalf of the Muslims in India, but found this leadership challenged by the likes of Azad. Meanwhile, the Arya Samajists had also launched the Shuddhi Movement, aimed at bringing those who had converted back into the Hindu fold, which Azad felt was not in the larger national interest. 'I am convinced that those who have started such a thing have simply ignored the national interest. They were duty-bound to have avoided raking up issues such as this since the attention is diverted from national unity to communal discord.'[85]

It is intriguing that the communal forces—the Hindu 'nationalists' and Muslim 'separatists'—were keen to pursue their narrow divisive agenda, ignoring the larger objective of national independence. One could see the agenda of the latter when they began speaking for a separate Muslim homeland but the Hindu communalists, who raised issues like shuddhi (purity), were aiding the British while claiming to fight the Muslim fanaticism. The colonial regime consciously used the strategy of religious divide, instigating the Muslims to provoke the Hindu communalists. Both the factions were openly patronised by the British and they responded by doing their bidding. Azad engaged with these divisive forces using his deep understanding of Islam and emphasizing Hindu–Muslim unity, as seen through his study of the Quran.

As we saw in the previous chapter, Azad went through intense churning to discover his own understanding of Islam. He was committed to Hindu–Muslim integrative politics to fight the colonial regime and he found enough resources in the Quran to take this indispensable fighting tool forward. He had to convince both the Hindus and Muslims to come around to the view that religious distinction was no impediment to creating a composite nation.

Azad had already begun striving for composite nationalism when V. D. Savarkar composed his essentialist text, *Hindutva*, in 1923 where he defined nationalism as the prerogative of the majority alone. The rest of the Indians, which included Muslims and Christians, were pushed to the margins in this xenophobic vision of Hindutva. Muslim communalists at this time were preoccupied with the fear of majority rule after independence. This was an incredibly potent tool for almost two and half decades in the hands of the League. Maulana Azad had to question both these narratives to make his composite nationalism acceptable to all, particularly to Muslims. In both the cases, religion was being transformed into political ideologies, where Hinduism became Hindutva and Islam turned into a political creed. One emphasized majoritarianism while the latter used the fear of the majority.

Azad countered them both in his writings and speeches. And he began doing that as early as 1912 when he wrote in *Al-Hilal* that he condemned the widely held fear that Muslims constitute a political minority and should, therefore, be wary of losing their individual and communal rights in a democratic India. This false image, he said, was created by the genius of the British sixty years ago to use the Muslims to counter the new political awakening that was stirring among Indians.[86] This was a collaborative effort of the League and the British, which Azad had to counter to make his case for composite nationalism. Defining the term minority, Azad describes it as a group of people who find themselves both numerically and 'qualitatively' ineffective. By this definition, he says, the Muslims of India cannot call themselves a minority.

> They number between eight and nine crores. Unlike other communities they are not divided on cultural and racial grounds. The powerful bonds of equity and brotherhood informing the Islamic life have, to a large extent, saved them from the weaknesses that flow from social segmentation. True, their fraction is no more than one fourth of the total population of the country, but the question is not of the fraction, but of the number of its quality. Can such a vast mass of humanity have any legitimate reason for apprehension that in free and democratic India it may not be able to protect its rights and interests?[87]

Reacting to the divisive and exclusivist politics of the League and other communalists, Azad repeatedly wrote that one can be Muslim as well as Indian at the same time—these identities are not mutually exclusive or contradictory. This was a response not only to League propaganda but also to the Hindu communalists who were imputing religion to nationalism, defining it exclusively as a majority Hindu prerogative.* However, we did not know that after rejecting the League's idea of Islamic nationalism in 1947, we would be stuck with majoritarian nationalism after keeping it at bay for seventy years. The parliamentary majority rule is a democratic prerogative of any political party elected to the parliament but majoritarian politics through majority in the parliament is a perversion of the Constitution and not democratic at all.

*Azad's writings and speeches are replete with this sentiment of inclusive nationalism, many I have quoted here make clear his idea of united India.

Maulana Azad wrote and spoke about his idea of composite and indivisible nationalism during the 1920s soon after he decided to be a follower of Mahatma Gandhi. He consciously declared that he will be more concerned with integrative politics and not merely Islamic issues anymore, although he had been writing about such matters in *Al-Hilal* since 1912–13.

Azad delivered the historic presidential address at the Ramgarh Congress session in 1940, which reflected his love for 'Islam and of liberty, his confidence that the qaum would be secure in a free India, and his faith in India's oneness'.[88] Azad underlined that it was 'India's historic destiny that its soil should become the destination of many different caravans of races, cultures, and religions. Even before the dawn of history's morning, they started their trek into India and the process has continued since. This vast and hospitable land welcomed them all and took them to her bosom.'[89] Tony Joseph, in his recent work *Early Indians*,[90] has done this more scientifically, using advances in DNA sequencing from people of various ethnicities as well as remains of ancient people to emphasize the origins, migration, and intermixing of people throughout history. He has distilled the results of recent research and has put on record the history of the waves of migration and intermixing that resulted in the rich tapestry that forms today's India. Azad argued in his address that Islam was the last of the caravans that came into India, following the footsteps of many who settled down here before them. Bringing in the compositeness of our nation, he pointed out that 'for a time they flowed along their separate courses, but Nature's immutable law brought them together into a confluence. This fusion was a notable historic event.' We need to be conscious of the fact that Azad was stressing on the inclusiveness of India at a time when the Muslim League's divisive politics had reached a crescendo following the Pakistan Resolution in

March 1940 in Lahore. At the same time, there were Hindu communalists who were aggressively pushing for a Hindu nation, claiming themselves to be true nationalists.

Before coming to the League's idea of nationalism, let me digress a bit to contrast the Hindu nationalist narrative, which progressed simultaneously with other events to weaken the composite nationalism of the Congress and Maulana Azad. And we do not have to go back to the 1940s for a better understanding of this—this narrative is being re-enacted daily in today's India. Savarkar, who articulated Hindutva in 1923 in a book with the same title, identified the characteristics of the Hindu nation—a marked geography, a common language, a common culture, and a belief that this land is a holy land. An intellectual genealogy of Hindu nationalism, however, reveals that there is nothing uniquely 'Hindu' about it.[91] Savarkar was deeply influenced by Italian thinker Giuseppe Mazzini who vouched for an 'akhand'—unified—Italy. Even his Abhinava Bharat was inspired by Mazzini's Young Italy. Savarkar derived from 'these Europeans their obsession with identifying a common fatherland or motherland, blood, civilization, and holy land.'[92] He argued in *Hindutva*:

> A Hindu...is he who looks upon the land that extends from Sindhu to Sindhu—from the Indus to the Seas, as the land of his forefathers—his Fatherland (Pitrbhumi), who inherits the blood of that race whose first discernible source could be traced to the Vedic Saptasindhus...who has inherited...the common classical language Sanskrit and is represented by a common history, a common literature, art and architecture, law and jurisprudence, rites and rituals, ceremonies and sacraments, fairs and festivals; and who above all, addresses this land, this Sindhustahan as his Holy land (Punyabhumi), as the land of his prophets and seers, of his godmen and gurus, the land of piety and pilgrimage.[93]

Maulana Azad, on the other hand, did not look to Western models in his fight against colonialism, but instead based them on the ideals of normative Islam. His concept of composite nationalism or Ummat-i-Wahida questioned the demand for a separate entity of South Asian Muslims through separate electorates. As Azad based his argument on normative Islam, he remained committed to the guidance of the Holy Quran and the traditions of the Prophet to address the problem of politics against colonialism and communalism.[94] Azad, as a theorist of Muslim nationalism or wataniyat, attempted to give it an alternative understanding through religion, history, and culture. Despite Islam being his source and inspiration, Azad never emphasized the exclusivity of the nationalism he espoused. Instead, he stressed on the indivisibility and compositeness of it and not, like the Hindu and Muslim fanatics, its incompatibility. Jinnah spoke of the same exclusivity as Savarkar when he said that Hindus and Muslims had 'different civilizations, different epics, and different heroes' and that 'very often the hero of one is a foe of the other'.[95] Azad responded to both when he said:

> Providence brought us (Hindus and Muslims) together over a thousand years ago. We have fought, but so do blood-brothers fight.... No, it is no use trying to emphasize the differences. For that matter no two human beings are alike. Every lover of peace must emphasize similarities.[96]

Maulana Azad had a serious challenge from all such forces and he responded to all of them with exemplary erudition, empathy, and grace. One of the most evocative responses came again in his 1940 address where he spoke with passion, saying:

> I am a Muslim and profoundly conscious of the fact that I have inherited glorious traditions of the last thirteen hundred years. I am not prepared to lose even a small part of that legacy. The history and teachings of Islam, its arts and letters, its civilization and culture, are part of

> my wealth and it is my duty to cherish and guard them. As a Muslim I have a special identity within the field of religion and culture.... But, with all these feelings, I have another equally deep realization, born out of my life's experience, which is strengthened and not hindered by the spirit of Islam. I am equally proud of the fact that I am an Indian, an essential part of the indivisible unity of Indian nationhood, a vital factor in its total make-up without which this noble edifice will remain incomplete. I can never give up this sincere claim.[97]

This was Azad's response to the exclusivist and faith-based nationalism of Savarkar, which aided the Muslim communalists led by the League to instil fear among Muslims about their future in united India. For communalists of all hues, the composite and indivisible nationalism was a chimera, which nationalists like Gandhi, Patel, Azad, Nehru, and others were using to dupe the masses. However, Azad ended his presidential address evocatively, saying:

> Our shared life of a thousand years has forged a common nationality. Such moulds cannot be artificially constructed. Nature's hidden anvils shape them over the centuries. The mould has now been cast and destiny has set her seal upon it. Whether we like it or not, we have now become an Indian nation, united and indivisible. No false idea of separatism can break our oneness. We must accept the inexorable logic of facts and apply ourselves to fashioning our future destiny.[98]

We will talk about some other significant initiatives that promoted the idea of composite nationalism, adding significantly to Azad's relentless campaign against the League's divisive politics. To take this mission forward and attract a larger number of Muslims to the Congress, Nehru formed a Muslim Mass Contact Programme (MMCP) at Anand Bhawan in Allahabad under his communist lieutenant

Kunwar Mohammad Ashraf.[99] Ashraf was a Meo from Alwar, a community famous for being neither fully Muslim nor Hindu, borrowing from the traditions and practices of both these religious communities.[100] It was this distinctive background of the community that attracted the attention of Maulvi Muhammad Ilyas, who decided to launch his Tablighi Jamaat to Islamize the Meos. Maulana Azad did not have that sort of eclectic family background but he did express similar universalist theological interpretation in his *Tarjuman al-Quran*. Ashraf was initially a believer and even practised Chilla Kashi, which involves fasting and praying for forty days. He even reminisced that 'he had already had visions of the Prophet Muhammad and Hazrat Ali during his school days and was convinced that this arduous practice would allow him to "perceive the Holy light of God".'[101] However, a dream one night shook him and the murshid in the dream firmly told him that spiritual development was not part of his destiny. Ashraf gradually moved away from spirituality and closer to more secular pursuits. He went to London to finish his education, met some future Muslim communist ideologues like Z. A. Ahmad and Sajjad Zaheer there. They all became a part of the MMCP and spent their lives striving to bring the poor and working-class Muslims into the Congress fold and also attracted poets and intellectuals with socialist and communist leanings. I brought this up to show that there were diverse groups of Muslims, besides Maulana Azad, who were trying their best to challenge the communal politics of the League as well as of the Hindu communalists and most of them joined the Congress Socialist Party. Sajjad Zaheer, an Urdu writer and Marxist, reminisces: 'Nehru was very proud of our group. He introduced us to Gandhiji and Sardar Patel saying, people say Muslims are not coming to the Congress. Here is this brilliant group of young Muslims which went to England and took degrees there and had come back and joined the Congress.'[102]

Despite all the sincerity at their command, this mass contact programme fizzled out due to the lack of funds as well as lack of support of the Provincial Congress Committees. K. M. Ashraf himself was not convinced of approaching Muslims separately.[103] The Muslim League turned more combative as it saw this as a direct attack by the Congress on its support base among Muslims. In the same year, the annual session of the Muslim League was held in Lucknow and Jinnah, in his presidential address, accused the Congress of 'pursuing a policy, which is exclusively Hindu and...that the Musalmans cannot expect justice or fair play at their hands.'[104] The Congress Muslim leaders were described as Mir Jaffars, in a nod to the historic betrayal during the Battle of Plassey. People like Maulana Azad and organizations such as Khudai Khidmatgars* too were subjected to severe criticism: 'with Congress money, Congress propagandists, and with the help of such persons such as Maulana Abul Kalam Azad, the Muslims of the Frontier were being de-Muslimized...the Khudai Khidmatgars were an all-India danger.'[105] The tenor of this vitriolic reaction was indicative of the threat which the Muslim League perceived against its demand for a Muslim homeland. Even the Jamiat ul-Ulema-i-Hind, which strongly supported the cause of Azad's united India, was split to form Jamiat ul-Ulema-i-Islam by Shabbir Ahmad Usmani in 1945, who was the disciple of Ashraf Ali Thanvi.† His aim was to oppose the ideology of composite nationalism (muttahida qaumiyat) espoused by Jamiat ul-Ulema-i-Hind under the leadership of Hussain Ahmad Madani, and in the process, support the All-India Muslim League. For Usmani, Pakistan was the 'new Medina', the 'first Islamic state in history that

---

*Khudai Khidmatgar was a body of nationalist Pathans of the Frontier region, which was formed by Khan Abdul Ghaffar Khan, popularly known as Frontier Gandhi.

†Ashraf Ali Thanvi (1863–1943) was a Deobandi scholar and Sufi. He wrote several treatises but *Behishti Zevar* is one of his most prominent works. Though the majority of the Deobandi ulema supported the Congress, Thanvi was one of those who was with the Muslim League.

would attempt to reconstruct the Islamic utopia created by the Prophet in Medina.'[106] The League became more aggressive about its idea of communitarian nationalism based on Islam while Azad vociferously questioned it and used Islam and its history to visualize a composite nationalism based on togetherness not otherness.

ALLAH BAKSH SUMROO AND AZAD MUSLIM CONFERENCE

In 1940 two other major political developments took place, one was the Pakistan Resolution passed by the League on 23 March and another less known but important event was the All-India Azad Muslim Conference held in Delhi 27–30 April. Maulana Azad was surely the strongest voice for a united India and composite nationalism but he was not alone. We also had leaders like Allah Baksh Sumroo, who remains relatively unknown, yet played a significant role in articulating the cause for a united composite India. He emerged as a major challenge to the Muslim League and its two-nation theory. Allah Baksh was the moving spirit behind the Delhi Conference, which he presided over and gave a call for a composite India in front of more than hundred thousand Muslims, according to some estimates.[107] Most of these came from a large number of political and social organizations, largely representing the backward and artisanal sections of the Muslim society. The representation at the conference was an indicator confirming the historical fact that the Muslim League spoke for the ashraf or the privileged sections of the Muslim society while the majority of Muslims, the ajlaf, remained almost untouched by the League rhetoric. The British identified a collaborative section of the Muslim community, which helped in forming the Muslim League, but this section largely represented the affluent zamindars and business families and professional classes. The leadership that emerged in the League had little idea about the highly segmented Muslim society they claimed to represent. Maulana Azad could see this early on and wrote in *Al-Hilal* that:

> Muslims and highly blessed Muslims of India are today probably such a community who will find no equivalent with any other human beings; for they are non-conformists to shariah, friends of taqlid-blind worshippers, not found to be welcoming reform and reinterpretation. Again, the most unfortunate part of their life is that they have a section of elite who are in the forefront and leading them. Those are the self-proclaimed leaders of the community. They have put the crown on their own head, with their own hands, instead of the masses doing the same. They indulged in all sorts of exhibitionism of power and the worst is show of their wealth. And by so doing they had converted the millat (class) of downtrodden men in their community as their slaves and camp followers. And now if anyone tries to question their validity as leaders or defy them, they are successfully suppressed and annihilated by those selfish leaders; as they have the power of money.[108]

The presidential address of Sumroo exposed the misplaced arguments of the League, particularly in the name of religion and culture. He spoke extensively on the shared history and heritage of Hindus and Muslims, which Maulana Azad also talked about in his Ramgarh address. All through his speech, Sumroo stressed the compositeness of the Indian nation, nationalism, and the compact between diverse communities, which cannot be severed. In a strongly worded condemnation of the two-nation theory exponents, he said:

> A majority of the 90,000,000 Indian Muslims who are descendants of the earlier inhabitants of India are in no sense other than the sons of the soil with the Dravidian and the Aryan and have as much right to be reckoned among the earliest settlers of this common land. The

> nationals of different countries cannot divest themselves of their nationality merely by embracing one or another faith. In its universal sweep Islam, the faith, can run in and out of as many nationalities and regional cultures as may be found in the world.[109]

Sumroo underlined the long history of shared heritage of Hindus and Muslims when he said:

> It is a vicious fallacy for Hindu, Muslim, and other inhabitants of India to arrogate to themselves an exclusively proprietary right over either the whole or any particular part of India. The country as an indivisible whole and as one federated and composite unit belongs to all the inhabitants of the country alike and is as much the inalienable and imprescriptible heritage of the Indian Muslim as of other Indians....[110]

Sumroo made these detailed references to the intermixing of Hindu and Muslim cultures over the centuries to counter both the Muslim League as well as those who were arguing for Hindutva majoritarianism. He was aware, like Maulana Azad, of the forces which threatened the future of united composite India. When Pakistan was being created, he said:

> It was based on false understanding that India is inhabited by two nations, Hindu and Muslim. It is much more to the point to say that all Indian Mussalmans are proud to be Indian nationals and they are equally proud that their spiritual level and creedal realm is Islam. As Indian nationals, Muslims and Hindus and others inhabit the land and share every inch of the motherland and all its material and cultural treasures alike according to the measures of their just and fair rights and requirements as the proud sons of the soil.[111]

Maulana Azad derived huge strength from such popular leaders, who were committed to a united India and composite nationalism. He sent a message of support to the Azad Muslim conference as he was not able to attend it. He expressed his solidarity with the conference and wished that the deliberations would be fruitful for the great cause of the freedom of the country and the Muslims.[112] Coming back to Sumroo's address, he strongly defended the idea of composite Indian culture, which was derided and mocked by the Muslim League. He said:

> When they talk of Muslim culture they forget the composite culture which the impact of Hindus and Muslims has been shaping for the last 1000 years or more and in which is born a type of culture and civilisation in India in the production of which Muslims have been proud and active partners. It cannot now merely by creating artificial states be withdrawn to segregated areas. To art and literature, architecture and music, history and philosophy and to the administrative system of India, the Mussalmans have been contributing for a thousand years, their share of coordinated, composite, and syncretic culture which occupies a distinctly distinguished place in the types of civilisations which hold a prominent place in the world.[113]

This fight for composite and inclusive Indian nationalism, which looks so beleaguered today, is more than few decades old. Azad and Sumroo challenged these regressive and divisive forces in the 1930s and 1940s. They almost took the battle to the enemy's camp by organizing a huge conference in Delhi, which unnerved the Muslim League leadership. A Bombay English daily was euphoric in its report about the conference when it said:

> Scenes reminiscent of Khilafat days, two decades ago, were seen today on the eve of the Muslim Conference. Bands of Muslim volunteers in bright uniforms are going about the city in buses with big placards; 'Freedom

> Is Our Birthright' and singing patriotic songs. The arrival of large number of leaders has naturally led to informal consultations. Organisers of the Conference are immensely satisfied with the response from all over the country. 'The response has been tremendous. It has surpassed all my expectations', said Dr. Ashraf (a leading Muslim nationalist leader) in the course of a talk. The first great success lies in the fact that all important Muslim organizations all over the country with the exception of the Jinnah League have enthusiastically identified themselves with the conference and its objects.[114]

I need to reiterate this important chapter of our nationalist struggle, particularly to remind bigoted and divisive pseudo-nationalists who claim that the creation of Pakistan was the handiwork of all Muslims, implicating even those who consciously decided to choose India as their homeland. So far as anti-Pakistan euphoria of the conference was concerned, thousands of delegates and participants started arriving even before the inauguration of the conference from various parts of the country.[115] According to a press report, the conference was 'sure to be a tremendous success and which promises to create a fresh wave of genuine nationalism and political thought among the Muslims of India.'[116] The Muslim League planned a black flag demonstration against Sumroo but after witnessing the mammoth support of Muslims for the conference, this idea was dropped.[117] Sumroo was assassinated in 1943 and many suspected it was League handiwork.

We can comprehend his stature and the sense of loss at his death by reading some of the reactions in the contemporary press and also the pain expressed by several nationalist leaders.

His murder was seen as a national calamity by several papers, including the *Amrita Bazar Patrika*, which observed: 'A high sense of duty and rare courage of conviction, who easily commanded the respect and admiration of all, even of those who differed from him on some or the other public questions.... A life so full of promise has been cut short. And India is much poorer today by the death of the young man of forty-two whose sturdy patriotism and devotion to duty would be cherished long after the present unhappy situation has ended and India has come into her own.'[118]

It is necessary to know about such leaders from our past to challenge the ongoing communal rhetoric that paints the entire Muslim community with a single brushstroke. The right wing in India often say that Netaji S. C. Bose did not find his rightful place in our national history, but this assertion is insincere and politically motivated, especially in the face of the numerous literary works and screen adaptations of his life. It is people like Allah Baksh Sumroo who seem to be lost in our history records, even in the writings of the so-called liberal and Marxist historians. Another prominent Muslim voice, who can rightfully represent our composite nationalist ethos, is Saifuddin Kitchlew, whose arrest triggered the protests leading to the Jallianwala Bagh tragedy in 1919. Most of us are oblivious to his contributions as well. Kitchlew also mourned the loss of Sumroo:

> At this critical period of the freedom movement in the country, the death of a man like Mr Allah Baksh is a thundering blow to the forces of nationalism. Mr Allah Baksh was a thorough going nationalist. Mr Allah Baksh is dead but his work will remain.[119]

Maulana Azad was surely a prime political figure, an Islamic scholar who stressed the concept of composite nationalism, however he derived his strength from other important leaders such as Sumroo. Azad was not fighting a lone battle against the Muslim League as Mr Jinnah wanted the British and the Muslims to believe. He was hated and derided as a showboy of the Congress party precisely to create a facade that a majority of Muslim leaders supported the idea of Pakistan, which is actually a fallacy. Interestingly, Jinnah has also been called a secular leader by some supporters of Hindu nationalism who until now saw him as a divider of the country and rightly so. They do this only to undermine the Congress and its leadership, particularly Jawaharlal Nehru, holding him responsible for the partition of the country. Muhammad Ali Jinnah did have a secular early phase, when he was even called an ambassador of Hindu–Muslim unity, but this is not the reputation and legacy he left behind. He left behind a bitter and divisive legacy, which is still with us, and keeps tormenting us as a nation and even as individuals.

Maulana Azad's legacy, though, has bestowed upon us a vision of an undivided India, where all communities live peacefully. He wanted to achieve composite nationalism amongst the masses of India, which he prioritized even before the freedom of India in his Congress presidential address of 1923. He spent all his active political years during the freedom struggle as a whipping boy of the Muslim league, derided and mocked by Jinnah and the League as a collaborator of the Hindus and a mere spectacle in the Congress scheme of creating a Hindu India, but it was Azad's vision of composite nationalism which kept India together for several decades after independence. It is not the same anymore; the threats to India's plurality are real, which we need to combat to save the secular fabric of the nation. The composite nationalism we inherited was not the creation of Maulana Azad alone, true, but he was one of its foremost thinkers. This nationalism can be given different names—like indivisible nationalism, empathetic nationalism, eclectic nationalism, composite nationalism, and even cosmopolitan nationalism. It was a collaborative project that included Tagore, Tilak, Gandhi, Patel, Nehru, Bose, Bhagat Singh, and so many others. All these nationalisms stood for a united India, where there was no space for communal politics.

I will conclude this section with the words of Ruskin

Bond*, one of our most celebrated and respected authors, who, in a brief note titled, 'On Being an Indian', wrote that for him 'India is more than a land. India is an atmosphere. Over thousands of years the races and religions of the world have mingled here.... Race did not make me an Indian. But history did. And in the long run its history that counts.'

*Ruskin Bond chose to be an Indian. A Briton for whom nationality did not have any association with race or religion—for him India was home. Ruskin Bond, 'On Being an Indian', *Communicate in English*, Book 8, New Delhi: Ratna Sagar Publishers, 2018, pp. 47–48.

FOUR

GHUBAR-I-KHATIR: BEYOND FAITH AND POLITICS

Following *Tarjuman al-Quran*, this is another literary masterpiece of Maulana Azad's. It has been described as the 'tour de force of a literary craftsman'.[1] This was also his last serious piece of writing as after his stint at the Ahmednagar Fort prison, Azad was left with little time to engage in any serious intellectual task. These epistolary essays were written in the midst of his other celebrity co-prisoners and intellectual and political giants like Sardar Patel, Jawaharlal Nehru, Acharya Narendra Dev, J. B. Kripalani, and others who occupied our frontline political firmament. Many others used this period of incarceration creatively, Nehru wrote his *Discovery of India* here and J. B. Kripalani, Harekrushna Mahatab, Bhogaraju Pattabhi Sitaramayya, and Acharya Narendra Dev wrote books of their own. Sardar Patel spent most of his time playing chess and reading some of the books available in the fort's library.

Kripalani devoted a chapter to this time in their lives, 'Life in Ahmednagar Fort', in his autobiography *My Times*, and recounted some interesting episodes. They were twelve prisoners in all and only ten rooms, so two rooms had to be shared. 'Jawaharlal and Syed Mahmood occupied the same room. So did Shankarrao and Profulla. The rest of us, Azad, Sardar, Pant, Pattabhi, Narendra Deva, Asaf Ali, Mahatab, and myself had a room each to ourselves. We were given the barest of furniture.'[2] I will write about Azad's fixation with tea and its intricacies later in the chapter but what happened soon after they all arrived is worth sharing here. Kripalani says:

> When we arrived in the afternoon of the 9th, some kind of readymade tea was brought for us in an aluminium kettle, along with a few loaves of bread in a plate of the same metal. As for cups and saucers, we were supposed to use the glasses already kept in our rooms. As ill-luck would have it for the poor jailor, he took the tea paraphernalia to Azad's room. He, perhaps, thought as the President, he would call all of us in his room and tea would be served! This unceremonious method of serving tea sent Azad into a towering rage. He ordered the jailor to take away the things he had brought; if he had to serve us tea, he should do it in the dining room in the proper way with a proper tea pot and cups and saucers. The frightened jailor hurriedly took away the paraphernalia he had brought...'

This is how their life began in the fort prison, though they settled into a routine soon. All of them got engaged in different tasks, from writing and reading, to playing and gardening.

Azad chose a sedentary life and decided to write on some very unusual subjects. These miscellaneous essays were written on unrelated matters, with no thematic framework to bind them. They were letters addressed to Nawab Sadar Yar Jung Bahadur Maulana Habiburrehman Khan Sherwani*, one of

---

*Nawab Sadar Yar Jung Habiburrehman Khan Sherwani belonged to an eminent family which occupied a significant space during the medieval period. He was born on 5 January 1867 at Bhikampur, near Aligarh in Uttar Pradesh, where the family had settled in the early nineteenth century. Sherwani had an intellectual bent of mind and built a rich library of rare books at this own expense. On the basis of his erudition, he was appointed professor of Islamic Studies at the Aligarh Muslim University from where his reputation travelled to Hyderabad. Mir Usman Ali Khan invited him to head the Religious Affairs department of the state in June 1918. Next year in August, Osmania University was established and Maulvi Habiburreaman Khan Sherwani was appointed its first vice-chancellor. Maulana Azad met him first in 1906, probably through Maulana Shibli Nomani. With the passage of time, their relationship matured and they developed immense respect for each other. Sherwani died on 11 August 1950.

Azad's few friends who could be interested in such diverse matters. Except for a few which were in the form of a letter, most others were actually essays on subjects Azad was keen to write about. These letters were completely apolitical, written at a time when Azad was deeply immersed in politics. Once Azad tried to raise some political issues in a letter but soon realized the redundancy of such an undertaking and said, 'But I should not talk about this to you. Our conversation is not meant for these wailings.'[3] This speaks volumes about his capacity to keep his mind compartmentalized. Malik Ram says that Charles Montesquieu's *Persian Letters*, published in 1721, may have inspired Azad to write these letters, since they had been translated into various languages, including Arabic, which Azad may have had access to.[4] However, there is no documentary evidence to confirm this. Even the style of both sets of letters is very different.

This collection of letters depicts his capacity to pick a subject as remote as possible from his known interests like literature, philosophy, religion, ethics, and of course anything but politics. Azad used to call this quality of quick change 'tehmiz', the Arabic word for changing the taste of the mouth. He once told his secretary Mr Ajmal Khan that if he did not indulge in tehmiz, his brain would stagnate. 'Tehmiz provides for my mind the relaxation necessary for it to become refreshed and rejuvenated'.[5] This is visible quite clearly when we go through each of these letters, which range from subjects like the virtues of staying cheerful, to the philosophy of life and merits of solitude, to gardening, tea, and music, and even about some resident sparrows in his cell. A notable feature of these essays is that Azad writes about each one of these subjects as an expert. These letters were written by Azad to keep himself engaged creatively against the monotony of prison life. They exude his literary and scholarly prowess, yet we find several lighter moments in these when Azad expresses himself through sarcasm and humour. Azad was not keen on exercise or manual work of any sort unlike Nehru, who spent a lot of time gardening, besides writing *Discovery of India*. He preferred a sedentary life.

Douglas observes that *Ghubar-i-Khatir* adumbrates Azad's outlook during the last period of his life. According to Douglas, Azad wrote it with the realization that independence was on the horizon. He foresaw the time when he would be in a place of leadership in a free India, in which he would need the confidence of non-Muslims as well as Muslims.[6] I don't think Douglas is right in concluding any such change in Azad's attitude at this juncture, for Azad had actually taken an integrative approach from the 1920s onwards and had seen himself as a national leader and not just as the leader of Muslims. *Ghubar-i-Khatir* is an extension of Azad's inclusive approach towards an India he had fought for since the mid-1920s.

Douglas complains that Azad refused to complete his *Tarjuman* despite the insistence of his co-prisoners in the fort.[7] He assumes that Azad had enough time to complete the project—one that was very dear to him. But Douglas seems to be oblivious to the circumstances which Azad himself reports in one of the letters in *Ghubar-i-Khatir.* If we look at the *Tarjuman*, it becomes clear that the task to carry it further needed a huge scholarly input, which was impossible without access to scholarly literature for citations and explanations. Writing about the circumstances, Azad says in one of the letters that, 'I had nothing with me except two books that had been kept as travel companions. There was nothing for serious study. I thought if I call for some books and manuscripts from home it may be possible to use this free time in detention. Apparently there seemed to be nothing wrong with the desire.'[8] Of course Azad could not complete his *Tarjuman* but he did revise the earlier text that was completed in 1930, while he was in Meerut prison. The 1945 version of his *Tarjuman* was a revised version which he worked on in the Ahmednagar Fort prison.

He scribbled a list of books and gave it to the prison authorities, but regretted it soon after. Many of his co-prisoners received books and other necessary items from their homes, but Azad felt differently. Expressing his feelings he wrote, 'It was a weakness of mind that I had agreed to take advantage of a government facility. Why expect that from a government that deprives us of the facility of calls by friends and relatives...a facility that is not denied to criminals and murderers, would arrange to get things from home? In such circumstances self-respect demanded neither to express any desire nor entertain any hope.'[9] Thus, prison was not a suitable place for Azad to undertake working on the *Tarjuman*. He could dabble only in a dilettante-like manner in curious and recondite matters, which eventually became the theme of *Ghubar-i-Khatir.*[10] Kripalani did not know what Azad was busy writing, he says that, 'Maulana was busy completing his commentary on the Holy Quran, which is said to be the best',[11] though he was actually revising the earlier text.

Maulana Azad's mind touches upon diverse subjects in *Ghubar-i-Khatir*, ranging from the very complexities of life that can be approached through different angles to simple observations. He is concerned about the meaning of religious faith, cutting across religions, he delves into the philosophical questions related to life and death, and he also touches upon the centrality of happiness in human life. His own life and personality are vividly expressed in some of the letters. I must say that *Ghubar-i-Khatir* gives us the most reliable account of many autobiographical details from childhood to adulthood. Most other sources that have been used by scholars, including me, do not come straight from his pen but through interlocutors like Abdur Razzaq Malihabadi (*Azad ki Kahani Azad ki Zubaani*), Maulana Fazluddin Ahmad (*Tazkirah*), and Humayun Kabir (*India Wins Freedom*).

Another distinctive feature of *Ghubar-i-Khatir* is the extensive use of Persian and Urdu couplets, maybe over seven hundred of them, which again proves how remarkable Azad's memory was. Many of these he had memorized in his youth as a student, and they remained with him even now when he had crossed fifty-three years. Azad, being a very private person, decided to talk to himself about his past while writing these letters. He poured his heart out in the solitude of prison and reminisced about his past, engaged with many philosophical issues, his likes and dislikes, and of course, many of his passions.

In the first letter after reaching the fort, Azad decided to write something about the history of Ahmednagar as well as of the fort. He regrets that he had been to 'almost all historical places in the country but never Ahmednagar [f]ort.... It is one of those cities in the country with which stories of centuries of changes have been associated.'[12] Remembering Chand Bibi* he says that it is the same Ahmednagar Fort on whose walls Chand Bibi engraved the world-renowned legends of her determination and bravery.

Let me also recall a significant speech delivered by Bal Gangadhar Tilak in this town in 1916, where he referred to the Muslim rulers of Ahmednagar and made some pertinent comments, particularly relevant in our ongoing political context. He spoke about aliens and defined who should be called an alien—he is an alien whose 'point of view is alien, their thoughts are alien.... The Muhammadan kings who ruled here at Ahmednagar (I don't call Muhammadans aliens) came to and lived in this country.... The religion may be different.... By alien I do not mean alien in religion.

---

*Chand Bibi or Chand Sultana was the daughter of Husain Nizam Shah, ruler of Ahmednagar. She was the queen of Ali Adil Shah, ruler of Bijapur. On the death of Ali Adil, his nephew Ibrahim Adil succeeded him and Chand Sultana became the regent queen. In 1595 the army of Akbar invaded Ahmednagar under the command of Prince Murad. Chand Sultana fought valiantly and defeated the Mughal forces. Four years later, in 1599, Akbar attacked again with a stronger army and Chand Sultana was betrayed by her own companions. Cheetah Khan, the guard, conspired with the people in the fort and murdered the queen. The fort was thus captured by Akbar.

He who does what is beneficial to the people of this country, be he a Muhammadan or an Englishman, is not an alien. "Alienness" has to do with interest. Aliennness is not concerned with white or black skin. Alienness is not concerned with religion.... He may not perhaps go with me to the same temple to pray to God, perhaps there may be no inter-marriage and inter-dining between him and me. All these are minor questions.'[13] I don't know if Azad ever came across this speech of Tilak, delivered almost three decades before Azad arrived at the fort. Tilak's words provide salience to Azad's definition of composite nationalism, where Hindus and Muslims have equal claim over the destiny of India. All those who are obsessed today with religious identities should care to read Tilak, rightly called the father of Indian nationalism—and Azad was not far from this when he talked of indivisible nationalism just a few years later.

Azad continued to turn the pages of history in his writing as he reminisced about the six centuries of Ahmednagar Fort's history where Abdur Rahim Khan-i-Khana* fought a battle against Suhail Habshi and Abul Fazl found the moat around the fort that was forty yards broad and fourteen yards deep, though it was filled up over the centuries. Azad concluded this letter by calling it idle talk as he was unable to hold back the urge to weave tales. He ended the letter remembering Ghalib:

Magar sitamzada hoon zauq-e-khama farsaa ka[14]

But I am a victim of the passion for writing.

Strangely, he begins the next letter by counting his days of incarceration, beginning with the year 1916 and through 1921,

---

*Abdur Rahim Khan-i-Khana (1556–1627) was the son of Bairam Khan, the famous statesman in Akbar's court. Rahim was not only a military general but was an important literary figure of the seventeenth century. He was accomplished in several languages including Persian, Turkish, and Hindi. He is also known to be a patron of Tulsidas, who was his contemporary. He is buried in Nizamuddin East, Delhi.

1931, 1932, and 1940—bringing the total days to seven years and eight months. Azad spent one-seventh of the fifty three years of his life in prison. He is even more precise when he writes that 'one day of every week in my life was spent in prison.'* Azad was aware of the two options Indians had in those days of the anti-colonial struggle—to be indifferent or outspoken. An indifferent life can be spent anywhere and everywhere, while the other option will land you only in prison. Azad chose to be outspoken, since indifference did not come to him easily.[15]

He moves to some philosophical issues which he calls daily experiences of our lives and not just philosophical questions. He tries to explain the importance of context when we talk of pleasure and pain. In this world, he says, there is neither absolute pleasure nor absolute pain; all our feelings are relative. Azad writes:

> Change the context and the nature of pleasure and pain would change. Every mind and every situation cannot be assessed by the same criterion. The test for the pain and pleasure of a peasant cannot be the same as the one for an artist. The pleasure that a mathematician draws from solving a mathematical problem is beyond the indulgence of a hedonist. There are times when we find no comfort even on a bed of roses and there are times when every thorn on the path provides a special pleasure.[16]

He continued that pleasure and pain are not caused by any external inducement; it is our own sensibility that gives a wound and also acts as a healing balm. Pursuit of a passion

---

*He writes as a footnote: 'This letter was written on 11 August 1942. After that I remained in prison for another two years and seven months so the total period of incarceration came to ten years and seven months. I have no complaint against this enhancement of time period. My only regret is that the appropriateness of the seventh part and the idea of Sabbath has become irrelevant.' Asadullah Khan Ghalib, *Diwan-i-Ghalib*, cited in Abul Kalam Azad, *Ghubar-i-Khatir: Sallies of the Mind*, 2003, Kolkata: Maulana Abul Kalam Azad Institute of Asian Studies, p. 45.

is the highest pleasure of life provided it is a worthy passion. Azad also explained that what he is saying may look like philosophy but actually it is not. It is the daily experience of life. 'I may not refer to love and passion as not many people can encounter them in their lives. However, there are many who seek hedonist and carnal pleasures. Let all these people ask themselves whether bitterness of pain and pangs of living have ever yielded them a sweet pleasure or not?'[17]

Azad further questions the monotony of a life based on conformity and uniformity, and for him it merely makes life bland and tasteless. Any change, even when not for good like change from peace to disturbance, adds salt to life. He cites an Arabic saying 'keep changing the taste of your company'—hammizu majaliskum—life should be experienced both in its sweetness and bitterness. All mornings and evenings of life, if alike, will make it so boring. Only those who have experienced loss can truly enjoy gains. Those who have never faced loss will never understand the meaning of gain. His philosophical strides take him further when he says that disturbance is at the core of life and the peace of a graveyard has no meaning. 'A wave is alive as long as it is restless; the moment it is at rest it ceases to exist.'[18]

Maulana Azad loved solitude; this passion remained with him all his life beginning from his childhood days. He wrote about it thus:

> Boyhood is generally spent in fun and frolic but, at the age of twelve–thirteen, I used to sit in a corner, book in hand, and tried to avoid people's attention. In Calcutta you must have seen Dalhousie Square, opposite General Post Office, commonly known as Lal Diggi. There are trees all around but in the middle, there is a space and also a bench to sit. Don't know whether that cluster is still around but whenever I went out for a stroll I carried with me a book, and immersed myself in the study in one quiet corner. The personal servant of my late father

> usually accompanied me. He kept walking outside and fretted 'if you were only to read the book why did you come out?'[19]

Later in his life, if some people turned away from him due to his indifference towards them he never regretted it, rather he felt grateful. 'The crowds that provide exhilaration to others become, at times, unbearable for me. I tolerate people due to compulsion not choice.'[20]

After reaching the Ahmednagar Fort he realized that though the world of eye and ear is lost, a host of new worlds of thought and imagination have opened up with all their secrets and vastness. If the closing of one door can open so many other doors, which fool would be sorry for the deal. As on several occasions, he quotes a couplet to stress the point:

> Nuqsan naheen junoon mein bala se ho ghar kharaab
> Do gaz zameen ke badle biyabaan giran naheen[21]
>
> No harm if passion ruins the house, for
> Gain of whole wilderness against two yards of land is no bad bargain.

His search for solitude made him wake up at three o'clock in the morning and this schedule remained with him all his life. Azad liked to work while the whole world slept for the peace and quiet it accorded him—'nobody can interfere in my solitude.'[22] He writes, when the world 'is awake I sleep and when it sleeps I wake up.' He enjoyed being alone even in the midst of a crowd, lost in his own thoughts, indifferent to the people around. This was one of the habits he inherited from his father who was always early to bed and early to rise and believed this to be one of the primary blessings of life. Maulana Azad says, 'I developed such fondness for early morning that whenever I was late I remained disturbed the whole day.' Inside the fort, the early morning silence was pierced by just one sound, writes Azad in a lighter vein:

> Now there is nothing to disturb the perfect silence except the snoring of Jawaharlal. He is sleeping in my neighbourhood, only a wooden partition in between. When snoring stops he, as usual, starts muttering in sleep.... Muttering in sleep is a strange mental condition. It occurs in people who are highly emotional....[23]

Azad's observation underlines the closeness between the two where, after working together for several years now, Azad knew that Nehru does not function merely through reason but emotion as well, both, while awake and in sleep.

In one of his letters, Azad concedes that his search for solitude has also created many misunderstandings in his life. 'I cannot explain my mind to people and they attribute my habit to arrogance and intellectual vanity. Fact is that I am so heavily burdened under my own weight that I can hardly bother about others.' He reiterates his love for solitude in other letters as well when he says that, 'I had to traverse my path alone in all spheres—religion, politics, as well as common thinking. Nowhere could I keep pace with the caravans of time.'

In one of the letters, Azad says that he has reconstructed life in prison with two contradictory philosophies, one of the Stoics* and the other of Epicureans†. And later, he wonders how epicurean delights can be enjoyed in prison when prison life is quite in tune with stoicism, in the sense that it helps forget the pain and comfort of life. 'I would however like to remind you that real pleasure is the pleasure of mind and not of body. I take from the epicures their mental disposition and leave the sensual to them.'[24] For Azad, the prison house

*Stoicism is a school of Hellenistic philosophy which was founded by Zeno of Citium in Athens in the early third century BCE. According to Stoic philosophy, the path to happiness is found in accepting the moment it presents itself, by not allowing oneself to be controlled by the desire for pleasure.

†Epicureanism was founded around 307 BCE in ancient Greece by the philosopher Epicurus. It mainly opposed Stoic philosophy. Epicurus's materialism led him to a general attack against superstition and divine intervention. Epicureanism is a form of hedonism as it also declares that pleasure is the chief good in life.

is not bereft of nature's generosities, the sun and the moonlit nights do not discriminate between a prisoner and a non-prisoner. He says:

> Nature does not behave like man to make some happy and keep others in deprivation. When it unveils its face, it invites one and all to enjoy the sight of beauty. It is our own carelessness that we do not see it and remain lost in our surroundings.[25]

In the middle of describing nature and its beauty, Azad makes a serious comment about human nature, something that is intrinsic to the human psyche—to discriminate amongst people on various counts like religion, language, region, or culture. It is only nature which follows equity and equality in disbursing its bounties.

He cites an old Chinese proverb that raises the question 'Who is the wisest person' and the answer is 'The one who is ever cheerful', which means that the Chinese truly understood the philosophy of life. If you have learnt to stay happy in all situations then you have learnt all that needs to be learnt in life. Our life is a sort of mirrored chamber (aina khana). Each face is reflected in hundreds of mirrors. If one face is morose it will affect hundred other faces. Life is not just an individual affair, it is part of a collective. One wave on the river surface generates several other waves. Nothing in life is absolutely personal or individual. Azad continues that no pleasure would cheer us up if we are surrounded by distressed faces. He brings in Andre Gide*, a French writer and Nobel laureate,

---

*Andre Paul Guillaume Gide (1869–1951) was a French author and winner of the Nobel Prize for Literature in 1947. His career ranged from its beginnings in the symbolist movement to the advent of anti-colonialism between the two World Wars. He was also a communist for a few years between 1932 and 1939 but gave it up after his visit to Russia. He was known as a freethinker but did not get much recognition within France due to his Protestant faith. He was the author of more than fifty books and the *New York Times*, in an obituary, described him as 'France's greatest contemporary man of letters.'

who also wrote in his autobiography that staying cheerful is not only a natural need but also our moral responsibility. The ripple effect leads to societal cheerfulness, thus it is our social responsibility as well:

> Afsurda dil afsurda kunad anjumane ra[26]
> One man's depression causes depression to a whole group

There is something very insightful and of contemporary relevance that follows his comments about the need of cheerfulness for all. He says that the three disciplines—philosophy, ethics, and religion, that were out to solve the riddles of life have themselves acquired anti-life attitudes. It is generally believed that a more glum and downcast a man's face, the greater possibility of his being religious, philosophical, and ethical. As if mournfulness is a precondition for knowledge (ilm) and piety (taqaddus). Such contempt and denigration of life was not peculiar to the Cynics of Greece (kalbiya) alone, it was also rampant among the Stoics (ravaki) and Peripatetics (masshai) as well. As a result, dejection and surliness became a prominent feature of philosophical disposition. If ethics are divested of the concepts of eudemonism (mazhab-i-tamaniyat-o-masarrat) and hedonism (madayati mazhab-i-ishrat), their common natural disposition would not be free from the grumpy demeanour associated with the philosophic mind. In the world of religion and spirituality, dry piety (zohade khushk) and coldness of conduct (tabaye khunuk) have taken over to the extent that it is impossible to locate a smiling face with piety and truth.[27]

Azad goes on to make some more observations that are so apt even in the contemporary times across religions. He says that 'the merry company of men of taste is never narrow like the heart of the narrow-minded. It is capable of accommodating a lot.' Azad quotes a couplet from Nizami Ganjvi to make his point more explicit:

Har cheh dar jumla aafaq dareen ja hazir
Momin-o-Armani-o-Gabr-o-Nasara-o-Yahood[28]

Gathered together in this world of ours are all—
Muslim, Armenian, Zoroastrian, Christian, and Jew.

With his biting sarcasm, Azad concludes that 'despite such breadth of mind if there was something for which there could be no place it was the big dome like turbans. One such turban squeezes up the entire company so that the men of frank disposition had to shout:

Dar majlis-i-maa Zahid zinhaar takalluf ne-st
Albatta tu mee ganji, ammama namee ganjad.'[29]

In our company, o pious one there is no formality,
You are welcome but don't bring your turban along.

Azad's love for nature and its bounties comes up again when he concludes this letter extolling nature so poetically. He says that we will have to recognize that with the dry visage of a philosopher, a pious religious person, or an ascetic we cannot fit in with the frame that Nature's art has adorned with its brush—the frame that holds in it the bright broad forehead of the sun, the smiling face of the moon, the twinkle of stars, dance of the trees, the ditties of the birds, the rhythm of the flowing waters, and the colourful coquetry of flowers with all their grace. Only a person with some warmth in his heart and with a cheerful visage can find a place in the midst of this sparklingly beautiful nature.[30]

In one of the letters, Azad expresses his dislike for summer and says that 'however temperate the summer it upsets me and I am ever anxious for the arrival of winter. Coldness of weather is for me an asset. As this asset is over, it seems to me, all the pleasures of life are gone.'[31] He even shares that his idea of a luxurious day begins with winter, almost freezing cold temperature, and ends with him sitting by a flaming fire in the fireplace, reading or writing, forgetful of all other cares. He even talks of paradise, where he says we hear about canals, but fear it may not be summer.[32] Azad was also passionate about swimming, he writes that as a child he spent few months in Chinsurah because Calcutta was facing a plague. It is on the banks of the Hooghly river that, he says, 'I learnt swimming at that place. For hours I would continue swimming in the river and yet would not be satisfied. Even now I crave for an opportunity to swim.'[33] Coming back to his love for winter, Azad writes that 'People go to hills to spend summer season. I have often resorted there in winter, for in my view that is the right time to be there.'

There are many lighter moments, besides some serious philosophical questions, that Azad shares in these letters. He refers to one British officer, probably of the Imperial Medical Service, one Major M. Sendak, who was appointed superintendent of the fort. This name amused him but the Sendak-Bendak did not sound good, so immediately an different name cropped up from history. Azad had read about one Cheetah Khan*, who was the commander of the fort during Chand Bibi's time. He foisted that name on Major Sendak, which soon became very popular, even among his fellow officers in the fort.[34]

As I mentioned earlier, *Ghubar-i-Khatir* is the only source which comes to us directly from Maulana Azad, particularly when he speaks about his childhood as well as other experiences. In one of the letters written on 12 October 1942, Azad reminisces about his elders who were committed to a path (maslak) that was rigid and unbending, where even the slightest departure was perceived as infidelity and hypocrisy. 'All my childhood was spent in the midst of people who were tradition-bound (qadamatparast),' he notes, 'where there was

---

*Cheetah Khan was the eunuch valet of Chand Bibi, who, it is alleged, during the war with the Mughals, spread the rumour that Chand Bibi was a traitor. She was then killed by an enraged mob of her own troops. After her death, the Ahmednagar Fort was captured by the Mughals.

not even a slight opening for any outside influence. My family was so far away from all the revolutionary changes happening all around the world that even a trace of those reverberations could not pierce my environs. On this count I was living in an India of almost hundred years ago.'[35] Unfortunately, this malaise is not alien to us even now—a large section of Indians, of all communities, are trapped in the frozen past. As a public figure and a recognized Islamic scholar, Azad had to confront Muslims who were committed to looking backwards. Even his *Tarjuman al-Quran* did not receive the sort of acceptance it deserved only because it questioned the regressive mindset of his community and opposed conformity at all levels.

Azad believes that we resort to faith and God's existence as a solution to life's riddles. He talks about Albert Einstein, who, in one of his books, likened scientific research with the search for the ultimate truth as in the exploits of the detective Sherlock Holmes, which he calls a very meaningful (manikhez) simile.

To establish the existence of God, Azad goes further and raises some questions about the entire purpose of our existence. He wants to reaffirm that we cannot just presume that there is no intelligent power operating behind this perfect display of nature—that there is someone who takes care of our natural needs, a force which runs the show in such an orderly manner. It is clear that he is trying to use reason and intellect to answer most of the questions, but ultimately he also ends up at faith's door. For Azad, his faith in God is an intrinsic human need and not a later acquisition. While reiterating the belief in God and its antiquity, Azad begins with the Australian aborigines, moving to later human groups, to the ancient Vedandists, the Hittites from the dawn of history, and the pre-Christian Egyptians, all of them expressed faith in God in their own diverse ways. But, were there not atheistic philosophies and traditions in the world, including in India? Why should an erudite scholar like Azad leave them aside?

Is it not necessary to talk about those who have no faith at all? In India, we have several atheistic philosophical traditions which are seldom talked about as part of our rich cultural and intellectual inheritance.[36] We need to acknowledge the existence of diverse philosophical and religious traditions, which most of us refuse to do, and this erasure is not specific to Maulana Azad alone.

In one of the letters Azad talks about egotism and egotistical literature (ananiyati adabiyaat), defining it as a genre of writing in which the 'ego' or 'I' of the author dominates the work. For him anything ranging from autobiographies, personal experiences, and impressions to personalized mode of thinking fall in the category of egotistical literature. Most of our self-effacing behaviour is actually a manifestation of our egoism. He explains it further and I want to use his own words in translation:

> Only rarely does an author rise above this dilemma. Some that have been successful are people who have the ability of presenting their ego before others without any frills or adornment. Their ego did appear before the world but in a way that an informal person appears without any formal dressing up. Such informal appearance of a person has its own charm. As the spontaneous expression of reality, it involuntarily attracts every eye. The ego of the rare ones who have been able to accomplish it, may be however large for them and however small for others, has an undeniable attraction for the world at large. The world does not get time to measure their ego and is overwhelmed by its frank and informal appearance.[37]

Maybe Azad wanted to be seen in this category of people—he did leave behind three accounts which may be called autobiographical—though recorded by others. He refused to do a proper autobiography despite the insistence of close friends like Fazluddin and Malihabadi. He could agree to talk to them about himself and his family but did not feel comfortable treating himself as his subject, maybe his aloof and shy behaviour kept him away from such a personal project. I was also a bit puzzled at the idea of an autobiography, which Fazluddin initially floated in 1918, when Azad was merely twenty-eight. He had established himself as a religious scholar and as a young, fiery journalist, but his political career had not even taken off properly. Perhaps that was the reason why Azad speaks about his ancestors in *Tazkirah* and little about himself.

Azad writes, 'When a person wants to be photographed, his ego mildly expresses the desire in his subconscious, no matter whether he is conscious of it or not.' According to him, just like all the meaningful feelings of man, assertion of ego also takes different forms in different conditions, just as every man is not equally perceptive, individuality also does not boil at the same temperature in every utensil. He goes on to cite examples from global history and literature. For the genre of autobiography, he selects few people randomly—St. Augustine, Rousseau, Strindberg, Tolstoy, Anatole France, and Andre Gide—and says that their autobiographies represent different pictures, but all of them have acquired a permanent niche in world literature because of the spontaneity and authenticity of their work. Similarly, among the Oriental characters he picks the work of Ghazali, Ibn-Khaldoon, Babar, Jahangir, and Badauni—they are diverse in their expressions but in all of them egos appear naked and unveiled. However, he puts Badauni in a different category who, as a commoner, acquired the knowledge of the time, made a place among scholars, and gained access to the royal court. What emerges from Badauni's activities is his inflexible narrow-mindedness, unremitting fanaticism, and unrivalled faith. For us his ego is petty and invites reproach, and yet, why is it that we cannot resist his attraction?

Tolstoy for him is the most outstanding example of an

egoistic literature; Tolstoy's autobiography is as attractive to Tolstoy himself as it is to the readers. In the later part of the last century and early part of this century, no other author could utter 'I' with the same self-confidence as did this 'ajeeb-o-ghareeb Rusi' and he could do that because he unmasked himself before the world while writing his autobiographical account, his personal notes and impressions, his dialogues and diaries, his debates on art and literature, but also because the world saw it as writings of universal significance. His autobiography is as gripping as some of his finest works like *War and Peace* and *Anna Karenina*, and in both the novels one can see the voice of his ego.[38]

Azad ends this epistle with some brief comments about the Greek etymology of the word 'ego', which was later adopted by Farabi and Ibn Rushd. It is interesting that Azad had no hesitation or prejudice in conceding that 'ego' is more appropriate a word than 'anaa' in literary discourse and that Urdu should adopt it. Azad knew that languages grow and transform, he was not hung up on the purity of spoken words, and he believed that all languages have a hybrid past. Azad followed this unprejudiced approach when he took over the responsibilities of education and culture as a minister.

TEA FOR ONE

In one of the first letters, which Azad wrote before reaching the Ahmednagar Fort, he talks about tea, a passion which stayed with him all his life. Most of his letters begin with tea, its preparation and consumption. He writes:

> With the first sip of tea I light the cigarette and then follow up with use of this special compound. At short intervals I take a sip of tea along with a pull at the cigarette.... This process of synthesizing the sip of tea with a pull on the cigarette continues.... How should I describe the intoxicating pleasure of this combination of

two sharp and light ingredients.[39]

Further, in the same letter, Azad narrates an episode when he was arrested in 1921 in Calcutta and put behind bars for two years in the Alipore jail. He was told that smoking was not allowed in the prison, so he had to leave his cigarette case with the jailor. While inside he found many of his co-prisoners smoking and well stocked with cigarettes, 'the jail administration turned a Nelson's eye towards them. Some of them followed the maxim "sharbul yahood".' (In Islamic states the Jews prepared the wine; therefore, clandestine drinking was so referred). Azad quoted Zauq:

> Sharbul Yahood karte hain nasraniyon mein hum[40]
>
> Like the Jews, we drink on the sly.

But the real story is that he eagerly accepted the offer of a cigarette from the jailor the day he was released. 'No delay in renouncing nor any hesitation in indulgence. Neither was I sorry at deprivation nor elated with acquisition.' This shows how Azad could firmly and conveniently give up an addiction, which is not an easy task.

Later, he writes of his morning routine in Ahmednagar, which involved morning tea at four o'clock like a celebration. I am tempted to quote his own words to convey the flavour of his excitement:

> Instead of old wine (badaye kuhan) I open a box of fresh Chinese tea and make tea with all the care of an expert. After that I place the tea pot and cup on the right side of the table for that is its deserved place. Pen and paper are kept on the left as they have secondary place being work-a-day things. With these things in place I take my position in the chair. And don't ask of the mood into which that seat transports me. A hundred-

> year old Champaign* and Bordeaux† would not have provided the drinker the pleasure that every sip of tea provides me.[41]

Not just the preparation of tea but the consumption itself is described as a distinctive process that is simply out of the ordinary. He revels in describing the process in his own poetic Urdu, which sadly can't be reproduced here. He says:

> You know I take tea in Russian cups that are smaller than the ordinary tea cups. Crudely swallowed cup will empty in two sips. God forbid that I should indulge in such a crude behaviour. I sip slowly like the expert tasters of wine, small sips after intervals. At the end of the first cup I stop a while and try to prolong the interval as long as I can. Thus, I will proceed with the second and third cup too and, in the process, totally forget all about gains and losses of the world.[42]

But what exactly is tea for him? Maulana Azad clarifies to all tea drinkers that he takes tea for its own sake whereas others drink it for milk and sugar—for him, it's an objective while for others it is a means. 'The Chinese have been producing and consuming tea for the last fifteen hundred years,' he writes, 'but they never thought of the grossness of mixing it with milk.' It was the British who introduced this evil practice, which Azad calls bidat‡, of mixing milk and sugar—though they did try to distance themselves by saying that only a little milk should be mixed, the consequences of their mischief could not be controlled. Gradually, people began mixing tea in their milk instead of the other way round. Azad rues this tragic turn of events with Daagh Dehlvi:

---

*Champagne is a French sparkling wine, an alcoholic drink produced from specific types of grapes grown in the Champagne region of France.

†Bordeaux wine is any wine produced in the Bordeaux region of France. Bordeaux is the on Garonne river.

‡Bidat in Islam means heretical doctrine, innovation, or heresy.

Haye kambakht tu ne pee hi nahin

O unfortunate wretch, you have never drunk it!

Among the prisoners in the fort, none appreciated tea, most of them were fond of milk and curd. You can understand the distance between the world of tea and that of milk and curd. Even a lifetime is not enough to cover that distance. Jawaharlal, of course, was a tea addict and preferred it in the style of the European elite, without milk but not very different in quality from others; he is content with his Lopchu-vopchu.* Obviously, inviting such people to tea was not only useless but also quite inappropriate. Azad uses Ghalib's Persian couplet to explain it further:

Mae beh zuhhad m'kun arza keh een jauhar-e-nayab
Pesh-e-een qaum beh shorba-e-zamzam na rasad[43]

Don't offer wine to the ascetic, as this rare substance
For them is no better than the slimy zamzam water

As Azad said in the beginning of the last letter we discussed here—he had run out of stock and was somehow coping with the usual black tea. This caused a bit of a comic situation as Cheetah Khan tried to secure the tea Azad drank, when a rumour began that a VIP must be visiting from China for whom this tea is required. The warden tried his best to convince people that no VIP visit was due but the morning papers were screaming with headlines that Madame Chiang Kai-Shek† was coming to meet the prisoners in the fort and the tea is for her. Azad ends the letter with the statement that 'I only wanted to say that my tea is finished but I have not been able to say that, though I have finished writing twenty-two pages.'[44]

*Lopchu is a commercial tea brand while vopchu is just a meaningless addition to rhyme.

†Madame Chiang was the daughter of Dr Sun Yat-Sen. She was married to General Chiang Kai-Shek in 1927 and had visited India in 1942 with her husband.

There are three letters that bring out an unknown aspect of his persona, his love for flowers with all the details about them and then his enchanting engagement with the resident birds. His prose is particularly lucid and poetic when he is narrating the colour and beauty of flowers and also when he is weaving stories about his winged friends. The titles of the first two letters were derived from Persian folklore, 'Hikayat-i-Zaagh-o-Bulbul' (The Story of the Crow and the Nightingale) and 'Chidiya Chidey ki Kahani' (The Story of Male and Female House Sparrow). The Persian classic *Manteq-ut-Tair* of Fariduddin Attar provided the title and the framework of these letters.

When Maulana Azad and his co-prisoners entered the fort, they found it desolate and barren, with no trace of colour or vegetation in sight. It is clear from his several other letters that Azad opted for a sedentary life but he was bored with the colourless surroundings and longed for some greenery, some flowers. After a discussion among fellow prisoners, the idea of a garden came up. He writes:

> We thought why not take up the hobby of gardening; it would also serve to break the monotony. The hobby would serve the dual purpose, providing pleasure to those interested in sensuous beauty and spiritual satisfaction for seekers of truth.[45]

One of the most enthusiastic participants in the gardening project was Jawaharlal, who was up in the morning with his spade and axe, 'digging the mountain' like the legendary lover Farhad; Nehru himself wrote that 'I took to gardening and spent many hours daily, even when the sun was hot, in digging and preparing beds for flowers.'[46]

Ultimately the flower beds were ready, with some earth and manure brought from outside. It took weeks for Jawaharlal, with shovel and spade in hand, to finish this difficult task. Now Cheetah Khan was requested to arrange for flower seeds from Poona. There was the issue of irrigation and as I said earlier, Azad refers to a suggestion by his fellow prisoners that chicken blood, which is easily available in the kitchen, should be used for irrigation. That spurred Azad's mind into a couplet though he had given up on poetic exercise long back:

Kaliyon mein ahtazaz hai parwaz-i-husn ki
Seencha tha kis ne baagh ko murghi ke khoon se

The buds are fired with a desire to fly;
Who has irrigated the garden with chicken blood?

The seeds were sown in September–October and by December the scene around the fort changed. By the beginning of January 'the courtyard was full like the sack of a gardener's wife and every bed looked like the bag of a flower-seller.'[47] Azad knew that most of the flowers were seasonal and he gave a long list of forty varieties—morning glory, which Azad calls bahare subh, was the first among them which brightened up the drab colourless ruin (kharabaye berang). As the sun rays glistened in the sky, the morning glory buds burst into laughter on the earth. There were also zinnias, which appeared with their colourful turbans on and hollyhocks, which stood like holding colourful wine glasses in their hands. Petunia also lent colour to all corners of the yard though its simplicity went generally unnoticed. There were also small clumps of aster, cornflower, sweet pea, poppy, phlox, calliopsis, and cosmos. But it was pinks, salvia, and pansy that provided delight to both sight and sensitivity. 'These flowers', writes Azad, 'are called seasonal because their life is confined to one season. As soon as the season is over, they bid goodbye to life. As if they were gifted only with one garment which also served as the coffin.'[48]

From the aesthetics of flowers, Azad moves to some miracle-making (ajaib aafreeniyon) attributes of flowers.

Gloriosa Superba is extraordinary according to him for it first blooms like the palm of a hand, then overturns in the shape of a cup, and then becomes spherical like a lampshade. Azad was not a trained botanist yet had so much to share about horticulture, he was not an ornithologist either but again it was his keen sense of observing, reading, and expressing which made him look like an expert bird watcher. While writing the letter he suddenly becomes conscious and says that writing about gardening etc. is just an interpolation, which got unintentionally prolonged. He actually wanted to write about the sparrow families that shared the room with him and also about nightingales, which fascinated him to no end. He comes to the subject of the title of this letter, which he called 'Hikayat-i-Zaaq-o-Bulbul', when he is elated to hear a nightingale singing, sitting among the hollyhocks with their raised head.

Once, sitting in the veranda, Azad heard the warbling of the bulbul (nightingale) and wanted his fellow prisoner, who was around, to enjoy the sweetness of bulbul's song. He waited for a while to hear and said:

> Yes, some bullock-cart is passing by the Fort and this screeching sound is of its wheels. God be praised! Look at the sense of discrimination, this one can make no distinction between the warbling sound of the nightingale and the screeching of a cart's wheels![49]

He was amazed at the fact that God Almighty has put together two types of people—one who has his ears filled with the sweetness of the bulbul's songs, while the other whose ears tell him that this is the creaking sound of a bullock-cart. He is locked up with people who can't discern the difference between the sweet and grating sounds. Azad's assumption that India has always been identified with the parrot and mynah and not with the exotic nightingale may not be true. Of course, 'Tooti-i-Hind' rather than 'Bulbul-i-Hind' was the title chosen by Hazrat Nizamuddin Auliya for his favourite disciple Amir Khusrau.[50] I am sure that Azad cannot be totally oblivious of the fact that his own fellow Congress stalwart and admirer Sarojini Naidu was widely known as the nightingale of India.

Azad admires Iran and calls it a good fortune that the Iranians have a taste for the songs of nightingale. The cold temperate climate of Iran is exuberantly intoxicating, and in its midst the various strains of nightingale songs emerge and the songster sings with such rapturous self-absorption that it seems the music is emerging from nature's own instruments. In India, only Kashmir comes anywhere close to this but here also people start visiting only after spring when the fruit season sets in. Azad is surprised 'why we all have turned into such gluttons although we were gifted with heart and mind besides belly!'[51]

Azad ends the bulbul story by describing the diverse varieties of nightingales found in the hills and plains of India. He could identify here in the fort the white-cheeked bulbul, which is also found in parts of western Uttar Pradesh and Punjab. One white whiskered couple had made a nest in one of the flowery creepers and would often break into a song as Azad finished his siesta and began writing—as if the bulbul wanted to share its own wounds of complaint and prayer.

'Chidiya Chide ki Kahani' (The Story of a Sparrow Couple) almost turns him into an ornithologist as he narrates the detailed life and behaviour of these birds. The sparrows are known to live in both urban and rural spaces, mostly in the company of humans, building nests in the crevices and holes in the walls. Here in the fort they lived with Azad, in the nineteenth-century building, with wooden beams in the ceiling and ample space to build nests. There were colonies of sparrows which kept chirping the whole day. Azad is reminded of his home in Calcutta*, with its many trees and cornices that were under attack by the gangs of sparrows. It is sad

---

*Azad's residence was at 19-A Ballygunge Circular Road, Calcutta. Now it is a museum developed and run by the Maulana Azad Institute, Kolkata.

that this once ubiquitous bird has almost disappeared due to the severe loss of habitat, it can hardly find crevices and cornices in the modern multi-story apartments and pollution has added to its struggle to survive.

When Azad arrived in the prison cell of the fort it was already occupied by a colony of sparrows, who had been residents here for years, and he was an intruder into their space. A battle ensued between them for days, weapons like umbrella and a bamboo were used to drive them out, and though he felt victorious many a time, after a short respite he would see the enemies chirping around again. Azad writes about this engagement with sparrows with wry humour and gentle irony. Azad was reminded of a couplet from Meer:

> Shikast-o-fateh naseebon se hai, vale ai Meer
> Muqabila to dil-e-natawan ne khoob kiya[52]

> Victory or defeat is a matter of luck but, O Meer,
> The feeble hearted faced the enemy with courage.

Now the challenge was to devise a strategy to coexist with these unlettered guests. He had to move his bed away from the constantly falling dust and scrapings of the old building but the washbasin had to stay there under the nest. It was decided, writes Azad, 'that we buy some towels and keep the basin covered. They also got some brooms to get the room swept, the sweeper prisoner did clean the rooms but we couldn't ask him to keep the room cleaned the whole day.' So, to keep it clean, Azad swept the room twice a day himself. His friendship with his winged friends reached the height when he became a host to hordes of them who came and ate rice from his palm while Azad was busy writing. Gradually his friendship became so intimate that sometimes one of them would get on to the back of the sofa; another would jump on to the books, and at times they mistook his shoulder for a bent branch of a tree where they could jump around. Azad ends this letter philosophically saying that finally these birds are convinced that this man on the sofa is not dangerous like human beings despite being human himself.[53]

His sparrow story did not reach its conclusion, so he wanted to write more on 'Mantaq-al-Tayyar'* or 'Bird Logic', though unsure about whether his friend enjoyed the story at all or not. Here Azad identifies three sparrows and introduces them in the story, all named according to their characteristics. He names one peculiar aggressive male sparrow Mullah and describes its characteristics thus:

> One of the sparrows has a very stout build, aggressive cock sparrow, which was extremely contentious. It is always chatting away; its gait has a swagger and it picks up fight whoever it sees. No neighbourhood sparrow can set foot in his domain; several brave ones tried but were laid down in the first encounter. Whenever a gathering of the company is held on the floor it comes with its peculiar swagger, casts glances all around, and jumps up on the high seat and starts an unending 'choon-chaan'.[54]

After describing its demeanour and characteristics, Azad asks whether any other name would suit it if not Mullah? Azad had watched this class from close quarters for very long and knew them in and out, he could see in this cock sparrow all the distinctive features of an arrogant and self-righteous mullah.

Azad identified another male sparrow with some unusual features, someone who was always quiet, enjoyed its solitude, and most of the time, remained absorbed in himself. He was like a man who only occasionally raised the head to utter a 'ha'. Azad called him Sufi—other sparrows noisily jumped around him as if tired of his silence but to no avail. Sufi was the most appropriate name Azad could imagine for a bird so preoccupied with its own feelings.

Azad ends the sparrow tale on an emotional note, with

Mantaq-al-Tayyar is the famous work of Khwaja Fareeduddin Attar in which temporal and spiritual wisdom is presented through birds.

a brief description of Moti and her young one. Moti, a hen sparrow, was the most beautiful one among all the sparrows around and could be easily named as Madame Ahmednagar Fort. He also narrates the struggle of the infant sparrow and its realization that it can fly. Moti's intense engagement with her little one to take to the air and join the others in the sky, this self-awareness of the baby sparrow, despite repeated hints from the mother, took days to materialize. Then, one day, writes Azad:

> The moment its 'self-awareness' awoke and it realized that it is 'a flying bird', every dead faculty came alive. The lifeless body that could not stand, stood erect like the cypress; the knees that could not carry the weight of the body, were straight; the fallen wings that showed no movement, began to flutter; the whole body was shaken by the lightening zeal to fly. It could be seen that all the shackles of helplessness were broken and the enterprising bird was measuring the boundless extremes of the sky like an eagle.[55]

Azad ends with a lesson here—no external stimulus can awaken a person till his self-awareness does not wake up. The moment he discerns his inherent nature and realizes his truth, the transformation occurs instantaneously and in one leap he rises from the dust to reach the heavenly heights.

ON LIFE AND DEATH

Azad did not write any letters for almost a month, this was a sad phase of solitude for him in the fort prison. Normally, he would always seek solitude, but this was more of an isolation and therefore not an enjoyable one at all. Azad got the news of his wife's illness and loneliness back home and his own inability to be by her side at this critical juncture affected him. He wrote after a month on 11 April, simply to unburden his heart and to inform the reader that sleep had eluded him for six nights. In it, he shares some intimate moments of relationship with Zuleikha, his wife of thirty-six years. Azad admits that she married someone who was a prisoner of his circumstances and had little time for himself or for her. She had been sick for the past few years and Azad recalls that she wrote many letters to him while he was in Naini jail in 1941 but did not write a word about her sickness. He explains this restraint of hers:

> How well she understood me. She was aware of the fact that if she betrayed her emotional distress at this critical moment it would intensely enrage me and its bitterness will last for long. In 1916, when I was arrested for the first time, she had not been able to hold back her emotions. This kept me displeased with her for several days. This incident completely transformed her life forever and she always tried to gracefully compromise with the conditions of my life.[56]

Azad describes his final parting with his wife when he had to leave for Bombay on 3 August 1942: 'She came up to the gate to bid me goodbye. She did not utter a word more than a goodbye. Even if she had spoken she could not have said anything more than what her perturbed face was communicating. Her eyes were dry but face was tearful.' We have seen through all his writings that Azad reluctantly shared his solitude with anyone, he didn't allow that space even to his wife but now, when she was almost on the verge of parting, Azad was awfully disturbed. When he got the news of her critical condition the government asked him if he needed anything to be done and they used even Nehru to influence him. Despite the fact that he did not want to bend even at this critical juncture, he was emotionally shaken. Expressing his state of mind, he wrote:

> Yet I felt that my peace of mind was shaken and I will

> have to struggle to control it. Such struggle wears down the body more than the brain; one begins to internally pine away. I don't want to hide my mental and emotional condition of those days. My effort was to bear it all with perfect equanimity and patience. I did succeed outwardly, not inwardly. I felt that the mind was playing the same formal showmanship that we play in most of our actions when we do not allow our appearance to betray the inner self.[57]

He tried hard not to disturb his daily routine or let his pain interfere in his public life. He went out as usual to have tea and meals with his fellow prisoners and followed the punctuality he was known for despite the agony and inner discomfort. There was not much appetite left but he did swallow a few morsels and even continued to spend some time with friends as usual. Finally, it was on 19 April that his marriage of thirty-six years came to an end. 'Death became the partition wall between us. Even now we can see each other but from behind that wall.' Addressing his friend Siddiq-i-Mukarram, Azad ends the letter with a couplet from the famous Urdu poet Sauda:

> Sauda! Khuda ke vaaste kar qissa mukhtasar
> Apni to neend ud gayi tere fasane mein
>
> Sauda! For God's sake shorten your tale;
> It has robbed me of my sleep.

Almost a month after his wife's death, Azad wrote two short letters on 14 and 15 June, both about his philosophical engagements with life and death. In the first letter he tries to explain the changes life brings and he does that through an apt simile from nature—all the trees wait for the rainy season, this is when they discard the yellow apparel and dress themselves in cheerful spring clothes, but the broken twig shows no signs of life, it stays dry as ever. Azad continues:

> I began to think that human heart has the same landscape as nature. In this garden also grow numberless trees of hope and desire and wait for the onset of spring. But, the branches severed from the root remain unaffected by changes of spring and autumn. No weather can bring cheer to them.[58]

He goes to Ghalib once again to emphasize what he said above:

> Khizan kya! Fasl-e-gul kehte hain kisko! Koi Mausam ho!
> Vahi ham hain, qafas hai, aur matam baal-o-par ka hai
>
> What is autumn? What flower beds? Whichever the weather,
> We are the same, in the same cage, grieving for loss of freedom.

He writes what was probably the shortest letter on 15 June, which just talks about life, its ephemerality and the struggle humans have to go through to live this transient life. In fact, Azad observes that the entire tenure of human life is no more than a morning and evening.

PASSION FOR MUSIC

Azad wrote his last and longest letter of this collection on 16 September 1943, after a gap of more than two months, on the subject of music. Here, he launches into evocative prose about one of his life's greatest passions:

> I can always remain happy doing without the necessities of life, but I cannot live without music. A sweet voice is the support and prop of my life, a healing for my mental labours. Sweet music is the cure for all the ills and ailments of my body and heart.[59]

Expressing his pain, he writes about an army officer who stays close to him in the fort, and who seems to possess a radio set. 'Last night I could clearly hear a violinist playing the tune of Mendelsohn's* famous stanza "Songs without words" (naghma baghair lufz). It made a huge impact on me, and I felt as if a boil was about to burst, but soon I was back to my normal self.'

Before I go into Azad's detailed assessments of music in the East and West, let me record here what Azad says about the beginnings of his interest in music, which were purely incidental and a classic example of Azad's obsession with learning. He says that his interest in music began by accident when, in 1905, after completing his education he began teaching, and 'the taste for books took me to a bookseller called Khuda Baksh, who had a shop in Wellesley Street, opposite Madrassa College...One day, he showed me a beautifully calligraphed pictorial, 'Raag Darpan' by Faqirullah Saif Khan. He told me that it was a book on music.'[60] Saif Khan was an expert on music during Alamgir's (Aurangzeb's) time, who translated 'Raag Darpan' from Sanskrit.† He was an expert on the theory and practice of Indian music. While Azad was going through the foreword of the book, Mr Denis Ross‡, the principal of Madarsa-i-Aaliya in Calcutta, arrived. He was known to speak Persian in an Iranian accent, and was surprised to see a teenager like Azad avidly reading a

*Jacob Ludwig Felix Mendelssohn Bartholdy (1809–1847) was a German composer, pianist, organist, and conductor of the early Romantic period.

†Saif Khan was among the many scholars of seventeenth/eighteenth-century India who had mastered different languages, including Sanskrit. Most of these scholars were patronised by the Mughal nobility and encouraged to pursue translations of various important texts from Sanskrit to Persian. For some more details on this issue see an interesting and insightful work of Audrey Truschke, *Culture of Encounters: Sanskrit at the Mughal Court,* New Delhi: Penguin India, 2016.

‡Edward Denison Ross was a multilingual scholar who knew many languages of the East as well as of the West. He was a teacher of Persian at the London University when, in 1901, he was appointed principal of Madarassa-i-Aaliya in Calcutta on Viceroy Lord Curzon's recommendation.

Persian manuscript. Rather haughtily, he told Azad that it was a difficult book on music, not easy to comprehend, which Azad took as a challenge. He bought the book and read it page for page but soon realized that he needed a professional teacher to help him grasp the difficult subject. He found a teacher in Masita Khan*, who used to visit his home to enrol himself as a murid of Maulana Khairuddin. Initially, Masita Khan was hesitant but later agreed to be a teacher to the son of his spiritual guru. This music teaching programme continued for a few years, almost two–three hours every day. Among the instruments, Azad's maximum concentration was on sitar and his fingers soon got used to it. He wrote about his ecstatic experience thus:

> Looking back, I wonder at the mood of the time, the enthusiasm and the passion that possessed me. I was just seventeen but even then, my disposition was to go all out for whatever was taken in hand and go ahead up to the farthest possible limit. Whatever the job, I would never agree to give it up halfway. Every path that was adopted was fully and thoroughly explored, perfect if it was piety and equally perfect if sin. Ahead of all in boozing and behind none in abstinence.[61]

Azad emphasized the importance of music in everyone's life when he said that 'the mind should not remain ignorant of this field because balance of mind and delicacy of thought cannot be acquired without music.' During this phase Azad was preoccupied with music—he narrates several memorable experiences that remained with him all his life though he had no time to indulge in music as such. Once he visited Agra during this period and it was a moonlit night in April. He

*Masita Khan was from Sonipat, now a district in Haryana, close to Delhi. He was a musician, taught by the expert teachers of Delhi and Jaipur. In Calcutta, he would instruct nautch girls. He later got a job with a Bengali landlord that facilitated his becoming a disciple of Azad's father.

goes on to narrate the magical experience thus:

> Late into the night, the moon would peep through the veil of darkness. I had made special arrangement for going to the Taj with my sitar. I would sit on its roof with my face towards Jamuna. As moonlight began to spread itself, I would start a tune and lose myself in it. I don't have [an] expression to tell what magical experiences the imagination brought before the eyes.[62]

Azad continues to reminisce that during his early visit to Lucknow he met the late Mirza Hadi*. He also goes back to his childhood spent in the Arab world, and recalls the melodious voices (mutarannim sadain) of Hejaz, which his ears got used to so early. His house was close to Bab-ul-Salaam† in Qidwa, from where he could see the lamps of the minarets and hear the morning azaan. His observations about the Egyptian music tradition are also quite revealing. He talks about the troupe of Sheikh Ahmad Sallama Hijazi, which is also called 'jauq' in Egypt while here we call it 'mandali'. The troupe of Sheikh Sallama often performed at the Cairo Opera House and Azad watched his performance there and also met him afterwards to discuss Arab music.

Azad also refers to one of the most popular Egyptian aalema singers of those times, Tahira from Tantana. And

---

*Mirza Mohammad Hadi Ruswa was born in Lucknow in 1857/1858 and died in 1931. He lost his parents early so his education was also disrupted. Many people helped him in his education, including the Urdu poet Dabeer. Ruswa took an overseer's diploma from Thomson Civil Engineering School at Roorkee and served in the railways for some time, laying tracks in Balochistan. All through this period he continued his studies—he was passionate about astronomy and chemistry, and finally came back to Lucknow and taught at Christian College. He left Lucknow for Hyderabad and worked in the bureau of translation at Osmania University. His most well-known literary work is *Umrao Jaan Ada*, a novel on the courtesans of Lucknow. One of the most beautiful films, *Umrao Jaan* by Muzaffar Ali, is based on this novel.

†Bab-ul-Salaam is one of the gates of the Great Mosque in Mecca. This phrase in Arabic, when literally translated into English, means 'Gate of Peace'.

knowing our worthy ulema back home, who may surely misunderstand it, he made it clear that 'aalema' in Egypt is used for an expert singer with a thorough knowledge of the art. Azad calls her bewitchingly beautiful (balaye jaan) and her voice even more captivating. He heard her perform and also struck upon acquaintance with her—an incident that makes him remember Ghalib's words:

Jaana pada raqeeb ke dar par hazaar baar
Ai kaash jaanta na teri rahguzar ko mein

It has taken me to the rival's doorstep a thousand times;
I wish I had not known thy path.

The letter is replete with instances in history when music was central to Islamic culture, and referring to the Mughal period, Azad writes that 'music became a part of the culture of the wise; without facility in music, knowledge and culture were considered incomplete. Music became an integral part of the education and upbringing of the children of the nobles and gentlemen. Masters of the art were in great demand in all parts of the country.... The youth who came to the cities in pursuit of education sought out master musicians in addition to scholars and teachers; they learnt the art at their feet.'[63] Azad narrates the centrality of music in Islam from the early Abbasid period onwards, particularly emphasizing its role in the evolution of Indian syncretic culture during the medieval centuries. Indian music, he claims, has much greater depth than any other music. As for Western music, although our ears are not tuned to it, we cannot help acknowledging its greatness. European music of the eighteenth and nineteenth centuries, especially German music, is an extraordinary example of the human genius. It is surprising that the Arabs showed interest in all the arts and sciences of India, except music. Although Al-Biruni did not pay any attention to Indian music, that was the time, Azad says that Indian musical instruments were heard being played on the streets of Ghazni.[64] Maybe, he postulates, that the Arab ear for music was so different from that of Indians that they could not appreciate one another.

Rebutting all those who dub music as un-Islamic, Azad cited some more examples from Indian history where orthodox and prejudiced courtiers of Akbar like Badauni were expert flute players and Abdul Salam Lahori was as well-versed in music as he was in texts like the *Hidaya* and *Buzduvi*. Azad, in this letter, tries to establish that music is not prohibited in Islam rather 'music is one of God's graces; it cannot be forbidden to man because it has been created for man.'[65]

Azad does accept that the rigid orthodoxy of Aurangzeb adversely affected the future of fine arts but this cold shouldering was confined to the royal court alone. To quote Azad:

> The streams let loose by the past were not so poor as to dry up with the change in royal attitude. The royal patronage did stop during the Alamgiri period but who would close down the generous doors of thousands of private households.[66]

'Raag Darpan', which was mentioned in the beginning, was translated by a mendicant Saif Khan during this period. Sher Khan Lodhi, who also belonged to the same period, attained proficiency in both Iranian and Indian music and later wrote a book *Tazkira Marat-ul-Khyal*. A beautifully calligraphed copy of this book is available in the Asiatic Society Library of Bengal. Azad also gives a detailed account of the early colourful life of the later puritan Aurangzeb, which includes his interest in music. Azad says that like all other plans of Aurangzeb, this aversion also could not last long and died with him. Just as in England the peevish cynicism of the Victorian Age ended with the advent of modernity, royal aptitudes returned as soon as Aurangzeb was no more. The indulgences of the days of Farrukh Siyar* and Mohammad Shah† were just a reaction to the rigid denials of the Alamgiri period.

Coming to the end of this longish letter, Azad writes about an interesting intellectual from the Awadh region, Allama Taffazzul Husain Khan‡, who was also ambassador of Awadh in Calcutta. He was an accomplished mathematician and astronomer but his skills in music were exemplary. His interest in music is known by the fact that he could sleep only when some sleep-inducing music was played near his bedroom.

Azad ends with a few comments about the efficacy and practice of music in Islam when he writes that it is generally assumed that Islam is antagonistic to fine arts and that music is counted among the forbidden arts according to its religious laws. Azad was aware that the Prophet only denounced excessive music or poetry as corrupting, but music as such was not prohibited. The thing whose wise and balanced use is an ornament turns into a blot as evil and bad manners if excessively indulged.[67] Azad raises an important point when he says that even this excessive use is found in the chapter on punishment, not in the chapter on laws. Punishment, according to him, has a very broad use; anything that causes disorder by overuse can be prohibited as punishment but the real meaning of laws cannot be obliterated. While digging a trench around Medina in preparation for battle, the Prophet and his companions were singing songs.[68] It is clear that music is

---

*Farrukh Siyar was the grandson of Shah Alam I, the son of Aurangzeb, and was the fifteenth Mughal king (1713–19)

†Mohammad Shah was the brother of Farrukh Siyar. He was so fond of fun and luxury that he was called 'Rangeela'. He ruled from 1719 to 1748. It was during his reign that we saw Raja Jai Singh taking up the Jantar Mantar project. Nadir Shah's invasion took place during that period.

‡Tafazzul Husain Khan was an erudite scholar with a great reputation during the times of Nawab Asafuddaula in Lucknow. Besides being an administrative functionary, he was a man of astronomy and mathematics as well as literature. He translated Newton's *Principia* from the original Latin into Arabic. He also translated Emerson's *Mechanics* and a treatise on Algebra into Arabic as well as several other texts.

anathema only for the myopic, bigoted, spoilsport apostles of self-righteous Islam and regrettably, most of the Muslims have succumbed to their vicious campaign against this significant cultural expression.

Ghubar-i-Khatir brings before us many aspects of Maulana Azad's persona that we cannot get from other sources, mostly because Azad was a private person who seldom wrote or shared his likes and dislikes. It is the only text where Azad opens up in his solitude, a condition that he greatly treasured. Maybe he consciously decided to raise some difficult philosophical questions like the aim and purpose of life and death, egotism, the theories about the origins of life like evolution etc. He also talks about some serious issues in a lighter vein, like happiness and how it is the moral and social prerogative of all humans to stay cheerful.

Ghubar-i-Khatir is a simpler and a more accessible text in terms of language, it lacks the passion and emotion which is found in *Al-Hilal* and *Al-Balagh*. The reason is obvious—this was a more mature phase of Azad's life and he had also decided not to write about emotive political questions at all. Most of the letters were actually essays that Azad decided to write as letters to his friends. The subject of the essay depended on Azad's mood or choice. In some of the letters he is a philosopher explaining complex issues of life and death, another one turns him into a connoisseur of tea as well as its expert taster and historian. There are three letters where Azad is an ornithologist, writing about his fellow avian jail mates—sparrows and nightingales. In one of the letters he turns into an expert horticulturalist and a keen observer of nature. The last and the longest letter is of a music lover and a musician where Azad not only narrates his own deep love of music but also chronicles the music history of Asia and Europe. It seems he wrote this detailed essay to establish the compatibility between Islam and music—both through theological as well as historical facts and arguments. *Ghubar-i-Khatir* is interspersed with Urdu and Persian couplets, most of these Azad had stored in some assigned corner of his brain since his childhood. Maybe some of them were added before the book was sent for publication.

Ghubar-i-Khatir is an important text, a literary masterpiece, which deserves an exclusive and detailed study. It introduces us to the versatility of Azad, and shows us his immense diversities. Unfortunately, it has not attracted serious attention, either from the scholars of Urdu literature and language or historians or social scientists. I hope that happens soon.

FIVE

BUILDING A NEW INDIA: EDUCATION, CULTURE, SCIENCE, AND THE PLURALIST ETHOS

In addition to the economic cost to India, British colonialism also destroyed the development of an education system in the country. The empire's primary objective was of course economic exploitation; a secondary objective was to civilize the natives and turn them into law-abiding citizens. Writing in *The Citizen of India* in 1897, a school textbook that was in use for many years, Lee-Warner described the British empire as an educational experience for India. It did not matter that the system of education had remained rather limited, he argued, for it was wrong to judge the education of India merely by the development of the education system.[1]

Almost two centuries of colonization, first as the target of a private conglomerate's exploitative appetite and later as a much-touted jewel in the British crown left India deprived of its vitality on all fronts. An emaciated India crippled with the pain of Partition was our inheritance in 1947.

The immediate task before the new independent government of India was to rebuild the nation, apply a salve to the wounds of the suffering masses, build confidence among the people, and convince them that hate would not add to their happiness or well-being. There was a long of things that had to be done on a war footing with limited resources, and many others took precedence over education and culture—when a large number of people were without food and shelter, education and culture had to wait.

There were many challenges before India's education system could be swerved away from the colonial model—the shadows of Macaulay and company were too deeply ingrained. This was the difficult legacy inherited by the first independent government of India and Maulana Abul Kalam Azad took the responsibility to reconstruct the education, cultural, and scientific infrastructure in society. Dr Kapila Vatsyayan, who began her long bureaucratic career with Maulana Azad, reminisces about this early period saying that 'it was Maulana Abul Kalam Azad's public statements of establishing the system of "basic education" enunciated by Gandhiji that essentially clinched my decision, as it was a vital, national stake.'[2] J. C. Ghosh, one of our leading scientists and founding director of the Indian Institute of Technology, Kharagpur, put it well when he said that 'the problems which occupied [Azad's] mind till the last moment of his life were those of national unity, and of education for national prosperity, for developing balanced minds and for promotion of better understanding among the people of India.'[3] These were noble, if only intractable, ideals and continue to pester us even now.

Maulana Azad was not a run-of-the-mill politician—he was a scholar who brought with him decades of experience as a writer and thinker on different aspects of Indian public life. Nehru visualized him as 'a "bridge" between the cultures of the East and the West, as the man who magnificently spanned in his person the gulf between the past and the future. Without any English education, without speaking or writing in English, he was as easily and effortlessly at home in Western culture as in Indian or Eastern or Islamic culture. Nothing that was good was stranger to him.'[4]

Azad had no formal education himself and thus no exposure to an institution, but his forays into education began early in life when he started writing serious columns in his papers *Lisan al-Sidq*, *Al-Hilal*, and *Al-Balagh*, besides many other papers like *Al-Nadwa*, etc. He also touched upon some fundamental philosophical and ethical aspects of education in his magnum opus *Tarjuman al-Quran* in 1930. Thus, by the time he took over as minister, Azad had thought and written extensively about education, culture, and science and its challenges since the early twentieth century. One feature, which is reflected in all his writings, is the emphasis on adl or justice in the dissemination of education and its access to people. This Quranic concept of striking a balance in the formulation of policies, particularly education, was at the core of Azad's educational policy endeavours. In his translation and interpretation of the Quran he writes that 'every planet and every star is at work in space in balanced or just or right relation with one another. It is this principle which binds together a society.'[5] This idea underlines how he used Quranic concepts to democratize an education system that had been enslaved for centuries. Education as a means to social justice brings in a state of stable equilibrium between the antithetical entities of individual freedom and social control, the spiritual and the scientific outlook, the religious and the secular system, and the national and international aspiration. Indeed, justice commands a pivotal place in Azad's general perspective, which has influenced his educational outlook quite profoundly.[6]

We also need to be aware that Azad's educational perspective was fundamentally Islamic in inspiration, yet he was not 'exclusively an "Islamic" scholar or even an "Oriental" mind, unacquainted with, or insensitive to, the rich streams of influences emanating from other sources.'[7] It is generally believed that Azad's scholarship was based on Arabic, Persian, and Urdu literature, which is a fallacy. Azad, being an autodidact, taught himself English and French, his exposure to Sir Syed convinced him that modern science and philosophy cannot be pursued without these two languages. He wrote: 'I decided that learning English is essential for me. I discussed it with Maulvi Mohammad Yusuf Jafri...he taught me the beginnings of English language and gave me Pyare Lal Sarkar's first book to read.'[8] His trip to France in 1908 made him conscious of the richness and relevance of the French language in the pursuit of modern education. He learnt French as well and his interest in both the languages remained with him till the end. According to some, he always had a few English and French books piled up on his study table.[9]

One Maulana Asadullah Khan, who was with Azad in the Meerut prison, wrote about his experiences in jail and narrated one interesting episode. One of their fellow prisoners Mr Kishan Chand, MA, who was known as a philosopher in the prison, got a popular philosophy book from the Meerut College library and assumed that Azad wouldn't have a clue about the book. But Azad surprised everyone when he not only explained the book in detail but also pointed out some of the lapses of the author.[10] Another admirer of Azad in prison, Hafiz Ali Bahadur Khan, also confirmed that Maulana Azad used to read only English books in the jail and read translations of Voltaire, Rousseau, Goethe, and many others.[11]

Thus, we cannot assume that Azad was not exposed to Western educational philosophy and literature. He was deeply impressed by the advances made in the West in the realm of elementary education for children. He was firmly committed to what was scientific in the Western system, and the two factors that most inspired him were the idea of freedom as a technique of education, and the all-embracing importance of primary education.[12] He was particularly impressed by the French philosopher Rousseau and was in agreement with him about the innate goodness of man.[13] He even wrote about this in his paper *Al-Hilal*, where he looked upon Rousseau as one who revolutionized the entire intellectual and social life of his age.[14] Azad agreed with Rousseau in his advocacy of encouraging children to grasp the truth through their own insights.[15] Contrasting the centrality extended to education in the West, Azad was bewildered at the apathy towards it in the East, with mediocrity as its hallmark. He felt strongly that Indians were oblivious of the fact that education was of paramount importance for a nation's overall development. He considered planning for education on a national scale as more important than national planning in economic and industrial development. Addressing the Central Advisory Board of Education (CABE) meeting in 1952 he said:

> Economic and industrial development creates material goods. These can be used by people in different parts whatever be their source or origin. Education, on the other hand, trains the citizens, and if this training fails to inculcate the right attitudes and ideals or encourages fissiparous tendencies, the security and welfare of the community is at stake. Our reconstruction of national education must therefore aim at creating a unity of purpose among all our nationals and developing in them a common outlook which will transcend and harmonize in an attractive pattern the differences in history, background, language, and culture that exist among various sections of the people.[16]

There is a sizable opinion among scholars that Azad did not really have much to do with education personally, and the task was handed over to him by Nehru, who continued to play a key role in most of the policy formulations in educational and scientific matters. It is true that Azad accepted the responsibility on the insistence of both Nehru as well as Gandhi. But it is equally true that the task fell to him because Azad was the best available person for the job. Both Nehru and Gandhi were aware that Azad was passionately committed to education, culture, and scientific and technical progress. He surely had his limitations and Nehru was always available to provide help, but this not reason enough to dismiss Azad's contributions to early achievements in education in India. His erudition and high intellect led Nehru to compare him with 'the great men of the Renaissance, or, in a later period, of the Encyclopaedists who preceded the French Revolution, men of intellect, men of action.'[17]

Azad represented the idea of a composite India, which the nation developed over the decades of the freedom struggle. There could not have been a better choice at the time he took over the crucial ministry. No one else could say it better than S. Radhakrishnan, who clearly spelt out his role after Independence when he said:

> When once freedom was won, he again felt that we must use that freedom for promoting social welfare, cleanse this country of sickness, squalor, illiteracy, etc., and cleanse our minds of superstition, of obscurantism, of fanaticism. He stood for, what one may call the emancipated mind, the mind which is free from narrow prejudices of race or language, province or dialect, religion or caste. We had in Maulana Sahib a civilized mind.[18]

In his first press conference after taking over the responsibility in the interim government, Azad spoke with clarity of objectives thus:

> Nothing has a more important bearing on the quality of the individual than the type of education imparted. A truly liberal and humanitarian education may transform the outlook of the people and set it on the path of progress and prosperity, while an ill-conceived or unscientific system might destroy all the hopes which have been cherished by generations of pioneers in the cause of national freedom.[19]

He began by referring to the Macaulayan system, which was committed to promoting British colonial interests, yet he conceded that 'the great services which the existing system of education has rendered to the Indian people need not be denied.... There is equally no denying that this system has led to the creation of a small intelligentsia separated from the mass of the Indian people.' He was also conscious of the fact the education imparted at that time tended to distance the educated from the uneducated and even taught learners to look down upon India's national heritage. For Azad, the greatest charge against the Macaulayan system of education was 'that it has not led to the development of a national mind'.

He emphasized the need for a sound system of basic education. If the foundations have not been truly and firmly laid, no abiding superstructure can be built. Teacher education is a serious concern even today, where many of the teacher training institutions are mired in corruption and controversies, despite the significant role teachers have played and the respect they have commanded over many centuries. With great foresight, Azad lamented teachers' working conditions and their loss of social and economic well-being:

> In the past, the status of the teacher in Indian society was an exalted one. He might not have been wealthy but his comparative poverty was compensated by the need of respect and prestige which the profession of teaching carried with it. Today, unfortunately, all this has changed, and the teacher, especially in primary stages, is considered as hardly better than an inferior servant. Any programme for reconstruction of education must therefore place in the forefront the task of improving the status and condition of teachers, and I am confident that the new National Government of India will recognize this as its first and foremost tasks.[20]

He was aware of the fact that a sound basic education with good and well-trained teachers can build a sound and viable higher education system. He believed that a good foundation at the school level would enrich the university system with competent and committed students. Thus, he saw the education system from school to university level as an interlinked chain.

EQUITY AND EDUCATION

Before I come to the education policies that had to be reworked and redesigned in national interest, I want to briefly touch upon the issues of equity and access because we inherited a colonial educational structure which was based on diverse injustices. Thus, soon after Independence, one of the important issues for Azad was the democratization of education, particularly when India had emerged out of two hundred years of colonialism, going through varied forms of discriminations and deprivations. His commitment to a change in the British educational system can be seen in the 1920s during the Non-cooperation Movement. In a pamphlet published then, called *Talimi Taraqi-Mawalat*, he began with a statement that 'of all the bonds of association with the British government which needs to be broken forthwith, education is the most important one'.[21] Maulana Azad was not lacking in vision and emphasized several Quranic principles in the context of equity—he stressed on adl or justice, the supreme principle that brings the creative process to its completion.[22] Justice is all the more relevant to education as a process of harmonious nurture. Indeed, social justice commands a pivotal place in Azad's general perspective, which influenced his educational outlook quite profoundly.[23]

He was conscious of the fact that a class or caste-ridden education system needed to be replaced by a more inclusive and just educational order. In 1948, while addressing the educational conference, Azad again reiterated that 'education, at any rate, must be pushed forward as rapidly as possible. We must not, for a moment, forget that it is the birthright of every individual to receive at least the basic education, without which he cannot discharge his duties as a citizen.'* Azad also realized that equity in education is not conceivable merely through the expansion of school education. He was aware of the huge adult population that needed serious attention. For him adult literacy and education were crucial for any idea of inclusive and equity-based education in India.

As he was an Islamic scholar, he used Islam as a democratic and modernist movement, quite in contrast to what is being done in the name of Islam today all over the world. He saw Islam as 'a perfect system of freedom and democracy whose function consists in bringing back to mankind the freedom snatched away from it'.[24] He also defined Islam as 'the message of democracy and human equality to the world suffering from chronic type of class discriminations'.[25] Azad expanded Islamic values on a national scale, going beyond the narrow confines of faith, to explain and understand the problems of the newly-independent nation, particularly the access to education on a universal scale.

India's emergence on 15 August 1947 as the largest democracy in the world was itself a great political achievement and challenge. Azad, being a great democrat himself, took the challenge as an opportunity to make education a vanguard of democratic life in the country. With a view to gearing education towards the cause of democracy, he, in his very first official statement, referred to Disraeli's verdict: 'A democracy has no future unless it educates its masters.' In independent and democratic India, with universal franchise as the key principle, the voter was truly the master of democracy, and Azad wanted this voter to be educated and aware. He was conscious of the sad inheritance of colonial inequalities, where

*In taking the argument of inclusive education forward Azad also emphasized the issue of adult literacy. He said 'It is obvious that with the extension of democracy, the problem of adult education has become even more important than it was in the past.' Azad, *Speeches of Maulana (Abul Kalam) Azad, 1947-1955*, New Delhi: Publications Division, Min. of Information & Boradcasting, Government of India, 1956, p. 29.

85 per cent of the country's population was illiterate on the eve of Independence. Several class and caste discriminations and disabilities were never discussed before and had to be removed immediately. Azad was convinced that the state had to play a key role in combating such social afflictions and provide everyone with the means to 'the acquisition of knowledge and self-betterment';[26] however, the most disconcerting factor was the lack of necessary funds to carry forward the state's responsibilities. Azad conceded with a sense of guilt as minister of education that the central government had allotted only 1 per cent of the funds in the budget for education and he thus pleaded in the Constituent Assembly to raise the expenditure to 10 per cent.[27] He pursued the issue with passion and was able to raise the allocation from ₹20 million to around ₹350 million during his tenure as minister of education.

On 30 September 1953, Azad addressed the nation on All India Radio, reiterating that 'every individual has a right to an education that will enable him to develop his faculties and live a full human life'.[28] He felt that our objectives could not be realized unless we shake off our narrow-mindedness, which has been our greatest hindrance. Elaborating further, he said: 'like an actor it masquerades in disguise. In the domain of religion, it appears in the form of blind faith and wants to deceive us in the name of orthodoxy. In politics it wants to overpower us in the guise of nationalism. In learning and culture, it makes an appeal to us in the name of our nation and country. It behooves us not to be taken in by these fictitious names. We must remember that the root cause of all this is nothing but narrow-mindedness.'[29] Azad was inspired by the values of our freedom struggle and was convinced that those values would come in handy for nation building, where the universal right to education should be seen as true freedom for all the citizens of this newly-independent nation. In this context of age-old discrimination and deprivation, Azad also emphasized women's education, which had so far been nearly non-existent. He felt that the education of women was doubly purposeful: first that they need to be educated as citizens of free India, and second that their education facilitated the task of educating the younger generation.* He raised this issue in the Constituent Assembly as well in 1949, demanding greater educational opportunities for Indian women.[30]

In 1950 Azad spoke on the programme for national education at the third CABE meeting. He spoke extensively about equity and expansion of education in India, particularly to wipe out the deficiency in education created over a hundred years of colonial rule. He laid down four objectives to be met over the next ten years—two of the objectives were the provision of basic education on a universal, free, and compulsory basis for all school-going children and provision of adult education in order to wipe out the colossal illiteracy of our masses.[31] He further reiterated the two points in his 1952 address at another meeting of CABE.[32] While participating in the Constituent Assembly debates, he emphasized the overall significance of universal education as laid down in our Constitution and the role of social education in the implementation of basic education for children between the ages of six and fourteen. Underlining the principle of equity, he reiterated that educating the future citizens of India expeditiously and effectively is indispensable in shaping our future destiny.

His commitment to equity and the democratization of education is also reflected in his strident position in the Constituent Assembly where he talked of equalizing opportunities in the context of old caste, class, and gender prejudices. He thus spoke in 1948, 'If they have been left

*In his press conference on 31 May 1948, Azad remarked: 'If women take to education, more than half of our problems will be solved. Educated mothers will mean children who can be easily made literate' This was a progressive thought, which may not be acceptable to many in the contemporary context. Women need to be educated for societal and individual good and not just to bring up educated well-groomed children. Azad, *Speeches of Maulana (Abul Kalam) Azad, 1947-1955*, p. 41.

behind in the sphere of progress, it is not their fault. The society is to be blamed for this. It is all the more necessary, therefore, that the society, which has not until now placed them on an equal footing, should help in their advancement.'[33] Towards this objective Azad was successful in framing the official policy of instituting special stipends and scholarships for students coming from the depressed classes.*[34] This is all the more important today in the context of the Right to Education Act—a tribute to Maulana Azad when he took on this arduous task almost sixty years ago.

TAKING ON THE CHALLENGE: BUILDING A NATIONAL SYSTEM OF EDUCATION

Soon after Independence, 'one of the most stupendous tasks was the reconstruction and expansion of her system of education.'[35] Azad also faced a major challenge to the federal structure as education was a state subject according to the India Act, 1935. He had to formulate policies that did not undermine the authority of state governments and helped in constructively supplementing their efforts. Many steps were taken to provide free elementary education to all children of school-going age to ensure that they were not denied the facilities that their parents lacked. Steps had to be taken to reorganize secondary and higher education and promote rapid expansion of the scientific and technical education necessary for the development of industry and agriculture.[36] Maulana Azad also felt a deep concern for Indian languages, which had languished over the past two centuries, and also had to confront the subject of medium of instruction in schools and universities.

*In his survey of Azad's role in 'what he called democratization of educational opportunities' through the installation of scholarships for the students of backward classes, Saiyadain remarked that the provision on this head went up 'about 75 fold, from 3 lakh in 1944 to 2.25 crore in 1960'.

Another aspect of education that Azad was deeply concerned about was enriching our cultural life. For him, no education at any level was complete without art and culture. He repeatedly emphasized the significance of culture and heritage while formulating his educational policies. While opening an art exhibition in New Delhi, he said 'Art is an education of emotions and is thus an essential element in any scheme of truly national education. Education, whether at the secondary or at the university stage, cannot be regarded as complete if it does not train our faculties to the perception of beauty.'[37] He was also aware of the urgency to revive foreign relations with the neighbouring countries in the East and the West. For almost two hundred years, India's cultural contacts had been confined almost solely to Great Britain. An independent India could not remain insular or isolated in a continually contracting world.[38]

Our Constitution was sincerely ambitious in hoping to provide universal compulsory education to all children below the age of fourteen within ten years of its promulgation. However, we know that the existing facilities did not extend to even 25 per cent of population on the eve of freedom, thus this directive must be recognized as revolutionary in import. As I said before, the task was made even more arduous because India was shaken by a series of cataclysmic events at the time of Independence. We had to pay a heavy price for freedom with the division of the country, followed by massive violence and displacement of millions across borders. India also confronted a natural calamity in the form of a serious famine, leading to massive efforts to import food from outside. Thus, education, science, and culture bore the brunt of a massive financial crunch. Azad had to take forward the three crucial arms of future progress through the thick and thin of these financially and socially unstable times.

One more important challenge, as I have pointed out above, was the issue of language—the promotion and development of local languages, and of course the medium of instruction. Any future formulation of a national education policy had to resolve the language question and make modern education accessible to students in their own languages. Azad was conscious of the fact that the colonial education system, particularly the post-Macaulayan phase, had done tremendous harm to Indian education, most importantly the medium of instruction. He agreed with Macaulay's contention that Sanskrit and Persian were unsuited mediums of instruction, 'but English could serve the purpose no better'.[39] When the East India Company decided to introduce English as the medium of instruction, we made a beginning in an un-Indian way. Indians had to shape their minds in artificial and not in natural moulds. 'If the Indian languages had been made the medium of instruction a hundred and fifty years ago they would have come in line with the progressive languages of the world.' Here let me recall an attempt made in Delhi almost 150 years ago, when Master Ramchandra and Munshi Zakaullah at Delhi College tried to teach modern science through the medium of Urdu. There were similar attempts in different parts of India, particularly in Tamil, Marathi, Malayalam, and other such languages in the nineteenth century. Zakaullah very poignantly expressed his faith in the local languages, echoing Azad's views, more than a century before him, when he once said:

> ....the constant use of English even from our childhood, so that we begin to express our thoughts in it instead of in our mother tongue, will go far to denationalize us. If we wish to remain an Eastern people, we must not neglect the language which we learnt at our mother's knee.... To forget it, or to despise it, is to lose one of the strongest factors in the building up of national character.[40]

How close was Azad to Zakaullah's understanding when he said about English as the medium of instruction that 'now it became necessary for every child to shape an artificial mind and to tackle every aspect of learning from an unnatural angle of vision. He could not enter the sacred precincts of learning with a natural mind.'[41]

However, Azad was an intellectual and a freedom fighter who could articulate the reasons for this inadequacy, in particular the loss of sovereignty to decide on such policy issues. He compared colonized India with Turkey, China, and Japan, who had the choice to impart modern education through their respective languages. He said:

> Suppose this educational revolution had been brought about by our own hands, we should have certainly done what other countries of Asia and the East did in the nineteenth century. Egypt, Syria, Turkey, China, and Japan all felt the need of having western education. They established schools and colleges for modern learning, but none of them had the experience of undergoing the artificiality of giving up their own languages and receiving education through the medium of a foreign language.[42]

India lost this freedom very early, with the victory of the Anglicists in 1835, and since then had to cope with a foreign language where learning was never a pleasure. Before English took over, India had three classical languages: Persian, Arabic, and Sanskrit. Sanskrit was not the language of the masses and the other two were foreign languages, which were not spoken by people but had to be taught. But Azad spoke about the other side of the picture as well:

> Howsoever wrongly the English language made its way into our life, the fact remains that it has influenced our mental and educational outlook for the past one hundred and fifty years. This state of affairs though harmful in some ways has also benefitted us in many ways.... The greatest advantage that we gained from the adoption of English was that many of the obstacles were automatically

> removed from our newly born national life. It has led to the unification of the whole of the country. All the different parts of the country were brought together in spite of distances and different languages.[43]

Thus, he acknowledged the significance of English too, both nationally as well as internationally, in our lives as a nation. Yet, he also argued that the centrality of English in our educational and official lives cannot be sustained in the future. Azad reiterated his earlier position that he was brought up in a family which was hostile to English and his own education was in Arabic and Persian medium. He learnt English and even French through his own efforts later in his life

> You need not therefore suspect that I am in any way influenced in my opinion by my English education. I can make bold to say that my opinion is perfectly unbiased. I am not one of those who are the products of English type of universities. I am entirely disconnected with them and as such can take a detached point of view and understand your needs and requirements.[44]

Azad was also seriously conscious of the fact that there is an antipathy towards everything associated with the British, including the English language. In the prevalent milieu, soon after Independence, it was not an easy task to take a balanced view on a subject like language or even generally about culture. Yet Azad spoke candidly on the subject in this convocation address at Patna university:

> Man is always inclined to go to extremes in realms of thought and action. It is very seldom that he steers a middle course, and it is where he stumbles. He is like the watch of which the regulator has gone wrong. It goes either too fast or too slow.... It is not many years when our educated young men had lost themselves in imitating the English, in their language, dress, manners, etc. They

> were not mindful of their own heritage.... They were ever ready to quote Shakespeare, Milton, Goethe, and Wordsworth but they felt no love for Valmiki, Kalidas, Khusro, or Anis.[45]

Mahatma Gandhi's leadership brought about some change in the attitudes of people when the craze for imitation of British culture began to wane. But then Azad encountered another problem:

> But now I notice that a number of my countrymen are on the verge of making another mistake. Previously they were on the brink of the precipice and now they want to jump over to the other extreme. By Indian nationalism it is now meant that we should forget the English language and literature and that we should have nothing to do with Milton or Shakespeare. From certain quarters I hear that in order to be true nationalists we should have no tinge of modern civilization in us. I believe there is nobody here who holds these views. But if there is any I must remind him that just as the previous position was wrong, this latter position will also be in the same category.[46]

Azad firmly believed that Indian languages needed to be developed to serve the purpose of medium of instruction, and pointed out that 'the experiment of imparting instruction in the mother tongue up to the matriculation standard has already been tried with success and the time has come when the process must be extended further and all education in the land made accessible to the people in their own language.' His faith in the provincial languages, however, could not be properly introduced in our education system, leading ultimately to the growth of disparate generation of Indians, even alien to each other. We are still grappling with the issue and have no clear solution to resolve the problem. There is even a group among the Dalit population, which has been deprived over the centuries, that believes that learning English is the only panacea to compete and get ahead in this world. Chandra Bhan Prasad, who is a well-known Dalit writer and thinker, even talks of worshipping the English language as a Goddess, with a temple of her own.[47] 'She is the symbol of Dalit renaissance,' notes Prasad, 'in her right hand she holds a pen which shows she is literate.... In her left hand, she holds a book which is the Constitution that has given Dalits equal rights.'[48] So Azad could imagine the impact English language had on our lives and believed it was futile to be hostile towards it, though he never undermined the significance of regional languages—a rational and workable choice could not be made. We continue to engage with this emotive issue even now.

His convocation address at Patna university was prophetic in many ways, particularly in the context of educational and cultural policies being pursued today. He was critical of the British and their contempt and condescending attitude towards Indian civilization and languages, but he was equally uncomfortable with those Indians who espoused tunnel vision. He warned as early as 1947 that our education and culture need to be broadly defined, with a window open for the outside world. We cannot function under any illusion that we already have everything and that the world needs to learn from us—a claim that is often made today, but one that can only be partially true. Azad put it succinctly:

> Just as it was not proper for you to lose yourself in the slavish love of western civilization or literature to the extent that you might forget the grand and proud civilization of your own country, similarly it would be wrong to put yourself in a cage so that no ray of light of western learning and civilization may enter it. Do not forget that you can seal all your worldly possessions within national and geographical limits but no seal can be put on learning and civilization. They are outside the pale of boundaries, and seals are of no avail there.... They are above nationalities. They are free from the stains of

> race, colour or factions.... No doubt Shakespeare was born in England but the immortal works of Shakespeare are for all nationalities.... Do you think dramas of Kalidas were also Indian nationals just as Kalidas was? Do you think no foreigner has a claim on them?[49]

He evocatively appealed to the people to shun narrow-mindedness in their lives and blind faith in any religious belief. The future policies of the independent Indian government were ingrained in the spirit of Azad's concluding words:

> If liberality of thought and toleration are the most precious heritage of ancient Indian civilization, shall we not prove worthy inheritors of this great heritage? Shall we let that kind of narrow-mindedness raise its ugly head which is in the air today? ...Today, India is free. There is no outside pressure to check her. She can have any kind of mental mould she pleases. Will it be exclusive, of which the world is sick today, or will it be all-inclusive which has been the characteristic of Indian culture throughout the ages?

This was almost an inaugural speech by Maulana Azad, where he raised some foundational issues for future educational policies and the civilizational vision of independent India. He carried this vision forward till he left us in 1958.

One of the major lapses of the Nehruvian era is said to be the lack of focus on primary and secondary education, which is true to a great extent. Maulana Azad did try to cope with this challenge, faced insurmountable hurdles on the way, many of them circumstantial. Some hurdles came about because the newly-formed government was in a hurry to cover lost ground and catch up with the world in industrial and scientific development. As said before, there were millions of hungry and desperate mouths to feed, to provide comfort and shelter to. This is no explanation for such a serious lapse, and I agree with the critics that a more constructive way should have been found, because the foundational attempts to build our holistic educational network were not enough. This early weakness is palpably visible in the ongoing educational crisis because the system is weak at many levels. Now the attempts to mend the structure is merely a patchwork, not an organized effort to strengthen the foundations of the structure.

Maulana Azad outlined the framework of his national education agenda in a press conference on 18 February 1947, as a minister of the interim government. His lofty ideals and commitment to humanitarian and progressive values is the core of the national education policy he espoused. I will share some of those passionate words here as most of them are under serious threat today. Addressing a conference on the eve of Independence, Azad categorically said that 'a truly liberal and humanitarian education may transform the outlook of the people and set it on the path of progress and prosperity, while an ill-conceived or unscientific system might destroy all hopes which have been cherished by generations of pioneers in the cause of national struggle.'[50] He was voicing here the noble objectives shared by most of the leaders during the national movement, most of these issues of national education were debated and discussed by the nationalists and it was now time to implement them. He raised six points to be followed in the future, which included emphasis on fundamental research, which was essential for scientific and industrial development; he also stressed on teacher education and some generalized curriculum. In India the problem of mass education is of vast proportions and will require time for its solution. He was happy in 1947 that modern technology and other effective instruments were available to take this mass education project ahead.

Sadly, we are still grappling with this essential project despite better and diverse technologies to reach the masses. This confirms that mere technology is not enough—on its own it cannot do much. We need an essential push to take any such ambitious and difficult projects forward. Azad concluded his press conference by stressing that 'education should have the highest priority in our national budget and should take its place immediately after food and clothing. In fact, a proper system of education is necessary in order to tackle satisfactorily even these problems. I have every hope that we shall be able to make up our leeway by a determined and concerted effort and place education in India on par with education in other civilized countries of the world.'[51]

Unfortunately, we continue to have the same expectations from governments past and present, but to no avail. Despite Azad's call to see education as the highest priority after food and clothing, we have somehow ignored that essential commitment till now. The budgetary allocation has remained abysmally low. The experts in the education sector and many non-governmental organizations working in related areas have kept the pressure on but to no avail. Our expenditure on education has never crossed 5 per cent of our GDP and we rank sixty-second in total expenditure on education per student. Manmohan Singh's government in 2009–14 left the average expenditure at 3.19 per cent of the GDP while the current Modi regime has brought it down to 2.88 per cent.

I want to discuss another issue, one raised by Maulana Azad at a press conference on 31 May 1948, which is sadly relevant even now. Azad realized the significance of social education, for him 'social education may therefore be defined as a course of study towards the production of a consciousness of citizenship among the people and the promotion of social solidarity among them.'[52] Azad felt its need in our educational framework soon after Independence. For developing a sense of citizenship and producing an educated mind, he laid down few essential points, which I shall share briefly here, as they are aptly relevant in today's educational system as well:

(a) Every citizen must know the meaning of citizenship and the way democracy functions. He should have not only some knowledge of the history and geography of the country but also of its social conditions.... With the introduction of adult franchise, it is imperative for every voter to know the meaning of the vote....

(b) There must also be instruction in the laws of personal and public health. True citizenship implies knowledge of and respect for the laws which govern the health of the community.... One of the main purposes of social education must be to train people in clean and healthy living...disposal of refuse, some rudimentary ideas of drainage and consideration for the convenience of neighbours....

(c) Social education must also mean the imparting of such information to people as will enable them to affect some improvement in their economic status.... Arrangements will therefore be made for training in a craft or the introduction of better techniques in existing crafts....

(d) Social education, involving as it does the improvement of bodily and mental health, cannot ignore the proper training and refinement of the emotions. Art and literature are the instruments of this training. Folk music, drama, dance, poetry, and recreative activities must be included in a scheme of social education.

(e) Social education should also contain an element of instruction in a universal ethic, with special emphasis upon the necessity of toleration of one another's differences in a democracy.[53]

Questions about citizenship, rights, and civil society are as pertinent today, if not more so, as they were in 1947. Azad wanted a comprehensive programme of education to be followed on a national level. Keeping in mind the financial constraints, he advised to follow it selectively in parts of India. He was conscious of the fact that any such programme will ultimately depend on the proper education of women. If women take to education, more than half of our problems will be solved. I brought this up here precisely to comprehend our educational journey as well as the progress and regress of our democracy, keeping in view the foundational ideals laid down by Azad in 1948.

Within a year after assuming charge in the interim government, Azad called for an all-India educational conference on 16 January 1948, where he laid down 'A Plan for National Education'. Within a fortnight of this Mahatma Gandhi was assassinated, which impacted the functioning as well as the morale of the government and the nation. However, Azad clearly spelt out that 'even if other nation building activities of the government have to be slowed down or deferred on account of such difficulties, education, at any rate, must be pushed forward as rapidly as possible. We must not, for a moment, forget that it is the birthright of every individual to receive at least the basic education without which he cannot fully discharge his duties as a citizen.'* The task to educate was not only for the school-going children but also a large number of adults. Our population after Partition was 24 crore and school-going children between the ages of six to eleven years were around 29,372,000. The number of trained teachers needed at that time was nine lakh, which was an impossible task. In this context, Azad appealed in his address that young men and women should come forward to meet this deficiency. He said: 'I would urge upon every educated man and woman to regard it as a sacred national service to come forward and serve as a teacher for at least two years. They should regard it as a sacrifice to the national cause and accept for their services

*The nation building activity for Azad and other leaders at that time was education and alleviation of sufferings of the people at all levels. Look at the contrast today, the Central Vista project has to continue as an essential project while the citizens are gasping for breath and searching for vaccines to save their lives. A sad tale of lopsided priorities, where massaging an ego of an individual is more important than the responsibilities the leader is committed to fulfil. Azad, *Speeches of Maulana Azad, 1947-1955*, p. 29.

whatever allowance the state may afford.' Azad even proposed some kind of conscription for the purpose where educated young men and women may spend two years as teachers, which was of course an emergency measure. Unfortunately, none of these policies could be implemented, however, they remain passionate examples of Azad's commitment to the cause of national education and the sense of urgency he felt to ameliorate the deprived sections of our population.

In his national plan for education, Azad also stressed the education of illiterate adults. 'It is obvious that with the extension of democracy, the problem of adult education has become even more important than it was in the past.' As part of the national education for adults, Azad had two objectives: (a) illiterate adults to be made literate and more importantly, (b) provisions to be made to enlarge their outlook and enable them to take an intelligent interest in the affairs of the country.[54] He stressed more on the second objective and not mere literacy when he said, 'expansion of the mind of the adults can largely be [a]ffected today through the use of scientific methods and machinery which has made our task in this respect much lighter than it was before.' Unfortunately, this task remains unfulfilled even now, even those who are products of university education lack this 'expansion of the mind' and remain cooped up in their narrow world instead.

Azad raised the issue of national education again two years later in the CABE meeting on 8 January 1950 in Cuttack. He began with his commitment of having to build our educational structure afresh—both qualitatively as well as quantitatively. Thus, he said, our ministry of education should have the following objectives:

(i) The provision of basic education on a universal, free, and compulsory basis for all school-going children.
(ii) The provision of adult education in order to wipe out the colossal illiteracy of our masses.

(iii) The improvement and expansion of technical education in order to solve the problem of manpower for industrial and technical development.

(iv) The reorganization and improvement of university education from a national point of view.

Besides laying down these objectives, Azad again expressed the lack of required budgetary allocations as a major limitation but he did not restrict to just this limitation. 'A truly national system of education demanded the creation of a new spirit among our educated men and women, so that they would regard the spread of education as a national obligation for all.'[55]

As I hinted before as well, one of the major challenges before Azad was the provision of education for the displaced population. One Ishar Singh Grover of the All India Refugee Association wrote a desperate letter to Maulana Azad on 31 May 1952 saying, 'The situation in Delhi is really unfortunate. Schools have put up notices stating that registration for admission is stopped for years. Anxious parents wonder what they can do. They are prepared to pay the fees beyond their capacity to ensure a safe future for their children. But…they meet with an emphatic "No" from one school to another.'[56] Azad took it up as an urgent matter, called for a conference on 12 June 1952, involving the education ministry as well as the rehabilitation ministry as well as Delhi government officials like Mehr Chand Khanna, adviser to the rehabilitation ministry.[57] This meeting led to the formation of a committee at Azad's initiative which collected the data of students and deliberated on the founding of new schools.[58]

Coming back to the Radhakrishnan Commission, the priority of the government was clear with the establishment of the education commission two years before in 1948. The commission submitted its report in 1949 and gave precedence to higher education over school education in terms of its detailed recommendations. This focus on higher education or on scientific and technical education was an outcome of our government's initial thinking, where it was felt that independent India has to catch up with the world and also feed the hungry and deprived masses as quickly as possible. Both the above-mentioned needs were interlinked, and thus had to be taken forward simultaneously. The commission, while formulating its recommendations, took note of India's heritage in the realm of education, art, and culture and blended them well with the future. The objective the commission set before itself was:

> If India is to face the confusion of our time, she must turn for guidance, not to those who are lost in the mere exigencies of the passing hour, but to her men of letters and men of science, to her poets and artists, to her discoverers and inventors. These intellectual pioneers of civilization are to be found and trained in the universities, which are the sanctuaries of the inner life of the nation.[59]

The spirit of this objective permeated through Azad's tenure in the 1950s, where we see the deep involvement and dependence of the government on the experience and thinking of scholars, scientists, and cultural figures.* This is something that is significantly absent from the governance model today, where most such experts are many times derided and not involved in crucial decision making.

---

*Several names that figure in the early phase are scholars and scientists like Prof S. S. Bhatnagar, Prof Tara Chand, Humayun Kabir, K. G. Saiyadain, Prem Kirpal, Dr Radha Krishnan, Dr Zakir Husain, J. C. Ghosh, Homi Bhabha, Meghnad Saha, and many more. Maulana Azad even invited Prof Birbal Sahni, a foremost palaeobotanist at the Lucknow University, to come and join as secretary to the education ministry. Sahni took some time to ponder and sent his consent telegram to Maulana Azad. He felt uncomfortable soon after, as the prospect of being a bureaucrat in a ministry did not fit with his temperament. He woke up his wife to seek her opinion and she agreed that he should say no and continue to work as a researcher. Sahni went to the telegraph office late at night and sent his regret letter to Maulana Azad, explaining his inability. Shakti Gupta, *Birbal Sahni*, New Delhi: National Book Trust, 1978, p. 71.

Coming back to the recommendations of the commission, it went along with the ideas of Maulana Azad on the issue of medium of instruction when it said that regional languages should replace English. Azad had already articulated his position on this issue in his 1947 convocation address in Patna. He argues that:

> So far as education is concerned the following should be the programme: (1) We should decide that the medium of instruction throughout will be regional language; (2) So far as elementary and secondary education is concerned there is no obstacle in our way. But we have to make provision for higher education. We have to make a start straightaway. Here too we have to fix a time limit of five years.[60]

Another area of divergence between the recommendations of the commission and Maulana Azad's ideas was the imparting of religious education. Azad was keen that religious education be provided under government supervision, and referring to the widespread communal violence after Partition, Azad felt that 'our present difficulties, unlike those in Europe, are not the creations of materialistic zealots but of religious fanatics.'[61] Azad, thus, sincerely believed that people should not be left at the mercy of semi-literate mullahs, pandits, and priests and that children should be taught by erudite teachers, proficient in their respective religions. However, the commission took a slightly different position, it did not recommend that all religions be taught in the schools and colleges but religious thinkers like Buddha, Confucius, Jesus, Prophet Muhammad, Zoroaster, Nanak, Mahatma Gandhi, and others be taught. It probably realized that Indian religions are diverse, there is no one Hinduism, nor one Islam, or even Christianity. What particular choice will the government make to teach in schools? All of them were diverse, not only theologically but even culturally. In any case, the argument that it is not the task for a secular government to teach religion in schools, any religion for that matter, prevailed and it was probably a wise choice. It was linked to our choice to be a secular nation and not a theological state, like our sibling and neighbour state, Pakistan. A discussion on religious education raged again when an article on the issue appeared in the *Hindustan Times* on 30 October 1956—the education ministry took it up in one of its files where bureaucrats and others expressed their views. One P. D. Shukla summarized the views in a note saying:

> I feel it very important that all the children be taught the fundamentals of ethics, human behaviour, tolerance, human values, and teachings of great men including religious leaders and this should be taught to all children irrespective of the religious group from which they come. I would say that we should teach them the 'religion of humanity'. I am personally a believer in the existence of God but I would not desire the children to have blind faith in the same. On the contrary, we should encourage their critical sense of understanding and if it leads to faith in God, it is all right; and if it leads them to think otherwise, we should leave them there to seek confirmation or modification of their beliefs through their future course in life.[62]

Commenting on the article, Mr Lal Singh, a member of parliament, wrote to the ministry a longish note where he accepted the constructive role of denominational institutions of diverse creeds, but also conceded that 'it is a painful fact that many of them had rendered [the] greatest disservice in spreading the cult of religious hatred against one another of which, we frequently taste the fruit in abundance in the form of communal riots...it cannot be denied that the products of these Sectional Institutions in general, represent [the] worst form of bigotry—all praise for their own religion and intense hatred for others. This suited our foreign masters but is ill-becoming in free India.'[63] He continued with his comments that are sadly relevant even today, when he reiterated that 'India is, and should be, secular in the sense that its government is not guided by any religious dogmas and all people, irrespective of their religious belief, can enjoy equal opportunities for advancement.' He ended his note by underlining the fact that 'our present generation of Indians, bred and brought up and drenched in bigotry of the worst kind, may not shake off their religious fanaticism but the coming generation reading in common schools and studying common religious books, are bound to have a far better outlook on moral and spiritual values, which must form the foundation of Indian character.'[64] I have recalled this incident to highlight a time in our early history when a member of the parliament could freely take the floor of the house to make such observations about religion in the formative phase of our educational development. We can see how far we have travelled from these ideals today. Most of the issues he raised so passionately in 1956 are not only rejected but mocked by many people in power.

I will not go into the details of the commission's report but will attempt to highlight some of the points which are relevant in our present-day context. Our universities are in a turmoil today; the deterioration began years ago, however, they have reached a new low in the recent past. In a section discussing the functions of a university the commission said that the objective of a university is to 'prepare individuals who seek guidance from the past but give up fatal obsession of the perfection of the past.... They must train intellectual pioneers, seeking guidance from the past but providing dynamics to realize new dreams.'[65] It also said that the universities 'must also develop value of democracy, justice, and liberty, equality and eternity—ideals of the Indian society.' It also wanted to develop appreciation for cultural unity and diversity; some of these are under severe strain today. It said 'India is like a palimpsest in which new characters do not entirely efface the old. In a single social pattern fragments of the different ages are brought together. It would be impossible to think of Indians where no Mughals ruled, where no Taj was built, no Macaulay wrote his Minute on education.'[66] Another issue, which resonates almost daily in our university and academic lives today, is related to the crucial question of liberty. The commission, talking about university autonomy, said that the 'freedom of individual development is the basis of democracy. Exclusive control of education by the State has been an important factor in facilitating the maintenance of totalitarian tyrannies.... Higher education is, undoubtedly, an obligation of the State but State aid is not to be confused with State control of academic policies and practices. Intellectual progress demands the maintenance of the spirit of free inquiry.'[67] This vital feature of our university life had been under severe stress for some time, it is almost redundant now when the state is slowly withering away, passing on most of the obligations of university education to several private players. The state-run universities had been languishing for years but now the grip of the state is tightened to an extent that most universities are gasping for breath.

One of the most important and concrete steps suggested by the commission was to set up University Grants Commission, though a University Grants Committee had been in existence since 4 June 1945. However, after the Higher Education Commission was set up, this committee almost ceased to function. Finally, the ministry issued a press release announcing the setting up of the Interim University Grants Commission with Dr S. S. Bhatnagar, as chairman, Dr A. L. Mudaliar, Acharya Narendra Dev, and Mr Wadia as non-official members. Mr Wadia was the vice-chancellor of Bombay university. K. G. Saiyidain and K. R. K. Menon represented the ministries of education and finance.[68] After this interim step, the government looked for some competent members to be part of the UGC, which led to a huge campaign among probable aspirants.[69] The UGC was constituted in 1953 but the Act in the parliament was passed in 1956, which provided the commission a statutory status. Maulana Azad took keen personal interest in constituting the commission. He carefully chose people who would constitute it.* This was a major step in the direction of organizing the higher education sector, it was established with a broader perspective where merely funding was not the objective but also an agenda to promote higher education across the country.

After the setting up of the UGC, Maulana Azad took few more significant steps regarding institutions like the Visva Bharati. This unique institution, founded by Gurudev Rabindranath Tagore, was declared an institution of national importance and Humayun Kabir wrote a note to the cabinet supporting the move to recognize it as a central university. The Visva Bharati authorities approached the Indian government in August 1948 to declare it a central university but the government decided to wait till the university commission was constituted. In his note Kabir stated 'when Tagore was alive, the Visva Bharati derived advantages both in prestige and financial assistance from the esteem in which he was held by people in India and outside.'[70] A memorandum on the reorganization of the Visva Bharati spoke about the poet's ideal of university education. From the beginning, Tagore was deeply conscious of the defects of the present system of university education in India. He found that 'our universities are not vital centres of intellectual life where high standard of learning is maintained, where the minds of the people are naturally attracted, where they find a genial atmosphere in which to prove their worth and contribute their share to

*The UGC was constituted as follows: Dr C. D. Deshmukh as chairman with three vice-chancellors nominated by the government: Dr John Mathai, Dr A. L. Mudaliar and Prof N. K. Sidhanta. There were distinguished academics like Dr Zakir Husain, Pt H. N. Kunzru, and Dr M. S. Thacker and K. G. Saiyidain and P. C. Bhattacharya as representatives of the ministry of education and finance. Ministry of Education, National Archives of India, New Delhi.

the country's culture.'[71] Tagore set up Visva Bharati with this comprehensive ideal in view. He called it 'an Eastern university as he wanted it to be a university in which the study of the Eastern humanities could be given a predominant place. India in the past was connected with all the neighbouring countries: Iran, Afghanistan, Eastern Turkestan, Mongolia, Tibet, China, Japan, Indo-China, and Indonesia. None of these countries grew in isolation. India played a leading part in developing the civilization of many of these neighbouring countries. Hence Indian history and culture are inseparable from the history and culture of those countries.'[72] This vision of Tagore was dear to Azad as well and thus he set up the Indian Council for Cultural Relations, initially with an emphasis on relations with the countries in our neighbourhood. Thus, an institution founded by Tagore in 1921 became a central university in 1951 and was inaugurated by Maulana Azad on 22 September 1951. While delivering the inaugural address, Azad said 'the thing which has always stuck with me about Gurudev was his lofty humanism which arose above all sectarian and communal limitations.... This sense of kinship with the whole world is the essence of Indian culture, and perhaps its greatest contribution to the world.'[73] He spoke with immense passion, invoking Tagore, when he said that 'It was this consciousness of the fundamental spiritual unity of man that led Gurudev to found the Visva Bharati where the world could unite in common brotherhood and realize the ideals of peace, goodness, and unity.' We can see very distinctly that Azad's educational as well as cultural policies were quite a bit inspired by Gurudev's vision, as I have tried to explain in the earlier chapter, his nationalism was also close to the humanist vision of Tagore. He continued in his address, emphasizing the use of three terms by Tagore: shantam, shivam, advaitam (we have a conception of God which rises above all narrow limitations of race, religion, or creed). Azad was struck by another Tagore ideal, which was read out before any ceremonial function of the Visva

Bharati: yatra visyam bhavatyekaneedam (the whole world has here become one home). 'I can think of no higher conception of humanity than that expressed in this beautiful phrase. I will appeal to everyone of you that whenever you have any function, you will never forget to start it with this proclamation of faith in the unity of mankind.'[74] This was the conception of a university which Azad shared so eloquently with Gurudev Tagore and expected the universities to follow this ideal in their campuses and teaching programmes. No better time to invoke Tagore and Azad than when our universities are desperately struggling to retain their intellectual and academic freedom as well as a cosmopolitan vision.

Jamia Millia Islamia was an institution that came up in the wake of the Non-cooperation and Khilafat movements in the 1920s. Thus, it was instilled with nationalist ideals and vision. Several eminent Muslim leaders like Hakim Ajmal Khan, Dr M. A. Ansari, and Dr Zakir Husain etc. were involved in laying the foundation of this institution—it began in Aligarh but soon moved to Delhi, first to Karol Bagh and later to its present location in Okhla. This initiative was not as privileged as Visva Bharati, it had to struggle to get even its degrees and diplomas recognized by the education ministry. A letter had to be written to remind the government that as far back as 1944, a committee had been appointed which recommended the recognition of all the degrees of Jamia, but the government of India recognized only the matriculation and diploma of Basic Training.[75] The letter also says that the matter was taken up with Dr Sargent and Dr D. M. Sen and they advised not to pursue the matter further. However, the letter writer insisted that 'I would request you to have the question of recognition taken up now, as the further development of our work now depends entirely upon the recognition given to it by the Government of India.'[76] Maulana Azad made some positive comments on the file and the issue was later pursued, but he could not resolve the matter of recognition of degrees and funding of Jamia, so a committee was formed to look into further details.[77] Finally when the committee was formed it included the joint educational advisor to the Indian government; Mr G. C. Chatterji, member FPSC; Principal Gurmukh Nihal Singh of Ramjas College, Delhi; a representative of the Ministry of Home Affairs; and Mr H. S. Verma, under secretary of education, who was also the secretary to this committee.[78] The details of the deliberations of this committee are not available in the files but the matter became public when Aligarh Muslim University (AMU) decided to recognize Jamia degrees in History, Politics, Economics, Urdu, Education, and Law and sought the ministry's approval. The approval could not be given as Jamia was not yet established by law—it took yet another decade before Jamia was given the deemed university status in 1963 and finally made a central university in 1988.

There is a thick file in the archives which deals with the shifting of many of the colleges that now constitute the Delhi university to its present campus in north Delhi. The most interesting case here is of the Hindu College, where Maulana Azad seemed to have been keenly involved, particularly in dealing with the corruption of the contractors and the lack of enquiry into the matter. The whole episode sounds so contemporaneous, though it began during the pre-Independence phase. The college was allotted land in 1939–40 and the construction of its hostel began in 1941, but the contractor stopped work and the incomplete building collapsed during the rains. Hindu College alleged that the plan of the building was prepared by the architect of the Delhi university and payments were made with the Central Public Works Department's approval. Even the reports submitted by the college raised doubts as to whether the foundation work had been done properly.[79] A detailed note on these colleges, particularly on Hindu College, was prepared by the ministry, where Maulana Azad gave an extensive reaction. He wrote that 'it appears the building was given a weak foundation and was not made according to the specifications.... The P.W.D in their report dated the 10 January 1949, have on the one hand brought out in detail all the technical defects.... On the other hand, this is clear that the P.W.D. did not object to the work of the contractor.... Their engineer inspected the building and gave a 'certificate' on the strength of which the amount was paid to the contractor.'[80] Azad wondered why an enquiry was not conducted into the whole affair despite the fact that Sir Shri Ram sent a note regarding the condition of the building and insisted that an enquiry should be initiated. I refer to this episode not merely to reflect upon the history of one of the foremost colleges in Delhi but also to remind ourselves of the functioning of various departments, particularly those involved in the construction activities, and how they got away then and continue to do the same even now.

There is an insightful document in the archives, which is 'A draft-outline for educational development in the second five-year plan' dated 25 April 1955. The document gives us an idea about the priorities of the government and its overall focus on educational development. The second plan proposed an increased emphasis on industrialization, which meant even more attention to education, as 'large scale industrialization cannot be carried out unless there is a considerable increase in literacy.'[81] For this, the plan stressed that 'better organization of education at all levels is necessary and provision for such improvement forms an important feature in the proposals.... No improvement of education is however possible without an improvement in the quality of teachers.... In the vast majority of cases, people come to the teaching profession only after they have failed to find any other avenue of employment.'[82] Though we generally assume that elementary and secondary education did not acquire the requisite place in the educational policies, it is not so if we look at the second plan. The plan, in 'formulating the proposals, the greatest emphasis has been placed on the expansion and improvement of elementary and secondary education, but it is obvious that programmes in these fields cannot be carried out without improvement of university education.'

The proposals for the second five-year plan assumed that by the end of the first plan period, the facilities for elementary education would be accessible for about 50 per cent of the children of the age group 6–11, though the situation would vary from state to state. By 1961, it was projected that there would be facilities for 75 per cent of the children in the age group of 6–11 and 30 per cent of the children in the 11–14 age group. This target could be met by hiring good teachers with enhanced salary structures and by opening new schools. Thus, it was estimated that there will be about 240,000 elementary schools in the country by the end of 1955–56. On the basis of proposals, this number would have to be increased by another 120,000 new schools. Regarding adult education, the draft proposal stated, 'There is no need to stress the importance of social education. Without the support of the adults—and in India about 90 per cent of the adults are illiterate—no programme of education or indeed any national development can be sustained.' Keeping such dire needs in view, the second plan proposed 'the establishment of a community centre in each Community Project Block, a literacy centre on a somewhat more modest scale in each National Extension Block and one Janta College in each Division.'[83] To make all this possible, the plan visualized that 'it will be necessary to establish or enlarge facilities for training social education workers and considerably strengthening the Social Education organization in the district and State Headquarters.'[84]

The second plan has been at times described as a plan for the industrialization of the economy. Thus, it proposed that a 'provision must be made for the technical training of far greater numbers.' A large number of junior technical schools need to be established in different parts of the country and a provision be made for the 'apprenticeship-training-cum-Schools of Industry' for high school dropouts. It was felt necessary to upgrade the quality of teachers in these technical institutions.[85] The plan also said that 'provision has been made for continuing the development of the Kharagpur Institute and the establishment of the Western and the Southern Higher Institutes.' It was also suggested to increase the plan outlay from ₹25.2 crores to ₹80 crores.[86] In university education, there was a proposal in the plan to finally agree for a three-years degree course which had been under discussion for some time. They also realized that 'the change in duration is important but cannot by itself bring about the desired result, unless the quality of teachers is improved.' The plan refers to the malaise that corrodes our good universities and colleges even now when it says that 'at present majority of such teachers are rejects from other services. Even if a brilliant student takes up a university career, it is only for a few years as a marking time while he awaits more profitable employment in government or industry.' It acknowledged that 'unless university teachers (and this will include teachers in affiliated colleges) are of a first-rate ability, the students do not get proper instruction and guidance. There is thus a danger that every succeeding generation of students will be poorer in quality.'

The second plan also talked of rural education at all levels, which suffered due to the lack of adequate facilities. 'This deficiency must be overcome both in the interests of democracy and to check the drift to town of the able and energetic among the villagers.' Despite such sincere early awareness of this problem we have not been able to curb rural–urban migration.

I have already referred to the equalization of opportunities in the beginning of this section. However, the second plan stressed on the issue when it said that 'one of the main criticisms against our educational system is that only children whose families are well off enjoy the privileges of higher education.' It also referred to the discrimination based on caste, language, or domicile.' The government, it said, is committed to remove disabilities based on such extraneous considerations. I need to quote a longish passage from the plan document as it will add to the ongoing debates and politics on this issue:

> The democratization of education also requires that there must be general provision of scholarships and other assistance to deserving pupils at all levels from the primary to the university, including technical education. The institution of scholarship to Scheduled Castes, Scheduled Tribes, and Other Backward Classes has led to an enormous increase in the number of students from these groups. From outside these communities also, there are many children who are meritorious but because of lack of resources are compelled to give up studies prematurely. In a rich country like the United Kingdom, as already pointed out, 70 per cent of all university students are in receipt of public support. In a university like Oxford, about 85 per cent students are scholars or stipendiaries. In India, on the other hand, perhaps not more than 10 to 15 per cent of the students receive public assistance.... For all these miscellaneous projects, an ad hoc provision of 40 crores is proposed for the second plan period.[87]

Despite all the statements and intentions expressed in the second plan document, the government was now conscious of the fact that education was not in the central list or even in the concurrent list and the states must be involved in formulating educational policies. The education ministry proposed some changes in the Constitution to bring higher education or even coordination of facilities and maintenance of standards at all stages of education in the concurrent list. However, the law ministry did not consider that such an amendment was in order in the larger context. The law ministry further said 'would it not be better to limit it to higher including technical and scientific education and research.'[88] Azad reflected upon all such issues while evaluating the past ten years of his responsibilities as education minister during his address at the CABE meeting on 6 February 1958, just a few days before he passed away on 22 February. He talked about the B. G. Kher Committee and its recommendations, regretting that 'we have not been able to give effect to this scheme. India is a democracy where the cabinet has joint responsibility. I am therefore equally responsible with my colleagues....'[89] Azad candidly accepted that 'when the first draft of the First Plan was made, education was almost completely ignored. There seemed to be a general view that we should take up only subjects which would give quick returns. Since they held that education could not do this, education was left out of this first draft.'[90] He went on to comment that 'this approach was basically wrong. In my view education is basic for the success of every sphere of planning. Industrial progress cannot be achieved without technical education.' Surely, some realization dawned and 'in the final draft of the First Plan, some provision for education was therefore made but it was totally inadequate to the needs.' The second plan brought additional difficulties before the central and state governments like the reorganization of territories etc., thus education suffered due to such urgent tasks before us. However, Azad concludes that the education ministry made progress despite the circumstances and it is reflected by the fact 'that when I assumed charge, the central budget for education was only about 2 crores and is today considerably more than 30 crores...', and it is not just 'financial allocation which has been increased but there has been expansion in all types of activities.' Azad talked of many difficulties that the education ministry faced but the most crucial matter was that, 'some of my colleagues have regarded education to be purely provincial subject and did not therefore think it necessary that the central government should provide adequate funds for education.'[91] I will end this section with the introductory remarks of Azad at his last CABE meeting where he began with some confessions about his ten-year tenure saying:

> There are two ways in which we can assess any programme of work. The first is to look at what has been done from the point of view of what was desirable. The second is to do so from the point of view of what was possible in the circumstances. If we take the first criterion and judge our progress from the standard of what was desirable, I confess that the results are not satisfactory. If, however, we consider the situation in which India attained her freedom and the difficulties which we have had to face since then, I am glad to say that there is no need to be apologetic for what has been achieved during the past ten years.[92]

SCIENTIFIC AND TECHNOLOGICAL DEVELOPMENT

As we know by now, Azad was an Islamic scholar who firmly believed in the power and role of reason in human progress. He was conscious of the fact that huge parts of the world, including India, were colonized mainly on the strength of the colonizer's scientific and technological ability. India had to cultivate scientific and technological capabilities to overcome hunger, deprivation, and poverty. It also needed to excel in scientific research, for which institutions of excellence and universities will have to be founded.

One of the first significant moves by the interim government was the decision of the cabinet meeting on 26 February 1947 to set up a Scientific Manpower Committee.[93] Its terms of reference were laid out and the committee was supposed to submit its report within six months. The terms of reference were:

1. To assess the requirements for different grades of scientific and technical manpower, taking a comprehensive view over a period of the next ten years, of the needs of the government (civil and defence), of teaching and research, and of industry, agriculture, transport, medicine, and other fields dependent on the use of scientific and technical manpower.
2. To make recommendations regarding action to be taken during the next five years to meet these requirements, in particular with reference to:
    a. The immediate improvement and expansion of facilities for scientific and technical training in Indian universities and special institutions,
    b. Training overseas in scientific and technical subjects,
    c. The promotion and development of scientific and technical research,
    d. The utilization of scientific and technical manpower, and
    e. The maintenance of a register of scientific and technical personnel to facilitate their utilization to the best advantage.[94]

Initially, Maulana Azad suggested a committee of eleven members[95], most of whom were scientists but Sargent, the education secretary, in his comments suggested the inclusion of a few prominent industrialists. There was an animated discussion on the composition of the committee and finally many names were dropped and new names included from the education and business sector. Azad initiated this on the note written by Jawaharlal Nehru, stressing the advisability of such a committee. Nehru felt that 'all our projects and plans for development, in whatever sphere they might lie, are likely to be affected by the number and quality of scientists available. This is a basic matter and the earlier it is tackled the better.' He also observed that 'we have some first-rate scientists. It is true, however, that their number is limited considering the size and the demands of the country. There is not only a lack of opportunity for training but also 'wastage' and 'leakage'. Many young men who show great scientific talent in the universities drift to the civil or other services where this talent and experience is not employed.' This is true even today when we see skilled young men and women from the IITs, medical colleges, and other highly professional institutions opting for the civil services. In most such cases their training and talent is not effectively utilized.

Nehru also referred to the close relationship between pure science and the various branches of engineering and technology. Defence depends on the growth of technology and the expansion of scientific research. These early statements in February 1947, on the crucial aspects of scientific and technological expansion, should be seen as foundational, upon which were built our superstructures in the 1950s and 1960s in the form of IITs, IIMs, and various other institutions of science and universities. Nehru also added that 'we are thinking in terms of starting several technical institutes on a big scale. This is of course desirable but it is not enough. These institutions cannot stand by themselves. They can only function properly with the growth of scientific education all over the country.' He also realized that we needed training institutions. Thus, the Scientific Manpower Committee was needed to advise and guide the newly independent India to carry forward its development—it should not be the responsibility of education department alone but the whole cabinet should give the weight of its authority.[96]

Maulana Azad took this agenda forward and was visibly satisfied with the progress of technical education, when he said:

> You will be glad to see that there has been a remarkable expansion both in quality and quantity of education in this field. In fact, this is perhaps the area where the most remarkable progress has been achieved.... We can confidently say that if this rate of progress is maintained, India will soon be able to meet all her requirements

for technical personnel and perhaps help some of our neighbouring countries.[97]

Keeping the spirit of the Scientific Manpower Committee alive, Azad was delighted on the occasion of the inaugural ceremony of the Indian Institute of Technology, Kharagpur on 18 August 1951. Maulana Azad played an important role in its establishment at a time when resources were scarce. It is not surprising that even today the IIT at Kharagpur recalls his services with a fine sense of gratitude: 'Maulana Azad was not only one of those who established this institute, he also retained to the last day of his life, kind and affectionate interest in its affairs.'[98] The IIT at Kharagpur was initially known as the Eastern Higher Technical Institute, founded in March 1950 in Hijili campus on the recommendations of the Nalini Ranjan Sarkar Committee in 1946. Dr J. C. Ghosh was its first director and soon the name was changed to IIT, Kharagpur. Dr B. C. Roy, the chief minister of Bengal, donated 1,200 acres of land, and the institute was modelled on the Massachusetts Institute of Technology, USA. Azad, while speaking at the inaugural event, reiterated the fact 'that the prevailing system of education in the country has been mainly literary and academic. It has not supplied us with the high level of scientific and technical personnel that is necessary to develop economic and material resources and improve the standard of life of our peoples.'[99] Azad was hopeful that the institute would provide training and education of the highest quality and wanted to ensure that we follow the two main principles in their functioning:

a. Properly qualified and experienced personnel had been secured to run the course, and
b. That the industrial and technical development of the country supports the provision of such a course.[100]

Besides ensuring constant government support to maintain the highest possible standards, Azad also appealed to business houses to come forward with their contribution at diverse levels. While making this appeal he said:

> I would like to make a special appeal to our industrial and business magnates to take an active interest in the development of this Institute. They can help in many ways. Industry can assist financially by establishing chairs in subjects in which it is especially interested.... I have no doubt that industrialists will also help to make the training in this institute more practical and concrete by permitting students to visit workshops and factories and allowing them to go through organized courses of practical training in the industry.[101]

Azad touched upon essential technical and professional aspects in his speech but did not forget, even while speaking at such an occasion, to say that students will be drawn from all over the country but 'their close association in a fellowship of study and research in some of the most formative years of their life will, we earnestly hope, develop in them *a consciousness of their common Indian nationality and culture*'[102] (emphasis mine). He ended his address by thanking Ardeshir Dalal for mooting the idea and Nalini Ranjan Sarkar for drawing up the plan for the institute.

The Council of Scientific and Industrial Research was another large scientific and industrial research organization that Azad focused on. It was founded before Independence in 1942 as an arm of the British government to meet wartime requirements. The Council was set up as an autonomous body through the efforts of Ramaswamy Mudaliar and Shanti Swarup Bhatnagar under the Registration of Societies Act XXI, 1860. Its constitution enunciated some of the functions as follows—the promotion and coordination of scientific and industrial research in India, including the institution and the financing of specific research; the establishment or development and assistance to special institutions or departments of existing institutions for specific studies of problems affecting particular industries and trades; and the establishment, maintenance, and management of laboratories, workshops, institutes, and organizations to further scientific and industrial research and to utilize and exploit any discovery or invention likely to be of use to Indian industries—apart from many other functions.[103] After Independence, the prime minister and minister of science took over as president and vice-president of its governing body—that arrangement continues even now.

Quite a few laboratories of CSIR came up during Azad's time and he enthusiastically participated in their inaugural events. He was conscious of the fact that expanding the network of diverse research labs will expedite the process of national reconstruction. Azad, while speaking at the inauguration of the Central Road Research Institute (CRRI) in Delhi, conceded that we could not take forward the national reconstruction at the level we expected to due to the prevailing conditions, yet 'we can, however, look back with satisfaction on the beginnings made in almost all fields of national reconstruction and welfare activity.'[104] While speaking at the inauguration of the Central Building Research Institute (CBRI) at Roorkee, Azad spoke with pride that CBRI is the last of the eleven laboratories planned by CSIR and these laboratories 'represent the first systematic and planned attempt to apply science and technology to the growth and development of India's national industries.'[105] Azad also stressed that the reason for the splendid success of CSIR and its diverse laboratories is that the council 'is an autonomous body with its own budget and free from formalities and red-tape which slow down the administrative machine of the Government.' He also expressed great admiration for the scientific and administrative skills of its founding director, Dr Shanti Swarup Bhatnagar, and also asked him 'to convey my appreciation to his colleagues without whose co-operation his work could not have been accomplished.'[106]

However, this huge network of laboratories did confront some complications in relationship with the university research programmes—large sums of money for scientific and industrial research was diverted towards the CSIR network of labs while universities began to languish financially. This early trend had serious implications later and is reflected even now when we look at the marginal role of many of the university departments. There was a debate and disagreement between scientists like Meghnad Saha and S. S. Bhatnagar on this issue, which is reflected in this criticism of Saha's of the government and particularly of Bhatnagar:

> The National Laboratories which you have erected will not satisfy our needs. You have erected a temple, but you have not made any provision that there should be a constant influx of qualified votaries into the temple which will bring life into it. If you want to instill life into this country, if you want to train a band of workers for the great work of reconstruction which has been the dream, I would appeal to you to give up this policy of indifference, this policy of denial. You must gird up your loins and find money so that we render sufficient assistance to the universities and revitalize their activities.[107]

Despite these disagreements, the dynamism and tenacity of S. S. Bhatnagar led to the much-needed foundational work in scientific research and industrial progress. Bhatnagar had a direct relationship with Nehru and Azad, which facilitated his decision making and speedy implementation of vital plans in the early years.

CULTURAL RECONSTRUCTION

This was another major challenge before Maulana Azad—the cultural profile of India as a nation was no priority of the colonial regime. Azad was conscious of this inadequacy and believed institutionalization of the various cultural features of India, including its art, music, literature, and much more, was the need of the hour. He knew that we had lost precious historical art objects during colonial rule, which had become part of museums and private collections of many in Europe and America. However, he believed that there was still a lot which could be done to collect and preserve the huge corpus of precious art objects that were in possession of the people of India.

The ministry initiated a process of collecting art objects in the 1950s and finally the National Art Treasures Fund was inaugurated by Prime Minister Jawaharlal Nehru on 23 February 1952. The note circulated by the ministry made it clear that 'during the last 200 years some of the finest specimens of art have gone out of the country. There are, however, still some objects in the possession of private collectors and unless efforts are made to recover them and arrange for their proper preservation, these national treasures may be lost forever.'[108] Even before the fund was established, Azad emphasized the importance of art objects when he said that 'No scheme of national education can claim to attain perfection unless art education finds a place in it. Unfortunately, our art treasures are scattered in various collections and are lying in the most neglected condition. It is therefore absolutely essential to bring together all such art treasures and display them in a scientific manner.'[109] We will briefly track a few more aspects of Azad's commitment to art and culture in the forthcoming pages.

One of the first few steps in this realm of culture was the issue of the national anthem, an issue which rocks our country even now. For Azad, the challenge was to institutionalize the singing of the national anthem once we had finally opted for Gurudev Tagore's 'Jana Gana Mana'. He prepared a two-page note in Urdu, available in his own handwriting, on the singing of national anthems all over the world: 'In almost all countries of the world it is the practice that national anthem of the country is learnt by all the children in the school and all of them sing it with great enthusiasm. There would be hardly any child in France who won't memorize "La Marsellaise"... and be able to sing it solo as well as in chorus.'[110] The British regime did not adopt any national anthem though the Congress did use 'Vande Mataram' in its sessions and in its connected institutions. 'But now,' Azad continued, 'that the government have adopted Tagore's "Jana Gana Mana" as the national anthem, there is no reason why our schools should remain deprived of the pleasure and effect of the tune. I don't know whether the state governments or the universities have taken any suitable step in this direction, but because the matter is of great importance from a national point of view, I am of the opinion that such a matter could not be left to the discretion of the state Governments.'[111]

The concerned file on the national anthem carries some interesting responses from different provincial governments as well as from some directorates of education. For example, the Delhi Directorate of Education responded by admitting that, 'The position with regard to this is that so far no training is given in any systematic or uniform manner. Actually, there is still confusion in many places about the position of the song "Bande Mataram" and in schools the headmasters and headmistresses have been making use of one or the other according to their whim in the matter.'[112] However, it took some time to settle this situation and finally the information and broadcasting ministry promised to bring out a record of the national anthem, 'which will give the standardized vocal version as approved by the prime minister.'[113]

Let me also recall here, before I talk of the institutionalization of art, music, and literature, Azad's interaction with Sardar Patel, which will convey to us Azad's serious commitment to music and aesthetics. Soon after he joined the interim government a few months before independence, Maulana Azad felt that not enough was being done to promote Indian classical music on All India Radio. He shot off a letter to Sardar Patel, who was formally in charge of broadcasting: 'You perhaps do not know that I have always taken keen interest in Indian classical music and at one time practised it myself. It has, therefore, been a shock to me to find that the standard of music of All India Radio broadcast is extremely poor. I have always felt that All India Radio should set the standard in Indian music and lead to its continual improvement. Instead, the present programmes have an opposite effect and lead one to suspect that the artists are sometimes chosen not on grounds of merit.'[114] Azad even proposed that he advise the person in charge of the programmes and suggest ways of improvement. This establishes Maulana Azad's commitment to matters of arts and aesthetics.

It was this spirit that moved him to conceive the idea to institutionalize music, art, and literature. The colonial regime neither promoted nor patronised anything related to art, literature, and culture, instead most of the worthwhile objects and books were transported across the seas. No concerted effort was made to provide a platform for any branch of culture, thus Azad had to begin the process in right earnest. The first institution was the Sahitya Akademi, founded in 1952, which was preceded by a Conference of Letters convened on 15 March 1951. The Conference of Letters was attended by the representatives of nineteen state governments. There were also representatives from diverse literary organizations representing languages like Assamese, Bengali, Gujarati, Hindi, Kannada, Marathi, Malayalam, Odia, Sanskrit, Tamil, Telegu, and Urdu.[115] Azad explained in depth the plans to establish an academy with the involvement of the Asiatic Society, Calcutta—even the first conference on art was held in Calcutta in August 1949. There were detailed discussions during this conference about the prospects of literature and art and finally the Sahitya Akademi was inaugurated on 12 March 1954 in New Delhi. While speaking on the occasion, Azad hinted that some people, including our prime minister, did not want these academies to be founded this way by the government. He said 'they regard it as an imposition from above. They hold that the growth of the academies should have been encouraged from below.... I am afraid I cannot agree with this approach. Since the Renaissance, many academies have been established in Europe.... All these academies were established by the governments under letters-patent of the sovereign or by legislation. There was therefore no reason why the government of India should not take the initiative for the establishment of the academies.'[116] Azad stressed on the merit of the academy members which, and that he believed, that the academies had to be exclusive, following the standards established by the various French academies over the years. The standards set were so high that even Descartes, Pascal, and Molière could not find a place among the academicians. Voltaire and Montesquieu were fortunate but Rousseau never achieved the distinction.[117] Maulana Azad believed that 'if the Indian academy of letters does not maintain similar standards and reserve its honours only for the immortals of literature, the academy will not be able to serve the object for which it is being established.'[118]

Azad was pleased when Jawaharlal Nehru agreed to become the first chairman of the academy. And he clarified that Nehru had been chosen not because he was the prime minister of the country 'but because he has carved out for himself a distinctive place as a writer and author.'

After the Sahitya Akademi, another important cultural institution was born in 1953 called the Lalit Kala Akademi. A small committee of experts was formed before its founding which, in its meeting on 4 April 1953, drew up a constitution for the academy. Azad, while speaking in its first meeting on 5 August 1954, was categorical that art could not flourish until there are strong non-official agencies working for it. The government should support it by all means but academies like the Lalit Kala Akademi should 'work as an autonomous body and without any interference from the government in its activities.' These were some of the founding principles for such institutions which we see being throttled almost every other day today. Azad expected that the academy 'must work to preserve the glorious traditions of the past and enrich them by the work of our modern artists. It must also seek to improve standards and refine public taste. If it serves this purpose, and I have every hope it will, the academy will have justified itself to India and the world.'[119]

The Sangeet Natak Akademi, the next important institution, was founded on 31 May 1952 and inaugurated by Dr Rajendra Prasad, the president of India, on 28 February 1953. A committee was given the task to draft its constitution which was called 'The Constitution of the Academy of Hindustani Music'.[120] However, it was finally named Sangeet Natak Akademi, to include both music and drama. Azad, while delivering his welcome address, made some fundamental points related to art, music, and our composite culture that are as relevant today as they were during those tormenting times soon after Partition. 'India can be proud of a long heritage and tradition in the field of dance, drama, and music.... It is my conviction that in the field of music, the achievement of India is greater than that of even Greece.'[121] He stressed an important aspect that we need to recall today when he said that 'the essence of Indian civilization and culture has always been a spirit of assimilation and synthesis. Nowhere is this more clearly shown than in the field of music.' Azad used this opportunity to delve deep into the exchange of vocal as well instrumental music traditions of India and Persia and how they converged to create a refreshingly new Hindustani music, which surpassed both the old Indian as well as Persian traditions. He also spoke about Amir Khusrau, who was not merely a poet but also a seminal contributor to both vocal and instrumental music, combining Indian and Persian melodies. 'Aiman, Tarana, Qol, Sazgiri, and Suhla and other tunes, which are sung to this day by millions of Indians, are a living testimony to his genius and his power of synthesis.' Azad also spoke about the brilliance of Khusrau, who invented the sitar because he found the veena too complicated, and therefore reduced the strings to just three.

Azad also touched upon the simplification of the vocal music tradition, particularly the role of Sultan Husain Sharqi of Jaunpur, who introduced the khayal style in Indian music. We find a similar spirit of synthesis and assimilation, said Azad, in the evolution of musical instruments in India. He also spoke about the tradition of drama, not only in India but in ancient Babylon, Egypt, as well as Greece. He said 'comparisons in such fields are invidious, but we can still say that Kalidasa may be compared with the greatest among the Greek dramatists. We have also the works of Bhasa, Bhavabhuti, and Banbhatta, who raised the Indian drama to a level which is perhaps not inferior to that attained by the Greeks.'[122] He also referred to the dance traditions of India and for him the 'most remarkable is the continuity of these traditions and the vigour they display to this day.' Azad concluded by saying that 'This precious heritage of dance, drama, and music is one which we must cherish and develop. We must do so not only for our own sake but also as our contribution to the cultural heritage of mankind.'

Art historian Kapila Vatsyayan remembers the time when the three academies were being set up—most of which are documented in the biography *Afloat a Lotus Leaf: A Cognitive Biography of Kapila Vatsyayan* by Jyoti Sabharwal. 'What Kapila found most instructive was Maulana Sahab's insistence that these institutions should be spelled as "akademi" and not "academy", to underscore the Arabic–Greek origins, and also to conform to the Hindi pronunciation.'[123] There is an interesting episode related to this which Kapila proudly shares. Once in her official note, she misspelt 'akademi' and the file came back with a note from Azad in Urdu, 'Kapila ko yeh hidayat di jaati hai ki woh "academy" ko 'akademi' sau baar likh ke bhejen'—Kapila is instructed to write 'academy' as 'akademi' a hundred times and send it to me. She did write 'akademi' a hundred times, carrying 'it out with both pleasure and some sense of humiliation.' This is something not imaginable today, neither do we have ministers of that calibre nor many bureaucrats who would learn with humility. She shares another memorable lesson when she was asked to seek some advice from the director-general of the Archaeological Survey of India on some issue. In her ignorant and arrogant manner, Kapila said, 'I will ask DG Chakraborty to come over.' Maulana Sahab looked at her sternly and said, 'Aap Hindustan ki tehzeeb ke raja ke paas jayengi, unko nahin bulayengi. Thanda paani pijiye aur left-right kijiye—You will go to the epitome of Indian culture and not call him here. Have a glass of cold water and walk across.'[124]

His approach to the relationship between the central ministry and the subordinate offices was a great learning for Kapila, something which we have left behind for years, now that we have hardly anyone to teach nor a generation of bureaucrats ready to learn. She realized that 'just because she was in the central ministry, those who were in-charge of museums, archaeology, or libraries were not to be treated as subordinates. They were never made to walk the corridors of the ministry, notwithstanding the North Block superciliousness and the systemic paradoxes.'[125]

After institutionalizing the diverse cultural traditions of India, Azad wanted a platform for cultural exchange with West Asia and other parts of the world. Azad wanted to 'deepen our friendship and contact not only with Iran but also with Turkey and the countries of the Middle East and China and our neighbours in South-East Asia.' He spoke about this at a conference for cultural cooperation between India and Asian countries on 21 August 1949. He also announced plans to create a platform which he tentatively called the Indian Council for Cultural Cooperation. The council was formally launched on 9 April 1950 and called the Indian Council of Cultural Relations. While delivering his inaugural address, Azad conceded the lack of resources, but he was still able to undertake many necessary actions like the setting up of the headquarters at Hyderabad House, building a library to which he donated his own personal collection, proposing to arrange for periodic meetings where specialists discuss aspects of the culture and civilization of India and neighbouring countries, and initiating an exchange programme of professors.[126]

Azad addressed the general assembly of the Indian Council for Cultural Relations on 14 February 1958 just a week before he left us forever. He spoke in detail about the eight successful years of the council, its cultural and intellectual achievements, as well as efforts to build relationships with overseas countries. He optimistically concluded saying 'I hope our contacts with all these countries will continue to increase and the council will play an increasing role in bringing our peoples closer to one another.'

This early phase of our educational and cultural development is instructive in many ways. It shows that national interest was of primary concern, and it was not merely rhetorical, as we see it now, but instilled with genuine national sentiment. Even culture and heritage were not subservient to someone's political prospects, rather its foundations were laid during politically and culturally divisive times to unite people. An effort was made to weave together an India beyond the trauma and violence inflicted by the Partition. It was indeed a difficult project which some of us deride today without making any attempt to improve upon it.

EPILOGUE

Azad did not live a long life. He passed away on 22 February 1958 while his admirers and colleagues were planning a commemorative volume for his seventieth birthday.* However, his had been an eventful life and he left behind a huge corpus of work. Azad began his creative career very early—he had achieved a lot by the time he turned fifteen, an age when most others had not even begun thinking coherently about larger issues. Not only did he break away from his father's rigid faith and come up with his own understanding of Islam, he tried his hand at journalism and editing—experiences that helped him launch his formal journalistic career with *Al-Hilal* in 1912.

The formative phase of his life was crucial for his future career as an Islamic scholar as well as for his other careers as a journalist and a politician. Azad did not attend any madrassa or university, his father was his first teacher and later chose teachers for him with strictly laid down parameters. This led to a secluded life that deprived him of a much necessary peer group; he grew up around adults where there was hardly any space or scope for childhood fun. Like many who are brought up in a stifling atmosphere, Azad rebelled. The first target of his rebellion against tradition was his faith, which led to him breaking away and carving a space for himself. He was attracted to Sir Syed Ahmad Khan's worldview, which was despised by his father Maulana Khairuddin. Azad was confronted and rebuked by Maulana Khairuddin for this

*This volume was one full of insights into Azad and it was published but as a memorial edition.

outrageous disobedience but he remained steadfast in his faith. Eventually, on his own terms, he distanced himself from Sir Syed and his political stance but the lessons Azad learnt from Sir Syed's rejection of tradition remained with him forever.

Azad's travels in West Asia, Egypt, and France in 1908–1909 convinced him that composite nationalism was indispensable in successfully battling the colonial regime. His mission in the freedom struggle was twofold—first, to fight against the colonial government and second, to confront the Muslim and Hindu communalists. He was also conscious of the nexus between these two forces, which were out to weaken and undermine the freedom movement and the foundations of an independent India. Azad was prescient when he argued that the demand for Pakistan was absurd; he wanted the Muslim community to know that such a move would be disastrous for the Muslims left behind in India as well as for those who opt for Pakistan. In this context let me quote part of the memorable speech delivered by Azad, addressing the Muslim community in the Jama Masjid, Delhi in October 1947:

> Today when I see your ashen faces and desolation in your hearts, my mind goes back to the past. Do you remember I called for you but you pulled out my tongue. I took up the pen but you severed my hands. I wanted to walk but you cut off my legs. I wished to turn on my side but you broke it. I had warned you how the forces of poisonous politics unleashed by sinister designs would lead to the tragedy of Partition but you refused to listen to me. You relied on your ignorance and today you feel as though you are threatened by new dangers.[1]

As we have seen through the book, Azad was a scholar and a solitary man who was uncomfortable in the midst of a huge crowd. Even Gandhi had to rely on leaders like the Ali brothers when Azad refused to be a frontline leader or was hesitant to sit in the front during a public meeting. He was a total misfit in the midst of communal rabble rousing of all hues and his serious scholarly engagements did not cut much ice with communalists. His idea of a composite nation or Ummat-i-Wahida appeared as a novelty in that hour of social, economic, and political turmoil. In this context, his political programme was too different from that of the Muslim League. In fact, it was the alternative understanding of nation states and God that Azad provided to the Muslims of South Asia which threatened the basic political philosophy of the Muslim League.[2] Despite being a reluctant public figure, Azad did succeed in weaning away a huge section of Muslims from the Muslim League trap, convincing them about their safe future in India. In the end, Azad could not keep India united, however, I have tried to argue here that he did succeed in convincing a large section of Muslims to stay back in India and participate in the nation-building process of the next few decades. Azad was able to convince of the Muslims to have faith in composite nationalism and the Jamiat ul-Ulema-i-Hind and the Deoband seminary also stood by Azad. The communal cauldron of Partition burnt everything reasonable and raging passions dumped the voices of sanity. At this juncture, Maulana Azad was joined by a large number of Muslims, particularly the ajlaf (backward sections), who questioned the notion of Islamic nationalism.

In the context of the communal politics of those years, we need to comprehend Azad's serious attempts to understand Islam as well as his engagements with the questions of identity and nationalism that have remained pertinent since. How far away has the world travelled on both these crucial issues? Maulana Azad left behind his nuanced understanding of the faith, a reading of Islam that was based on a comparative religious perspective. He had deep insight into the various religions of the world and could isolate the real and essential from the spurious.[3] This approach was commendable in the context of divisive politics, where both Islam and Hinduism confronted each other as inveterate foes. 'By his profound learning and rare intelligence, Azad did a real good job for Islam by clearing the dust of prejudice and bigotry which had gathered upon it during the long years of its history in India.'[4] Azad stressed the innate humanity that was central to Islam and its concerns regarding the destiny of man. Quite a few of these basic tenets of Islam had almost taken a backseat or have even disappeared from the understanding of the believer. Azad's prolific writings on Islam provided new vigour to a faith that appeared exhausted since the nineteenth century.

Maulana Azad, as I have said before, interpreted and defined nationalism as inclusive, he even used Islam and its history to reinforce his argument. He did this more aggressively to counter communal forces of all hues, which were determined to supplant the spirit of anti-colonial struggle with communal self-interests. And today do we want to pursue the divisive politics of the communalists who caused havoc in our lives during the freedom struggle or espouse the composite nationalism which was the foundation of our independent India? Maulana Azad failed to keep India united despite his unbridled faith in indivisible nationalism. However, he remained committed to the fact that religion alone can never be the basis for nationhood. This fact was never as relevant in the past seventy years as it is today.

I have also referred briefly to Azad and Allama Iqbal's enigmatic relationship in the context of the debate on nationalism. Both of them were inspired by the Quran, shared many literary and other intellectual concerns but never met or referred to each other's work. I agree with Datta that 'the Azad–Iqbal relationship needs further examination from the literary angle to see how far Azad's writings had influenced Iqbal's thinking and poetry.'[5]

One of his most creative and interesting literary works was *Ghubar-i-Khatir*—a collection of letters from Ahmednagar Fort prison, which he was not allowed to post. During his time at the fort prison, he wrote epistolary essays which were never intended to be published but his secretary Ajmal Khan took the initiative to publish them in 1946. All of them were addressed to his friend Maulana Habibur Rahman Khan Sherwani, and Azad took care to stay apolitical as Sherwani was not interested in political matters. It was a challenging task for someone who was deeply immersed in politics. However, Azad accomplished this task by opening his heart and mind as he had never done before. He wrote about his childhood and early education and delved deep into many complex philosophical issues and his likes and dislikes as well. *Ghubar-i-Khatir*, as I have tried to show, revealed many unknown facets of Azad's life.

I conclude with Azad's crucial role after Independence, when he was assigned the task of reconstructing our education system, building our scientific and technological institutions, and revamp our cultural policy. It was an arduous task in the aftermath of Partition violence and the ensuing bitterness in society, however, a new India had to be built. These tasks were crucial for development, as India had opted for a secular democracy where 85 per cent of the citizens were illiterate and unaware of democratic governance. A huge section of the adult population was also not literate which made the challenge even more daunting. There were millions of mouths to feed while food was hardly available. Thus, scientific and technological institutions had to be set up and the colonial agenda of scientific and technological production and research had to be redone in the national interest. A lot was accomplished on all these fronts in the decade of the 1950s though much still remained to be achieved.

There was no institutional platform for any cultural or intellectual expression like literature, music, or fine arts. The British government did not care to use resources on such 'wasteful' projects, so Azad had to begin almost afresh. I have briefly traced the origins and the ongoing challenges in the founding of several such institutions. The three 'akademies' of arts, literature, and music were established during this short phase of ten years. Azad also had a passion for cultural relations beyond national borders, particularly with countries in West Asia and Europe, thus the Indian Council of Cultural Relations was founded to facilitate cultural exchanges between India and the world. This was no mean achievement in the trying times Azad was placed in.

Maulana Azad was never a very healthy man. He always had serious health issues, mostly related to his heavy smoking and his addiction to tea, which used to begin at 3.30 or 4 a.m. in the morning. He woke up early even when he was a child though his father did warn him of serious implications of this habit on his health. Azad was also fond of drinking, as I mention in the book, and remained a solitary drinker all his life—no one ever saw him indulging. Gandhi said to Nehru once, 'I hear that Maulana drinks.' In his characteristic fashion Nehru said, 'What of that. I too drink.'[6] Azad also spent a sedentary life, never showing any interest even in a morning walk or in any form of exercise. He always remained glued to his books, confined to a room, seldom ventured out of his own house, and rarely invited guests home. The lack of physical exercise stiffened his legs, he walked with a slight lurch, and even suffered a couple of falls. His final stumble was in his bathroom on 19 February 1958, when he broke his hip bone and fell unconscious. Very briefly he regained consciousness when Nehru came to enquire about him. On seeing him, Azad said 'Jawahar, Khuda hafiz (May God protect you).[7] Despite all efforts, he could not overcome this terrible shock and injury and finally left us on 22 February 1958 at 2 a.m.

Azad (and other of his ilk) were not merely political leaders but also scholars and men with vision—we can keep their ideas alive if we care to follow their ideals. We need to understand Azad more than ever, not only in the context of Islam but also as a means to create conditions that are conducive to living happily together with our fellow countrymen in one composite India.

REFERENCES

PREFACE

1 Mushirul Hasan (ed.), *Islam and Indian Nationalism Reflections on Abul Kalam Azad*, New Delhi: Manohar Publishers and Distributors, 1992, p. 5.

2 Ibid, p. 6.

INTRODUCTION

1 V.N. Datta, *Maulana Azad*, New Delhi: Manohar Publishers and Distributors, 1990, p. viii.

2 M. Mujeeb, 'The Tadhkirah: A Biography in Symbols', in Humayun Kabir (ed.), *Maulana Abul Kalam Azad: A Memorial Volume,* New Delhi: Asia Publishing House, 1959, p. 136.

3 Abdur Razzaq Malihabadi (ed.), *Azad ki Kahani Khud Azad ki Zubani*, Calcutta, 1959, p. 173.

4 Ibid, pp. 203–204.

5 Mohammad Habib, 'The Revolutionary Maulana', in Humayun Kabir (ed.), *Maulana Abul Kalam Azad: A Memorial Volume,* New Delhi: Asia Publishing House, 1959, p. 80.

6 Azad as quoted in Arsh Malsiyani, *Abul Kalam Azad,* New Delhi: Publications Division, 1976, p. 33, cited in Rizwan Qaiser, *Resisting Colonialism and Communal Politics, Maulana Azad and the Making of the Indian Nation*, New Delhi: Manohar Publishers and Distributors, 2011, p. 77.

7 J. B. Kriplani, 'The Voice of Reason', in Kabir, *Maulana Abul Kalam Azad,* p. 36.

8 Datta, *Maulana Azad*, p. 106.

9 Malik Ram (ed.), *Khutbat-i-Azad,* Delhi, 1974, pp. 47–55.

10 S. A. I. Tirmizi, *Maulana Azad A Pragmatic Statesman*, New Delhi: Commonwealth Publishers, 1991, p. 9.

11 Hiren Mukherjee, *Recalling India's Struggle for Freedom*, New Delhi: Seema Publications, 1983, p. 94.

12 *Hindustan Times,* 16 February 1940, cited in Qaiser, *Resisting Colonialism and Communal Politics, Maulana Azad and the Making of the Indian Nation*, p. 214.

13 Rizwan Qaiser, *Resisting Colonialism and Communal Politics, Maulana Azad and the Making of the Indian Nation*, New Delhi: Manohar Publishers and Distributors, 2011, p. 218.

14 M. A. Jinnah to Azad, as cited in Pattabhi Sitaramayya, *History of the Indian National Congress*, Vol. 2, 1935–47, Bombay: Padma Publications, 1947, p. 202.

15 Syed Abdul Latif, 'An Unfinished Masterpiece', in Kabir, *Maulana Abul Kalam*

Azad, p. 121.

16 Cited in Syeda Saiyidain Hameed, *Maulana Azad, Islam and the Indian National Movement*, New Delhi: Oxford University Press, 2014, p. xii.

17 Savarkar cited in V. D. Savarkar, *Samagra Savarkar Wangmaya: Hindu Rashtra Darshan*, Vol. 6, Poona: Maharashtra Prantik Hindusabha, 1963, p. 296, cited in Shamsul Islam, *Muslims Against Partition*, New Delhi: Pharos, 2018, p. 215.

18 Ibid, pp. 215–16.

19 Cited in B. N. Pande, 'Contribution to Indian Secularism', in Syeda Saiyidain Hameed (ed.), *India's Maulana*, New Delhi: Vikas Publishing House, p. 215.

20 Ahmad Saeed Malihabadi, 'Religious Ideology and Indian Nationalism', in Syeda Saiyidain Hameed (ed.), *India's Maulana-Abul Kalam Azad*, New Delhi: Vikas Publishing House, 1990, Vol. 1, p. 205.

21 Humayun Kabir, 'A Personal Testament', in Kabir, *Maulana Abul Kalam Azad*, p. 78.

CHAPTER 1: THE EARLY YEARS

1 Mujeeb, 'The Tadhkirah: A Biography in Symbols', in Kabir, *Maulana Abul Kalam Azad: A Memorial Volume*, p. 136.

2 Abul Kalam Azad, *Ghubar-i-Khatir: Sallies of the Mind*, 2003, Kolkata: Maulana Abul Kalam Azad Institute of Asian Studies, pp. 102–103.

3 Ibid.

4 Abul Kalam Azad, *Tazkirah*, New Delhi: Sahitya Academy, 2012, first published in 1968.

5 Azad, *Tazkirah*, p. 26.

6 Ibid, p. 27.

7 Ian Henderson Douglas, *Abul Kalam Azad: An Intellectual and Religious Biography*, Gail Minault and Christian W. Troll (eds.), New Delhi: Oxford University Press, 1988, p. 30.

8 Ira Mukhoty, *Akbar the Great Mughal: A Definitive Biography*, New Delhi: Aleph Book Company, 2020, p. 228.

9 Abdur Razzaq Malihabadi (ed.), *Azad ki Kahani khud Azad ki Zubani*, Calcutta: Daftar Azad Hind, 1960, pp. 19–23.

10 Douglas, *Abul Kalam Azad*, p. 31.

11 Amit Dey, *Islam in South Asia*, Kolkata: Parul, 2016, p. 102.

12 S. A. A. Rizvi, *Religious and Intellectual History of the Muslims in Akbar's Reign, 1556–1605*, New Delhi: Munshiram Manoharlal Publishers, 1975, p. 440.

13 Azad, *Tazkirah*, p. 36.

14 Ibid, p. 36.

15 Ibid, pp. 36–37

16 Mushir U. Haq, *Muslim Politics in Modern India 1857-1947*, Meerut: Meenakshi Prakashan, 1970.

17 Douglas, *Abul Kalam Azad*, p. 32.

18 Aziz Al-Azmeh, *Islams and Modernities*, London: Verso Books, 1993, p. 104.

19 Stephen Schwartz, *The Two Faces of Islam*, New York: Anchor Books, 2003, p. 74.

20 Wilfred Cantwell Smith, *Islam in Modern History*, Princeton: Princeton University Press, 1957, p. 49.

21 Ibid.

22 Eugene Rogan, *The Arabs: A History*, London: Penguin books, 2011, p. 68.
23 Schwartz, *The Two Faces of Islam*, p. 80.
24 Ibid, p. 81.
25 Rogan, *The Arabs: A History*, p. 68.
26 Ibid, pp. 68–69.
27 Ibid, p. 69.
28 Azad, *Ghubar-i-Khatir*, p. 103.
29 Azad, *Azad ki Kahani*, pp. 90–91.
30 Ibid, p. 63.
31 Ibid, p. 338.
32 Ibid, p. 362.
33 Abul Kalam Azad, *Azad ki Kahani*, translated by Gopal Krishna, New Delhi: Orient Blackswan, 2015, pp. 140–43.
34 Maulvi Abdul Haqq, *Marhum Dihli College,* New Delhi: Anjuman Taraqqi Urdu, 1989, pp.162–63.
35 Azad, *Tazkirah*, pp. 141–49.
36 Azad, *Azad ki Kahani*, pp. 171–72.
37 Ibid, p. 172.
38 Ibid, p. 173.
39 Ibid, p. 173.
40 Ibid, p. 177.
41 Ibid, p. 213.
42 Ibid, p. 269.
43 Douglas, *Abul Kalam Azad*, p. 36.
44 Abdur Razzaq Malihabadi, *Zikr-e-Azad*, Kolkata: Maktab-e-Isha'at-e-Quran, 1959, p. 389, quoted in Douglas, *Abul Kalam Azad*, p. 36.
45 M. Mujeeb, *Indian Muslims*, New Delhi: Munshiram Manoharlal Publishers, 2003, p. 441.
46 Malihabadi, *Zikr-i-Azad*, p. 389.
47 Azad, *Azad ki Kahani*, pp. 203–204.
48 Malihabadi, *Zikr-i-Azad,* p. 116–18.
49 Ibid, pp. 121–22.
50 Abul Kalam Azad, *Ghubar-i-Khatir*, p. 60.
51 Ibid.
52 Ibid, p. 194.
53 Azad, *Ghubar-i-Khatir*, p. 103.
54 Ibid.
55 Azad, *Azad ki Kahani*, p. 193.
56 Azad, *Ghubar-i-Khatir,* p. 106.
57 Ibid, pp. 106–107.
58 Ibid, pp. 386–87.
59 Ibid.
60 Ibid.
61 Azad, *Azad ki Kahani*, p. 388.
62 Azad, *Ghubar-i-Khatir*, p. 92.
63 Wilfred Cantwell Smith, *Modern Islam in India*, Charlottesville: University of Virginia Press, 1979, cited in V. N. Datta, *Maulana Azad,* p. 19.
64 Syed Ahmad Khan, *Maaqulat-i-Sir Syed*, Lahore: Majlis-i-Taraqqi-i-Adab, Vol. 1, 1962, pp. 97–98.

65 Douglas, pp. 56–57, n. 74.
66 Azad, *Azad ki Kahani*, p. 396.
67 Ibid, pp. 397–98.
68 Douglas, *Abul Kalam Azad*, p. 95.
69 Datta, *Maulana Azad*, p. 23.
70 Datta, *Maulana Azad*, p. 24.
71 Abdul Majid Daryabadi, *Maktubat-i-Sulemani*, Vol. 1, Lucknow, 1963, pp. 13–15, cited in Datta, *Maulana Azad*, p. 21.
72 Daryabadi, *Maktubat-i-Sulemani*, pp. 13–15.
73 Azad, *Ghubar-i-Khatir*, p. 256.
74 Mujeeb, 'The Tadhkirah: A Biography in Symbols', in Kabir, *Maulana Abul Kalam Azad*, p. 142.
75 Azad, *Tazkirah*, p. 330.
76 Ibid, p. 318.
77 Ibid.
78 Christian W. Troll, 'Abul Kalam Azad and Sarmad, The Martyr', in Hasan, *Islam and Indian Nationalism Reflections on Abul Kalam Azad*, p. 31.
79 Azad, *Azad ki Kahani*, p. 275.
80 Ibid, p. 276.
81 Ibid, p. 277.
82 Ibid.
83 Ibid.
84 Ibid, p. 280.
85 Ibid.
86 Hameed, *Maulana Azad, Islam and the Indian National Movement*, p. 3.
87 R. Nikki Keddie, *An Islamic Response to Imperialism*, Berkeley: University of California Press, 1968.
88 Some critical notes on the introduction of modern sciences to the Ottoman empire and the relation between science and religion up to the end of the nineteenth century, in Jean-Louis Bacque-Grammont and Emeri van Donzel (eds.), *Comite Internationale D'Etudes pre-Ottoman*, pp. 235–51, Istanbul: The Divit Press, 1987.
89 Keddie, *An Islamic Response to Imperialism*, p. 42.
90 Albert Hourani, *Arabic thought in the Liberal Age, 1798–1939*, Oxford: Oxford University Press, 1962, p. 108.
91 Keddie, *An Islamic Response to Imperialism*, p. 55.
92 Azad, *Azad ki Kahani*, pp. 255–56
93 Ibid, p. 309.
94 Ibid, pp. 309–10.
95 Ibid.
96 Altaf Husain Hali, *Hali's Musaddas: A Story in Verse of the Ebb and Tide of Islam*, translated from the Urdu by Syeda Saiyidain Hameed, New Delhi: Harper Collins India, 2003, pp. 158–59.
97 Habib, 'The Revolutionary Maulana', in Kabir, *Maulana Abul Kalam Azad*, p. 92.
98 Azad, *Azad ki Kahani*, pp. 312–13.
99 Ibid, p. 315.
100 Datta, *Maulana Azad*, p. 49.
101 Zia-ul-Hasan Faruqi, 'Orthodoxy and Heterodoxy in India', in Hasan, *Islam*

and Indian Nationalism Reflections on Abul Kalam Azad, p. 335.

102 Shibli Nomani, *Shibli Makatib ki Roshni mein*, Muinuddin (ed.), Karachi, 1967, pp. 98–99, cited in Muhammad Aslam Syed, *Muslim Response to the West: Muslim Historiography in India 1857–1914*, Islamabad: National Institute of Historical and Cultural Research, 1988, p. 78.

103 Ziaul Hasan Faruqi, 1981.

104 Ibid.

105 Sayyid Sulaiman Nadvi, *Hayat-i-Shibli*, Darul Mussannefin: Azamgarh, 1970, pp. 91–94.

106 Aziz Ahmad, *Islamic Modernism in India and Pakistan*, Oxford: Oxford University Press, 1963, p. 112.

107 Azad, *Ghubar-i-Khatir*, p. 259.

108 Datta, *Maulana Azad*, p. 30.

CHAPTER 2: MAULANA AZAD AND CRITICAL THINKING IN ISLAM

1 Mujeeb, *Indian Muslims*, p. 457.

2 Azad, *Ghubar-i-Khatir*, p. 49.

3 Ibid.

4 Ibid.

5 Ziauddin Sardar, 'Critical Muslim', *Seminar*, January, 2014.

6 Hameed, *Maulana Azad, Islam and the Indian National Movement*, p. 83.

7 Ibid.

8 Azad, *Tazkirah*, p. 149 and 256, cited in Datta, *Maulana Azad,* p. 97.

9 Ayesha Jalal, 'Striking a Just Balance: Maulana Azad as a Theorist of Trans-National Jihad', *Modern Intellectual History*, 4, 2007, pp. 95–107.

10 Mujeeb, *Indian Muslims*, p. 457.

11 Habib, 'The Revolutionary Maulana', in Kabir, *Maulana Abul Kalam Azad,* p. 81.

12 Ibid.

13 Fazlur Rahman, 'Muslim Modernism in the Indo-Pakistan Sub-Continent', *Bulletin of the School of Oriental and African Studies*, 1958, pp. 82–99.

14 Pervez Hoodbhoy, *Islam and Science: Religious Orthodoxy and the Battle for Rationality*, London: Bloomsbury Azademic, 1991, p. 56.

15 Khan, *Maqalat-i-Sir Syed*, 1961.

16 C. W. Troll, *Sayyid Ahmad Khan: A Reinterpretation of Muslim theology*, New Delhi: Vikas Publishing House, 1978, pp. 168–70.

17 Christopher De Bellaigue, *The Islamic Enlightenment: The Struggle between Faith and Reason*, New York: WW Norton, 2017, p. xxix.

18 Quran 59:14, Aisha Abdurrahman Bewley translation, cited in Mustafa Akyol, *Islam Without Extremes: A Muslim Case for Liberty*, New York: WW Norton, 2011, p. 52.

19 Maxime Rodinson cites Henri Lammen's comment in his *Islam and Capitalism,* London: Saqi Books, London, 2007, p. 115.

20 Bassam Tibi, *Islam Between Culture and Politics*, London: Palgrave Macmillan, 2005, p.187.

21 For a more detailed discussion on this see S. Irfan Habib, *Jihad or Ijtihad: Religious Orthodoxy and Modern Science in Contemporary Islam,* New Delhi: Harper Collins, 2012.

22 *Al-Hilal*, 8 September 1912.
23 For more information: http://ziauddinsardar.com/2013/07/critical-muslim/
24 Azad, *Ghubar-i-Khatir*, p. 102.
25 Azad, *Azad ki Kahani*, in Malihabadi, 1960, p. 257.
26 Mushirul Hasan, *A Moral Reckoning: Muslim Intellectuals in Nineteenth Century Delhi*, New Delhi: Oxford University Press, New Delhi, 2005, p. 17.
27 Mohammad Zakaullah, *Uloom-Tabiya Gharbi ki Abjad* (*Beginnings of Western Physical Sciences*), Delhi, 1900, pp. 5–6.
28 Hasan, *A Moral Reckoning*, p. 61.
29 Azad, *Azad ki Kahani*, p. 319.
30 S. R. Kidwai, *Master Ramchander*, Delhi, 1963, p. 49.
31 To Bashiruddin Ahmad, *Mauiza-I Hasana*, 5 January 1876, p. 4.
32 Hasan, *A Moral Reckoning*, pp. 156–57.
33 Hoodbhoy, *Islam and Science*, p. 97.
34 Altaf Husain Hali, *Hayat-i-Jawaid*, Delhi: Idarah-i-Adabiyat, 1979, pp. 247–71.
35 Azad, *Azad ki Kahani*, pp. 397–98.
36 Ibid.
37 Ibid, p. 420.
38 Ibid, pp. 419–421.
39 Ibid, pp. 259–60.
40 Azad, *Ghubar-i-Khatir*, p. 50.
41 Ibid, p.51.
42 Keddie, *An Islamic Response to Imperialism*, p. 60.
43 Ibid.
44 Ibid, 106.
45 Scott L. Montgomery, 'Naming the Heavens: A Brief History of Earthly Projections, Part II: Nativizing Arab science', *Science as Culture*, 1996, pp. 73–129.
46 'On Teaching and Learning', cited in Keddie, *An Islamic Response to Imperialism*, p. 107
47 Akyol, *Islam without Extremes*, p. 170.
48 Azad's letter to Hakeem Mohammad Ali Tabeeb , 11 June 1902 in Malik Ram (ed.), *Khutoot Abul Kalam Azad*, New Delhi: Sahitya Akademy, 1991, pp. 22–23.
49 Abul Kalam Azad, *Speeches of Maulana (Abul Kalam) Azad, 1947-1955*, New Delhi: Publications Division, Min. of Information & Broadcasting, Government of India, 1956, p. 76. Convocation address at the Aligarh Muslim University, 20 February 1949.
50 Rashid Shaz, *Creating a Future Islamic Civilization*, New Delhi, 2008, p. 66.
51 G. Rasool Abduhu, *The Educational Ideas of Maulana Abdul Kalam Azad*, New Delhi, Sterling Publishers, 1973, p. 67.
52 *Al-Hilal*, 23 April 1913.
53 Moin Shakir, *Azad, Islam, and Nationalism*, New Delhi: Kalamkar Prakashan, 1969, p.11.
54 Douglas, *Abul Kalam Azad: An Intellectual and Religious Biography*, p. 151.
55 *Al-Hilal* cited in ibid, p.153.
56 Pankaj Mishra, *From the Ruins of Empire: The Revolt Against the West and the Remaking of Asia*, London: Picador, 2013, p. 70.
57 Ibid.

58 *Maqalat-i-Jamaliyyeh*, cited in Keddie, *An Islamic Response to Imperialism*, p. 130–31.

59 Azad, *Speeches of Maulana (Abul Kalam) Azad*, p. 185. Inaugural speech at the Symposium on the concept of man and the philosophy of education in the East and West, New Delhi, 13 December 1951.

60 Ibid.

61 Rogan, *The Arabs: A History*, 2009.

62 Ibid.

63 Akyol, *Islam Without Extremes*, p. 171.

64 Toby Lester, 'What is the Quran', *The Atlantic*, January 1999. Cited in ibid, p. 171.

65 Akyol, *Islam Without Extremes*, p. 171.

66 Moin Shakir in *Azad, Islam and Nationalism*, 1969, cited in Hameed, *India's Maulana,* p. 44.

67 Malikzada Manzoor Ahmad, *Maulana Abul Kalam Azad*, Lucknow, 1978, pp.109–19.

68 Douglas, *Abul Kalam Azad.*

69 Christian W. Troll, 'Abul Kalam Azad and Sarmad, The Martyr', in Hasan, *Islam and Indian Nationalism Reflections on Abul Kalam Azad*, p. 28–42.

70 Hasan, *Islam and Indian Nationalism Reflections on Abul Kalam Azad*, pp. 32, 35.

71 Douglas cited in Troll, in Hasan, *Islam and Indian Nationalism Reflections on Abul Kalam Azad*, p.29.

72 V. N. Datta, *Maulana Abul Kalam Azad and Sarmad,* New Delhi: Rupa Publications, 2007, p.4.

73 Ahmad, *Maulana Abul Kalam Azad*, p. 23.

74 Abul Kalam Azad, *Tarjuman al-Quran*, pp. xxv–xxvi.

75 Ibid, pp. xxix–xxx.

76 Ibid, pp. xiii–xliii.

77 Syed Abdul Latif, 'An Unfinished Masterpiece', in Kabir, *Maulana Abul Kalam Azad,* p.117.

78 S. Irfan Habib, 'The Forgotten Inheritance of Azad', *Hindu*, 22 February 2014.

79 Aijaz Ahmad, *Lineages of the Present: Ideology and Politics in Contemporary South Asia*, London: Verso Books, 2002.

80 Ibid.

81 Ibid, p. xii.

82 Azad, *Tarjuman*, p. x.

83 Ibid, p.xi.

84 Ibid, p. xxxiv.

85 Ibid, p. xxxvii.

86 Ibid, p. xxxviii.

87 Ibid, pp. xxxviii–xxxix.

88 Ibi, p. xxxix.

89 Akyol, *Islam without Extremes*, p.82.

90 Shaz, *Creating a Future Islamic Civilization*, p. 144.

91 Datta, *Maulana Azad*, p. 188.

92 Azad, *Tarjuman*, p. 8.

93 Ibid, p. 5.

94 Qazi Abdul Ghaffar, *Asar-I Abul Kalam Azad,* cited in Habib, 'The Revolutionary Maulana', in Kabir, *Maulana Abul Kalam Azad,* pp. 82–83.

95 Azad, *Tarjuman*, pp. 633–35 and 690 cited in Datta, *Maulana Azad*, p. 188.
96 Quran 5:48, Aisha Abdurrahman Bewley translation, with Arabic words anglicized, cited in Mustafa Akyol, *Islam Without Extremes: A Muslim Case for Liberty*, New York: WW Norton, 2011, pp. 83–84.
97 Datta, *Maulana Azad*, p. 189.
98 Habib, 'The Revolutionary Maulana', in Kabir, *Maulana Abul Kalam Azad*, p. 82.
99 Azad, *Tarjuman*, pp. 19–20
100 Ibid, p. 73.
101 Ibid, p. 8.
102 Ibid, p. 77.
103 Douglas, *Abul Kalam Azad*, pp. 201–202.
104 Ibid, p. 104.
105 Clair Carlisle, 'Is Religion Based on Fear', *Guardian*, 2 December 2013.
106 Tirmizi, cited in Abu Hamid Ghazali, *The Love of God and Its Signs*, translated by Syed Nawab Ali, 1921, https://en.wikisource.org/wiki/The_Love_of_God_and_Its_Signs.
107 Annemarie Schimmel, *Mystical Dimensions of Islam*, Chapel Hill: University of North Carolina Press, 1975, pp. 133–34.
108 Ibid, pp. 109–10.
109 Ibid.
110 Ibid, p. 148.
111 Ibid, p. 149.
112 Ibid, pp. 149–50.
113 Eric E. F. Bishop, 'Al-Shaf'I (Muhammad ibn Idris) Founder of Law School', *The Muslim World*, April 1929, p. 160, cited in Akyol, *Islam Without Extremes*, p. 89.
114 M. N. Roy, *Historical Role of Islam*, Allahabad: Kitabistan, 1938.
115 Ibid, p. 154.
116 Ram, *Khutoot Abul Kalam Azad*, pp. 275–76.
117 Ibid.
118 Azad, *Tarjuman*, p. 154.
119 Ibid, p. 155.
120 Ibid, p. 158.
121 Ibid, p. 159.
122 Ibid, p. 160.
123 Ibid, p.159.
124 Datta, *Maulana Azad*, p. 196.
125 Azad's statement on the reform of Islamic law from *The Hindustan Times*, 5 July 1945, also *Tarjuman-ul-Quran*, p. 143.

CHAPTER 3: AZAD, ISLAM, AND NATIONALISM

1 E. J. Hobsbawm, *The Age of Empire 1875-1914*, New Delhi: Rupa Publications, 1992, p. 142.
2 S. Irfan Habib, *Indian Nationalism: The Essential Writings*, New Delhi: Aleph Book Company, 2017, pp. 161–64.
3 Shashi Tharoor, *The Battle of Belonging: On Nationalism, Patriotism, and What It Means to be Indian*, New Delhi: Aleph Book Company, 2020,

p. 6.

4 Tharoor, *The Battle of Belonging*, p. 7.

5 Hobsbawm, *The Age of Empire 1875-1914*, p. 142.

6 Romila Thapar, *On Nationalism,* New Delhi: Aleph Book Company, 2016, pp. 10–11.

7 Ibid, p. 11.

8 Ibid.

9 Tharoor, *The Battle of Belonging*, p. 24.

10 Pranab Bardhan, 'How to Reimagine Nationalism', *Indian Express*, 11 October 2021.

11 Ibid.

12 Thapar, *On Nationalism*, p. 17.

13 Syeda Saiyidain Hameed, *India's Maulana, Abul Kalam Azad*, New Delhi: Vikas Publishing House, Vol. 2, 1990, p. 55.

14 Moin Shakir, *Azad, Islam, and Nationalism,* p. 58.

15 Abul Kalam Azad, *Muzamin-i-Abul Kalam Azad*, New Delhi: Hindustan Publishing House, 1944, p. 87.

16 Rajat Ray, 'Revolutionaries, Pan-Islamists and Bolsheviks: Maulana Abul Kalam Azad and the Political Underworld in Calcutta, 1905-1925', in Mushirul Hasan (ed.), *Communal Politics and Pan-Islamic Trends in Colonial India,* New Delhi: Manohar Publishers, p. 87.

17 Ayesha Jalal, 'Striking A Just Balance: Maulana Azad as A Theorist of Trans-National Jihad', *Modern Intellectual History*, 4, 1 2007, p. 97.

18 Syeda Saiyidain Hameed, *Islamic Seal on India's Independence: Abul Kalam Azad-a Fresh Look,* Karachi: Oxford University Press, 1998, pp. 42–43.

19 Farzana Shaikh, 'Azad and Iqbal: The Quest for the Islamic "Good"', in Hasan, *Islam and Indian Nationalism: Reflections on Abul Kalam Azad*, p. 62.

20 Ian Henderson Douglas, *Abul Kalam Azad: An Intellectual and Religious Biography*, Gail Minault and Christian W. Troll (eds.), New Delhi: Oxford University Press, 1988, p. 141.

21 Muhammad Ali, 'Nationalism and Islam: Perspective of Egyptian and Syrian Muslim intellectuals', *Indonesian Journal of Islam and Muslim Societies*, June, 2014, p. 51.

22 Albert Hourani, *Arabic Thought in the Liberal Age 1798–1939*, Cambridge: Cambridge University Press, 1983, p. 118, 152, 156; Azad took the name of his own paper from Zaidan's. Cited in Douglas, *Abul Kalam Azad: An Intellectual and Religious Biography*, Minault and Troll, p. 141.

23 Ray, 'Revolutionaries, Pan-Islamists and Bolsheviks: Maulana Abul Kalam Azad and the Political Underworld in Calcutta, 1905-1925', pp. 88–89.

24 Maulana Abul Kalam Azad, *India Wins Freedom,* New Delhi: Orient Longman, 2003, pp. 6–7.

25 Ahmad Saeed Malihabadi, 'Religious Ideology and Indian Nationalism', in Hameed (ed.), *India's Maulana-Abul Kalam Azad*, p. 205.

26 *Al-Hilal*, 18 December 1912, Vol. 1, No. 23.

27 Ibid.

28 Ibid.

29 Jalal, 'Striking a Just Balance: Maulana Azad as a Theorist of Trans-National Jihad', pp. 95–107.

30 Arsh Malsiani, *Abul Kalam Azad*, New Delhi: Publications Division, 1976, cited

in Rajmohan Gandhi, *Understanding the Muslim Mind*, New Delhi: Penguin Books, 2003, pp. 237–38.
31 Bipin Chandra Pal, *Nationality and Empire*, New Delhi: DK Publishers, 2002, p. 23.
32 Habib, *Indian Nationalism*, p. 75.
33 Hameed, *India's Maulana, Abul Kalam Azad*, p. 144.
34 Ibid, p. 145
35 Ibid, p. 146.
36 N. N. Mitra (ed.), *Indian Annual Register*, Vol.1, January-June, 1930, p. 333.
37 *Hindustan Times*, 8 August 1930, cited in Rizwan Qaiser, *Resisting Colonialism and Communal Politics, Maulana Azad and the Making of the Indian Nation*, New Delhi: Manohar Publishers and Distributors, 2011, p. 142.
38 Ibid.
39 Rizwan Qaiser, *Resisting Colonialism and Communal Politics, Maulana Azad and the Making of the Indian Nation*, New Delhi: Manohar Publishers and Distributors, 2011, p.143.
40 V. N. Datta, *Maulana Azad,* New Delhi: Manohar Publishers and Distributors, 1990, p.138.
41 Mitra, *Indian Annual Register*, p. 292. The institution of modern learning that largely kept away from the movement was Aligarh Muslim University.
42 Azad, *Speeches of Maulana (Abul Kalam) Azad, 1947-1955*, p. 20.
43 Ibid, p. 83.
44 Ahmad, *Lineages of the Present*, pp. 133–34.
45 Abul Kalam Azad, 'Khutbat-i-Sadarat-i-Iftitahia', in Malik Ram (ed.), *Khutoot Abul Kalam Azad,* New Delhi: Sahitya Akademy, 1991, p. 51.
46 Abul Kalam Azad, *Khutbat-i-Azad*, Lahore: Maktaba Jamal, 2004, pp. 38–39, cited in Jalal, 'Striking A Just Balance: Maulana Azad As A Theorist of Trans-National Jihad', *Modern Intellectual History*, p. 106.
47 Maulana Hussain Ahmad Madani, *Composite Nationalism and Islam (Muttahida Qaumiyat aur Islam)*, New Delhi: Manohar Publishers, 2005, p. 114.
48 D. R. Goyal, *Maulana Hussain Ahmad Madani: A Biographical Study*, Calcutta: Maulana Azad Institute of Asian Studies, 2004, p. 8.
49 Samina Awan, *Political Islam in Colonial Punjab: Majlis-e-Ahrar 1929-1949*, Karachi: Oxford University Press, 2010, p. 10, cited in Ishtiaq Ahmed, *Jinnah: His Successes, Failures and Role in History*, New Delhi: Penguin Random House India Private Limited, 2020, p. 71.
50 Habib, *Indian Nationalism*, pp. 101–19.
51 Cited in Goyal, *Maulana Husain Ahmad Madni,* pp. 170–71
52 Ibid.
53 Latif Ahmad Sherwani, *Speeches, Writings and Statements of Iqbal*, Lahore: Iqbal Academy Pakistan, 1995, p. 10–31, cited in Ishtiaq Ahmed, *Jinnah: His Successes, Failures and Role in History*, New Delhi: Penguin Random House India Private Limited, 2020, pp. 131–32.
54 Cited in L. R. Gordon-Polonskaya, 'Ideology of Muslim Nationalism', in Hafeez Malik, *Iqbal: Poet-Philosopher of Pakistan,* New York: Columbia University Press, 1971, p. 135.
55 Translated by K. G. Saiyidain.
56 Habib, *Indian Nationalism*, pp. 101–19.
57 S. M. H. Burney, *Iqbal Poet-Patriot of India*, New Delhi: Vikas Publishing

House, 1987, p. 48.

58 Figures from https://en.wikipedia.org/wiki/Western_Uttar_Pradesh also https://en.wikipedia.org/wiki/Islam_in_Uttar_Pradesh.

59 Qaiser, *Resisting Colonialism and Communal Politics*, pp. 109–10.

60 'On Teaching and Learning', in Keddie, *An Islamic Response to Imperialism*, pp. 101–102.

61 Sudhanva D. Shetty, 'There's a world of a difference between Patriotism and Nationalism', *Huffington Post*, 6 March 2016.

62 Abul Kalam Azad, 'Islam and Nationalism', cited from Hameed (ed.), *India's Maulana,* pp. 51–52.

63 Ibid.

64 Ibid, p. 52.

65 Ibid.

66 Ibid.

67 Habib, *Indian Nationalism*, pp. 119–135.

68 Rabindranath Tagore, *Nationalism,* London: Macmillan and Co Limited, 1917, p. 106.

69 Qaiser, *Resisting Colonialism and Communal Politics,* p. 111.

70 Hameed, 'Islam and Nationalism', *India's Maulana, Abul Kalam Azad*, p. 52.

71 Ibid, p. 53.

72 Qaiser, *Resisting Colonialism and Communal Politics*, p. 109.

73 Abul Kalam Azad, 'Presidential address at the special session of the Congress in 1923', cited in Qaiser, *Resisting Colonialism and Communal Politics, Maulana Azad and the Making of the Indian Nation.*

74 Mitra, *The India Annual Register*, p. 26, cited in Qaiser, *Resisting Colonialism and Communal Politics, Maulana Azad and the Making of the Indian Nation*, p. 116.

75 Qaiser, *Resisting Colonialism and Communal Politics*, p. 118.

76 Ibid, p. 119.

77 Maulana Azad, 'Islam and Nationalism', cited in Syeda Saiyidain Hameed, *India's Maulana*, p. 54.

78 Hameed, *India's Maulana, Abul Kalam Azad*, pp. 53–54.

79 'Quol-e-Faisal', cited in Hameed, 'Islam and Nationalism', *India's Maulana, Abul Kalam Azad*, p. 66.

80 Ibid, p. 66.

81 Ibid, pp. 66–67.

82 Ibid, p. 70.

83 *Al-Hilal*, 11 September 1912, cited in Rajmohan Gandhi, *Understanding the Muslim Mind*, New Delhi: Penguin Books, 2003, p. 222.

84 Ishtiaq Ahmed, *Jinnah: His Successes, Failures and Role in History*, New Delhi: Penguin Books, 2020, p. 14.

85 Abul Kalam Azad, 'Fitna-i-Irtidad aur Musalman', in Ghulam Rasool Meher (ed.), *Maulana Abul Kalam Azad, Ek Nadir Rozgar Shakhsiyat,* Lahore: Meher Sons, 1994, p. 169, cited in Qaiser, *Resisting Colonialism and Communal Politics,* p. 109.

86 Hameed, *Maulana Azad, Islam and the Indian National Movement*, p. 180.

87 Ibid, pp. 180–81.

88 Rajmohan Gandhi, *Understanding the Muslim Mind*, New Delhi: Penguin Books, 2003, p. 236.

89 Hameed, *India's Maulana*, p. 161.
90 Tony Joseph, *Early Indians: The Story of our Ancestors and Where we came From,* New Delhi: Juggernaut Books, 2018.
91 Pankaj Mishra, 'Hindu nationalism is more Italian and Christian than Sonia Gandhi', *The Times of India*, 22 January 2017.
92 Ibid.
93 V. D. Savarkar, *Hindutva: Who is a Hindu?* Bombay: Veer Savarkar Prakashan, 1969, p. 115–16, cited after Hilal Ahmed, *Siyasi Muslims*, New Delhi: Penguin Books, 2019, pp. 66–67.
94 Safoora Razeq, *Nationalism and Maulana Azad*, Kolkata: Pragatishil Prokashak, 2018, p. 72.
95 Allen Hayes Merriam, *Gandhi vs Jinnah*, Calcutta: Minerva Books, 1980, p. 68, cited in Gandhi, *Understanding the Muslim Mind*, p. 238.
96 Mahadev Desai, *Maulana Abul Kalam Azad*, Agra: Siva Lal Agarwala, 1940, p. 124.
97 Hameed, *Maulana Azad, Islam and the Indian National Movement*, p. 161.
98 Ibid, p. 162.
99 Venkat Dhulipala, *Creating a New Medina, State Power, Islam, and the Quest for Pakistan in Late North India*, Cambridge: Cambridge University Press, 2015, p. 52.
100 Ibid.
101 'K M Ashraf on Himself', in Horst Kruger (ed.), *Kunwar Muhammad Ashraf: An Indian Scholar and Revolutionary, 1903-1962*, Bombay, 1969, p. 393, cited in Venkat Dhulipala, *Creating a New Medina, State Power, Islam, and the Quest for Pakistan in Late North India*, Cambridge: Cambridge University Press, p. 52.
102 Oral History Transcript, Sajjad Zaheer, *Nehru Memorial Museum and Library*, New Delhi. Cited in Venkat Dhulipala, *Creating a New Medina, State Power, Islam, and the Quest for Pakistan in Late North India*, Cambridge: Cambridge University Press, p. 53.
103 For further details on the Muslim Mass Contact Programme see Mushirul Hasan, 'The Muslim Mass Contact Campaign: Analysis of a Strategy of Political Mobilization' in Mushirul Hasan (ed.), *India's Partition: Process, Strategy and Mobilization*, New Delhi: Oxford University Press, pp. 133–59.
104 'Some notes on the general approach and propaganda methods of AIML with special reference to inter-communal relations.' AICC papers, 1938, Nehru Memorial Museum and Library, New Delhi.
105 Ibid.
106 Raja of Mahmudabad, 'Some Memories', in C. H. Philips and M. Wainwright (ed.), *The Partition of India: Politics and Perspectives, 1935-1947*, London: Geo. Allen & Unwin, 1970, p. 380, cited in Francis Robinson, *Scholar, Sufi & Politician Maulana Jamal Mian of Farangi Mahall 1919-2012*, New Delhi: Primus Books, 2020, p. 114.
107 Shamsul Islam, *Muslims against Partition of India*, New Delhi: Pharos Media, 2018, pp. 92–93.
108 *Al-Hilal*, 1912, Vol.1, No, 15.
109 *The Sunday Statesman*, 28 April 1940.
110 *Hindustan Times*, 28 April 1940.
111 Private papers from Hafiz Mohammad Ibrahim, cited in Shamsul Islam, *Muslims*

against Partition of India, New Delhi: Pharos Media, 2018.

112 Ibid, p. 94.

113 Ibid, pp.101–112.

114 *The Bombay Chronicle*, 27 April 1940.

115 Islam, *Muslims against Partition of India*, p. 90.

116 *National Herald*, 21 April 1940; cited in Islam, *Muslims against Partition of India*, 2018.

117 *The Bombay Chronicle,* 27 April 1940.

118 *Amrita Bazar Patrika*, 17 May 1943, cited in Islam, *Muslims against Partition of India*, New Delhi: Pharos, 2018. p. 119.

119 Jagat S. Bright, *India's Nationalist No.1: Mr Allah Baksh*, Lahore: Hero Publications, 1943, p. 58–59, cited in Islam, *Muslims Against Partition of India*, pp. 119–120.

CHAPTER 4: GHUBAR-I-KHATIR: BEYOND FAITH AND POLITICS

1 Sheikh Muhammad Ikram, *Modern Muslim India and the Birth of Pakistan,* Lahore: Institute of Islamic Culture, p. 149, cited in Gandhi, *Understanding the Muslim Mind*, p. 242.

2 J. B. Kripalani, *My Times: An Autobiography*, Rupa & Co.: New Delhi, 2004, p. 484.

3 Azad, *Ghubar-i-Khatir,* p. 97.

4 Malik Ram, 'Introduction', in Azad, *Ghubar-i-Khatir*, p. 2.

5 Ajmal Khan in Azad, *Ghubar-i-Khatir*, 2003. Edition cited in Hameed, *Maulana Azad, Islam and the Indian National Movement*, 2014.

6 Douglas, *Abul Kalam Azad,* p. 226.

7 Ibid.

8 Azad, *Ghubar-i-Khatir*, p. 63.

9 Ibid, p. 63.

10 Datta, *Maulana Azad*, p. 201.

11 Kripalani, *My Times*, p. 488.

12 Ibid, p. 37.

13 Verinder Grover (ed.), *Bal Gangadhar Tilak*, New Delhi: Deep & Deep Publications, 1992, p. 249.

14 'Diwan-i-Ghalib', cited in Azad, *Ghubar-i-Khatir*, p. 44.

15 Azad, *Ghubar-i-Khatir*, p. 45.

16 Ibid, pp. 52–53.

17 Ibid, p. 53.

18 Ibid, p. 55.

19 Ibid, p. 90

20 Ibid, p. 93.

21 Ibid, p. 90.

22 Ibid, p. 94

23 Ibid, p. 61.

24 Ibid, p. 78.

25 Ibid, p. 80.

26 Azad, *Ghubar-i-Khatir*, p .84. The footnote in the book attributes the couplet to Hasabi Natanzi ('Safina-e-Ali Hazeen...'). Some people have attributed it to Mukhlis Khan Mukhlis (as in 'Behtareen Ash'aar').

27 Ibid, pp. 85–86.

28 Ibid, p. 86.
29 Ibid.
30 Ibid.
31 Ibid, p. 167.
32 Ibid.
33 Ibid, p. 168.
34 Azad, *Ghubar-i-Khatir*, p. 66.
35 Ibid, p. 103.
36 Debiprasad Chattopadhyaya, *Indian Atheism*, New Delhi: People's Publishing House, 2008.
37 Azad, *Ghubar-i-Khatir*, p. 176.
38 Ibid, pp. 178–79.
39 Ibid, p. 27.
40 Ibid, p. 29.
41 Ibid, p. 82.
42 Ibid.
43 Ibid, p. 159.
44 Ibid, p. 164.
45 Ibid, p. 186.
46 Jawaharlal Nehru, *Discovery of India*, New Delhi: Oxford University Press, 1991, first published in 1946, p. 35.
47 Ibid, p. 189.
48 Ibid, p. 192.
49 Azad, *Ghubar-i-Khatir*, p. 196.
50 Hameed, *Maulana Azad, Islam and the Indian National Movement*, p. 229.
51 Azad, *Ghubar-i-Khatir*, p. 199.
52 The note in English edition of *Ghubar-i-Khatir* says the couplet is wrongly attributed to Mir, it is in fact by Mohd Yar Khan Amir.
53 Azad, *Ghubar-i-Khatir*, p. 211.
54 Ibid, p. 216.
55 Ibid, p. 221.
56 Ibid, p. 225.
57 Ibid, p. 227.
58 Ibid, p. 231.
59 Azad, *Ghubar-i-Khatir*, p. 259.
60 Ibid, p. 238.
61 Ibid, p. 241.
62 Ibid, p. 244
63 Ibid, pp. 253–54.
64 Hameed *Maulana Azad, Islam and the Indian National Movement*, p. 251.
65 Ibid, p. 256.
66 Azad, *Ghubar-i-Khatir*, p. 258.
67 Ibid, p. 265.
68 'Is Music Haraam?', *Al-Balagh*, Vol. 28, No.1, Feb–March 2003, 5.

CHAPTER 5: BUILDING A NEW INDIA: EDUCATION, CULTURE, SCIENCE, AND THE PLURALIST ETHOS

1 Krishna Kumar, *Political Agenda of Education A Study of Colonialist and*

Nationalist Ideas, New Delhi: Sage Publications, 1991, p. 26.

2 Jyoti Sabharwal, *Kapila Vatsayayan: A Cognitive Biography Afloat a Lotus Leaf*, New Delhi: Steller Publishers, 2015, p. 179.

3 J. C. Ghosh, 'The Educational Leader', in Kabir, *Maulana Abul Kalam Azad*, p. 101.

4 Mahavir Singh (ed.), *Maulana Abul Kalam Azad: Profile of a Nationalist*, Kolkata: Maulana Abul Kalam Azad Institute of Asian Studies, 2003, p. 125.

5 Azad, *Tarjuman al-Quran*, p. 94.

6 Abduhu, *The Educational Ideas of Maulana Abdul Kalam Azad*, p. 42.

7 K. G. Saiyidain, 'Philosophy of Education', in Hameed, *India's Maulana,* p. 64.

8 'Hamari Azadi', cited in Ahmad, *Maulana Abul Kalam Azad*, p.33.

9 Ahmad, *Maulana Abul Kalam Azad*, p. 33.

10 Ibid.

11 Ibid, pp. 33–34.

12 Abduhu, *The Educational Ideas of Maulana Abdul Kalam Azad*, p. 24.

13 *Al-Balagh*, 25 February 1916, pp. 10–11.

14 *Al-Hilal*, 5 August 1927.

15 Abduhu, *The Educational Ideas of Maulana Abdul Kalam Azad*, p. 25.

16 Azad, *Speeches of Maulana (Abul Kalam) Azad, 1947-1955*, p. 208.

17 Jawaharlal Nehru, 'The Passing of a Great Man', in Kabir, *Maulana Abul Kalam Azad: A Memorial Volume,* New Delhi: Asia Publishing House, 1959, pp. 1–2.

18 S. Radhakrishnan, 'The Search and the Attainment', in Kabir, *Maulana Abul Kalam Azad,* p. 6.

19 Azad, *Speeches of Maulana Azad 1947-1958*, p. 1.

20 Ibid, pp. 2–3

21 Abduhu, *The Educational Ideas of Maulana Abul Kalam Azad*, p. 83.

22 Azad, *Tarjuman al-Quran*, p. 119 cited in Abduhu, *The Educational Ideas of Maulana Abul Kalam Azad*, p. 41.

23 Ibid, p. 42.

24 *Qawlii-faisal*, Calcutta: Al-Balagh Press, 1921, p. 50, cited in Abduhu, *The Educational Ideas of Maulana Abul Kalam Azad*, p. 94.

25 Presidential address, Indian National Congress, March 1940, Ramgarh.

26 Azad, *Speeches of Maulana Azad*, p. 260.

27 The Constituent Assembly, 1949, cited in Abduhu, *The Educational Ideas of Maulana Abul Kalam Azad*, 1973.

28 Azad, *Speeches of Maulana Azad*, p. 260.

29 *Ibid*, p. 20.

30 The Constituent Assembly, 1949, in Abduhu, *The Educational Ideas of Maulana Abul Kalam Azad*, 1973.

31 Azad, *Speeches of Maulana Azad,* p. 126.

32 Ibid, p. 201.

33 The Constituent Assembly, 1948, in Abduhu, *The Educational Ideas of Maulana Abul Kalam Azad*, 1973.

34 Abduhu, *The Educational Ideas of Maulana Abul Kalam Azad*, p. 96.

35 Humayun Kabir, *Education in New India*, Westport: Greenwood Press, 1955, p. 1.

36 Ibid.

37 Ibid, p. 48.
38 Ibid, p. 1.
39 Ibid, p. 2.
40 Charles Freer Andrews, *Zaka Ullah of Delhi*, New Delhi: Oxford University Press, 2003, p. 97.
41 Azad, *Speeches of Maulana Azad*, 'Education and Independence'. Convocation Address at Patna University, 21 December 1947.
42 Ibid, pp. 13–14.
43 Ibid, p. 15.
44 Ibid, p. 16.
45 Ibid, p. 19.
46 Ibid.
47 Geeta Pandey, An English Goddess for India's Down-trodden, *BBC India*, 15 November 2011.
48 Ibid.
49 Ibid, p. 21.
50 Azad, *Speeches of Maulana Azad*, p. 1. Press conference on 18 February 1947.
51 Ibid, p. 8.
52 Azad, *Speeches of Maulana Azad*, p. 38. Press conference on 31 May 31 1948.
53 Ibid, p. 39–40.
54 Ibid, p. 32.
55 Azad, *Speeches of Maulana Azad,* p. 127. Programme for CABE meeting, Cuttack, 8 January 1950.
56 Delhi State Expansion of Educational facilities in Delhi. National Archives of India, New Delhi, p. 8.
57 Ibid. Mehr Chand Khanna Market in Lodi Colony is named after him.
58 Ibid. Letter of Director of Education, Delhi State to Professor Humayun Kabir, dated 28 June 1952.
59 Report of the University Education Commission, Government of India, Ministry of Education (December 1948–August 1949), Vol. I, New Delhi, 1949, p. 33, cited in Qaiser, *Resisting Colonialism and Communal Politics,* p. 284.
60 Azad, *Speeches of Maulana Azad*, p. 18.
61 Ibid. Azad's presidential address at the 14th session of CABE, 13 January 1948, p. 25.
62 Note regarding religious education published in the *Hindustan Times*. National Archives of India, p. 5, New Delhi.
63 Ibid, p. 3.
64 Ibid, p. 5.
65 Radhakrishnan Commission or the University Education Commission 1948–49: https://www.tetsuccesskey.com/2016/12/radhakrishnan-commission-part-1.html
66 Ibid.
67 'The Report of the University Education Commission', Ministry of Education, 1950: http://www.academics-india.com/Radhakrishnan%20Commission%20Report%20of%201948-49.pdf
68 Ministry of Education, Government of India, File no. 30-4/52 G3 U2, National Archives of India, New Delhi.
69 Ministry of Education, Government of India, File No. 30-5/52 G3 (U2), National Archives of India, New Delhi. Cited in Qaiser, *Resisting Colonialism and Communal Politics,* p. 330, note. 48.

70 Ministry of Education, Government of India, National Archives of India, New Delhi.
71 Ibid.
72 Ibid.
73 Azad, *Speeches of Maulana Azad*, p. 163–64.
74 Ibid, p. 165.
75 Qaiser, *Resisting Colonialism and Communal Politics,* p. 295.
76 Ibid. A letter from Jamia Millia Islamia, dated 27 April 1949. It is not clear from the file as to who signed the letter. Ministry of Education, Government of India, File no. 73-216/49 D III A I.
77 Ibid.
78 Ibid, p. 297.
79 Ministry of Education, National Archives of India, New Delhi.
80 Ibid, p. 8.
81 Second Five Year Plan-Development of University Education, National Archives of India, New Delhi.
82 Ibid, p. 4.
83 Ibid, p. 8.
84 Ibid.
85 Ibid.
86 Ibid, p. 13
87 Ibid, p. 16–17.
88 Ministry of Education, National Archives of India, New Delhi. These comments were made by the law ministry on 14 October 1954, almost about a year after the original proposal was made by the education ministry. Cited in Qaiser, *Resisting Colonialism and Communal Politics,* p. 334, note. 101.
89 Azad, *Speeches of Maulana Azad*, p. 407–408.
90 Ibid, p. 408.
91 Ibid.
92 Ibid, p. 407.
93 Scientific Manpower Committee, National Archives of India, New Delhi.
94 Ibid.
95 Ibid.
96 Ibid.
97 Azad, *Speeches of Maulana Azad*, p. 412.
98 S. T. H. Abidi, et al., *A Walk Through History: 50 Years of IIT Kharagpur*, p. 31, cited in Qaiser, *Resisting Colonialism and Communal Politics,* p. 309.
99 Azad, *Speeches of Maulana Azad,* p. 159. Opening address at the Indian Institute of Technology, Kharagpur, 18 August 1951.
100 Ibid, p. 160.
101 Ibid, p. 161.
102 Ibid.
103 V. V. Krishna, 'Organization of Industrial Research: The Early History of CSIR, 1933-47', in Roy Macleod and Deepak Kumar (eds.), *Technology and the Raj: Western Technology and Technical Transfers to India, 1700-1947,* New Delhi: Sage Publications, p. 289.
104 Azad, *Speeches of Maulana Azad*, p. 210. Inaugural Speech at the CRRI, New Delhi, 16 July 1952.
105 Azad, *Speeches of Maulana Azad*, p. 240. Inaugural address at the CBRI, Roorkee, 12 April 12 1953.

106 Ibid, pp. 241–42.
107 S. N. Sen, *Professor Meghnad Saha: His Life, Work and Philosophy,* Calcutta: Meghnad Saha Sixtieth Birthday Committee, 1954, p. 129, 133.
108 National Archives of India, New Delhi
109 Azad, *Speeches of Maulana Azad*, p. 49. Inaugural speech at the annual session of the Museums Association of India, Delhi, 27 December 1948.
110 National Archives of India, New Delhi. National Anthem-Singing of the Song 'Jana Gana Mana' in all schools and colleges.
111 Ibid.
112 Ibid. Letter from the Directorate of Education, Delhi State, 28 September 1950.
113 Ibid. Circular issued by the Ministry of Education dated 31 May 1955 to the secretaries of Education.
114 Letter of Azad to Sardar Patel, 10 February 1947.
115 Ministry of Education, National Archives, New Delhi.
116 Azad, *Speeches of Maulana Azad*, p. 292. Speech at the first meeting of the Sahitya Akademi, New Delhi, 12 March 1954.
117 Ibid, p. 293.
118 Ibid, p. 294.
119 Ibid, p. 302.
120 File No. 4-5/49 G 2 AI, Ministry of Education, National Archives, New Delhi.
121 Azad, *Speeches of Maulana Azad*, p. 227. Welcome address at the inauguration of the Indian Academy of Dance, Drama, and Music, New Delhi, 28 January 1953.
122 Ibid, p. 229.
123 Jyoti Sabharwal, *Kapila Vatsayayan*, p. 197.
124 Ibid, p. 227.
125 Ibid, pp. 227–28.
126 Azad, *Speeches of Maulana Azad*, p. 133–34. Inaugural Address at the Indian Council for Cultural Relations, 9 April 1950.

EPILOGUE

1 Datta, *Maulana Azad,* pp. 219–20.
2 Razeq, *Nationalism and Maulana Azad*, p. 117.
3 Alam Khundmiri, 'Religious Philosophy of Azad', in Shakir, *Azad, Islam, and Nationalism*, p. 44.
4 Ibid, p. 43.
5 Datta, *Maulana Azad*, p. 225.
6 Datta, *Maulana Azad*, p. 227; his conversations with S. Gopal.
7 Ibid.

INDEX